Praise for

"In telling us in exquisite detail what has gone into the making of one particular instrument, James Barron has created a classic in its own right."

—CHARLES OSGOOD

"Barron deserves praise for leading us through the manufacturing maze with . . . clarity and grace [and] wonderful stops along the way."

—*The New York Sun*

"A succinct and captivating account of the craft that produces this supremely subtle instrument that dominates the world's concert halls. Fascinating, informative, and fun."

—THAD CARHART, author of
The Piano Shop on the Left Bank

"[Barron] combines a journalist's eye for exactitude with a musician's love of the instrument. . . . A treat not just for music-lovers, but for woodworkers, craftsmen and anyone who has ever mourned the passing of grand tradition."

—*Kirkus*

"Rewarding . . . Barron weaves an engaging narrative, and he rounds out the personalities of the workers."

—*BusinessWeek*

"Part Steinway family history, part adventure story, part character study of a factory run by people, not mechanized assembly lines."

—*Richmond Post-Dispatch*

"Barron is an old-time artisan . . . [who] has managed to squeeze a huge amount of storytelling into his biography of a pampered piano."

—*The Globe and Mail* (Toronto)

"Barron's flowing style and evident affection for the material enable him to convey the pride in craftsmanship of the Steinway family and their employees."

—*Library Journal*

"A thoroughgoing chronicle of how a New York immigrant family created an American cultural institution."

—*Publishers Weekly*

PIANO

PIANO

THE MAKING OF A
STEINWAY CONCERT GRAND

James Barron

TIMES BOOKS
Henry Holt and Company
New York

Times Books
Henry Holt and Company, LLC
Publishers since 1866
175 Fifth Avenue
New York, New York 10010
www.henryholt.com

Library of Congress Cataloging-in-Publication Data

Barron, James, 1954–
    Piano : the making of a Steinway concert grand / James Barron.—1st ed.
        p.   cm.
    Includes bibliographical references and index.
    ISBN-13: 978-0-8050-8304-0
    ISBN-10: 0-8050-8304-9
    1. Steinway piano—Construction.   2. Steinway & Sons.
3. Piano makers—New York (State)—New York—History.   I. Title.
ML661.8.N7B37   2006
786.2'1973—dc22   2005057172

Originally published in hardcover in 2006 by Times Books

First paperback edition 2007

Designed by Meryl Sussman Levavi
Photographs by Fred R. Conrad
Heinrich Engelhard Steinweg photograph: Collection of the New-York
Historical Society.
Cristofori grand piano-forte photograph: Courtesy of the
Metropolitan Museum of Art.
"Inside a Concert Grand" diagram by Mika Gröndahl

Printed in the United States of America

3   5   7   9   10   8   6   4   2

To Jane, for No. 252669—and everything else

Contents

Prelude

~~~

By These People,
in This Place

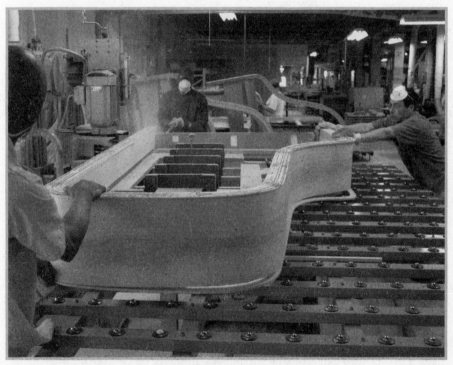

Steinway No. K0862 on its way to becoming a concert grand

*The piano being a creation and plaything of men, its
story leads us into innumerable biographies; being a
boxful of gadgets, the piano has changed through time
and improved at ascertainable moments and places. . . .
Indeed, for the last century and a half, the piano
has been an institution more characteristic than the
bathtub—there were pianos in the log cabins of the
frontier, but no tubs.*

—JACQUES BARZUN

Eighty-eight keys, two hundred and forty-some strings, a
few pedals, and a case about the size of—yes—a bathtub:
every piano has pretty much the same curves outside and
the same workings under the lid. But the biography of a piano is
the story of many stories. It is the story of the fragile instruments
from which all pianos are descended. And it is the story of con-
trasts. It is the story of nineteenth-century immigrants who
struck it rich making pianos, and of more recent immigrants from
Europe and Central America who are paid by the hour. It is the
story of the family that virtually invented the modern grand piano, of brothers and cousins who drank, who hated the United
States, or who dabbled in bulletproof vests and subways and land
deals and amusement parks and the earliest automobiles. It is the
story of a few workers who have exceptionally good ears and
many who have never read a note of music or set foot inside
Carnegie Hall. It is the story of men with a passion for motorcycles who have taught themselves snippets of Beethoven and
Chopin and of others who tack photographs of Frank Zappa
above their workbenches. It is the story of workers who have
brought in special radios that receive the audio portion of television broadcasts so they won't miss their talk shows while they
drill out the bottoms of keys and shove in tiny lead weights. It is

the story of the place where they work, of factory floor camaraderie, of pleasant, unhurried work.

This book is the biography of one piano that was made by these people in this place. It is a concert grand that was built at the Steinway & Sons factory in New York City in 2003 and 2004. The main character will not make a sound for months. A big supporting cast—the most experienced workers in a factory with a payroll of 450—will fuss over it and fume at it.

Like all Steinways, that main character goes by a number, not a name: K0862. Like all other newborns, K0862 comes with hopes for greatness and with fears that it may not measure up to the distinguished family name it wears, and not bashfully. On its right arm the Steinway name is stenciled in big gold letters that an audience cannot miss; on its cast-iron frame the name is stamped in black letters that a camera closing on the pianist's face cannot miss. There is no mistaking K0862 for a Baldwin or a Yamaha or a Bösendorfer.

Yet K0862 looks just like every other Steinway concert grand. It is eight feet, eleven and three-quarters inches long. It contains the same bewildering assortment of moving parts, thousands of tiny pieces of wood and felt and metal that bend and twist and rise and fall on command.

Pianists always say that a good piano has "personality," but the workers know that a piano is a machine, or the eighteenth century's idea of one. Talented tinkerers refined it later on— improvisational wizards of hand tools who, little by little, made a good thing stronger, tougher, and, above all, enduring. But the piano remained an invention from an earlier time. Nineteenth-century inventions had mechanized guts and world-changing goals, like doing in an hour what human hands took days to do. By the beginning of the nineteenth century, Eli Whitney had invented the cotton gin. In the middle of the nineteenth century, Robert Fulton made his steamboat, Cyrus McCormick his reaper, and Isaac Merrit Singer his sewing machine. No one would say that a sewing machine has a personality. It is just a machine.

What a different machine is a piano: a machine with emo-
tions, if that is possible, or at least emotional attachments. There
are pianists who kiss their pianos every day, who touch the case as
tenderly as they would touch a lover's cheek, who talk to their pianos in a way they talk to no one. Musicians regularly talk about
the individual characteristics of this or that piano, the traits that
make one a pleasure to play and the one next to it an agonizing
slog. They dream of one that can deliver what Beethoven's pupil
Carl Czerny called a "holy, distant and celestial Harmony."

Even before its first note sounds, the question hanging over
K0862 is the question that hangs over every Steinway: How good
is it? Will it be a lemon or the piano-world version of a zero-to-
sixty delight? Will it sound like celestial harmony or "a squadron
of dive bombers," as the pianist Gary Graffman said of a Steinway
he hated on first hearing (but came to love)? Will it surprise the
Bach specialist Angela Hewitt, who considers Steinways made in
New York to be "powerful but rather strident, and in my opinion,
clumsy"? Will it match the piano that was the onstage favorite of
Rachmaninoff and later Horowitz and, after retiring from concert
life, became the living room piano in Eugene Istomin's apartment? Will it be anything like the piano that Van Cliburn discovered during a late-night practice session before a concert in
Philadelphia? That piano so captivated him that he offered to buy
it then and there. Steinway told him to wait—it was booked for at
least nine months. He waited, and took it home in February 1990.

Will K0862 be good enough for a place in Steinway's stable
of concert pianos, the three hundred or so instruments that dom-
inate the nation's concert stages and recording studios? Will it be
good enough to spend five years on a very fast track with a different rider every night?

$\maltese$

A Steinway's life begins far from center stage, in the gritty com-
plex of red-brick factory buildings that was laid out when Ulysses

S. Grant was president. The factory is dingy, just as it always was. At quitting time, the workers track sawdust home on their shoes, just as they always have. Many of the machines are older than the men who operate them—and most of the workers at Steinway *are* men. The factory floors are so worn that everyone has memorized where the dips are. If they open the grimy back windows, the workers can watch the airplanes taxi into position, nose to tail, at La Guardia Airport, on land that the Steinways once owned. A real estate ad would note that the factory has "partial rvr vus"—a narrow channel leading to the East River is just beyond the runways. Something a real estate ad would not mention is that New York City's largest jail is on an island a quarter of a mile from the shore.

The windows on the other side of the factory look toward Manhattan, a few miles away. Just inside those windows are the workbenches of the bellymen, called that because the only way to do their work is to climb inside a piano on their stomachs. The bellymen talk about how they watched the twin towers of the World Trade Center burn and collapse on the morning of the 9/11 attacks. The bellymen remember it as one of the few days when the world beyond their windows intruded on the timelessness of the factory.

In so many ways, the factory is a dusty leftover from the days before computers, televisions, even recordings—scratchy old 78s, not compact discs or MP3 downloads. It is nothing like the huge television soundstages that have filled the shells of old factories a few miles away, or the art galleries that have taken over other old industrial buildings. Nor is this the world of pristine white rooms and bright lights and smooth surfaces and the ultra-modern machinery that turns out computers. This plant remains rooted in a world that was. Old etchings combined this factory with a second Steinway plant a mile away, as if a composite image would be more impressive. The other factory has been turned into pricey condominium apartments.

The piano factory that still is a piano factory still has the shadowy old workrooms. And it still sends its products off to a life of white tie and tails in some of the swankiest concert halls in the world. The hands that will eventually touch K0862—the hands of the pianists who will play it—could not be more different from the hands that will build it and shape its character, its personality. These hands are calloused and chapped and cut, and there is dirt and grease under these fingernails—most of them, anyway. One worker, a woman, has half-inch-long painted nails.

These hands will shape, spray-paint, polish, and tune K0862, and then work on it some more. K0862's wooden parts will be aged in a room as dim as a wine cellar. Its 340-pound iron plate will be lowered in and lifted out ten or twelve times. It will spend long hours in rooms where workers wear oxygen masks to avoid getting headaches, or getting high, from smelly glues. It will be broken in by a machine that plays scales without complaint, unlike a student.

Someone walking through the factory, following a single piano as it takes shape, could forget a basic fact: Every Steinway is made the same way, from the same materials, by the same workers. Yet every Steinway ends up being different from every other—not in appearance, perhaps, but in ways that are not easily put into words: colorations of sound, nuances of strength or delicacy, what many pianists call—here's that word again—personality. Some Steinways end up sounding small and mellow, which is fine for chamber music. Some are so big and muscular and percussive that a full-strength orchestra cannot drown them out. On some, the keys move with little effort. On others, the pianist's hands and arms get a workout.

Why is one piano different from another? No one really knows.

In its first fifty years, Steinway made nearly one hundred thousand pianos (99,517 to be exact; No. 100,000, delivered to the White House in 1903, is now at the Smithsonian Institution). The next thirty-five years were Steinway's busiest. It made two hundred thousand pianos. No. 300,000, the Steinway that is still in the East Room, was delivered in 1938.

K0862 will be built the way those ancestors were built. The process is labor-intensive and has not changed much over the years. Nor has the design. Planned obsolescence is not a concept that came to the piano industry the way it came to the power-houses of the twentieth century that made cars and refrigerators and rubber boots. The wood in a piano does not rust or rot, and a sounding board can last seventy or eighty years, or maybe longer. There is very little to keep a piano from functioning long after it has been paid for, long after it has been passed on to the next generation, or the next. There are no annual model changes. The basic design of concert grands like K0862—their shape, their length, the layout of their strings—has gone unchanged since the 1890s. Steinway's newest model, a baby grand almost four feet shorter than K0862, has been on the market since the 1930s.

K0862 and the pianos next to it on the factory floor are products of one of the last outposts of hand craftsmanship in what was once a boomtown for piano makers. Steinway outlasted rivals like Sohmer and Weber, as well as apparel makers who turned to lower-wage factories in Asia and printers who turned to newer, automated plants in the South. Just by staying put, Stein-way became one of the last large manufacturing operations in New York City, which lost 666,400 factory jobs between 1962 and the end of 2002. Nowadays, the city's largest factories bake cookies and squirt soft drinks into cans and bottles that are made elsewhere, and Steinway is a relatively small concern in an industry dominated by foreign giants that can turn out as many pianos in a day as Steinway makes in a month. Some of Steinway's competitors also make everything from guitars to motorcycles to stereo com-ponents. But Steinway, for most of the twentieth century, remained focused on its pianos.

When the Steinway factory was new, barges loaded with raw lumber docked at the edge of the eleven-acre compound, and the company operated its own foundry to make the cast-iron plates it had patented. Anywhere but in New York City, a 440,000-square-foot factory like Steinway's would be horizontal, a sprawling single-story wonder. There would be no need to make appointments for the freight elevators to haul the pianos from floor to floor, as foremen do at Steinway. There might be mechanical booms to lower the cast-iron plate into the rim, instead of the heavily muscled arms and hand-cranked winches at Steinway. But this factory is a warren of interconnected structures, of bare fluorescent lights hanging from the ceiling, of workrooms where a mouse occasionally darts across the floor. It is a place where the day is paced according to the company's union contract, where workers sometimes spend their two fifteen-minute breaks napping on a storage shelf the size of a Ping-Pong table.

Once, the youngest workers were sent to a nearby bar on Friday afternoons to fetch buckets of beer. Fridays have been dry for years, but the timelessness of the factory remains. As Joe Gurrado, a foreman, says when showing off World War I–era photographs of Steinway workers, "The only thing you'd have to change is the clothing on those guys."

Over the years, the Steinways sold most of their land, and in 1972 they sold the company itself. But their name remains on Steinway Street, and the company wraps itself in its history. Its high-ceilinged showroom in Manhattan is filled with outsized paintings of the nineteenth-century matinee idol Ignace Jan Paderewski and busts of Franz Liszt and Sergei Rachmaninoff, and the company boasts that it produces "the instrument of the immortals." K0862 has a long way to go before it reaches the world beyond the factory, the world of concert stages, finicky impresarios, tantrum-throwing performers, dour critics, and perfection-minded tuners. This is its story.

PIANO

1

A Familiar Curve

March 11: Patrick Acosta and the team of rim-benders wrestle the maple case into shape.

Joe Gurrado pads across the cement floor, a big man in a big
room that smells of fresh lumber and just-made glue—caustic,
stinging glue that is all the more unpleasant for the lack of
ventilation. It is too early in the year to open the only windows,
near the ceiling, and let in the see-your-breath coldness of this
late-winter morning. For now, Gurrado is alone with the glue and
the hissing steam pipes in the too-warm basement of a gritty factory that opened soon after the Civil War. No one stands in front
of the battered workbenches that line the yellowish cinderblock
walls; tools have been set down and work has been left behind.
The men who set down those tools, Gurrado's men, are on their
midmorning break, gulping extra-strong coffee brewed in a silver
truck whose arrival is timed to the factory's schedule. It is 9:43
A.M. on Tuesday, March 11, 2003. "Two minutes to blast-off,"
Gurrado says.

Nothing could be more at odds with what is coming than
slang from the space age. What is coming is an old-fashioned contest between a giant sandwich of wood—seventeen glued strips
of maple, each a foot tall, an eighth of an inch thick, and about
half as long as a city bus—and half a dozen workers with muscles,
a pneumatic wrench, and Gurrado, their time-conscious foreman. The workers are supposed to bend and shove the seventeen
strips into a familiar-looking shape with two curves and a long
straightaway. It is a ritual of the early industrial age that is acted
out in this room several times a day, a ritual of pushing and
pulling and flexing and grunting that another boss calls "the Fred
Flintstone part of the operation." There is always a moment when
the wood seems to be winning this first round in building a piano:
the bending of the rim, the long, curved piece of wood that will
eventually hold the sounding board and thousands of smaller
parts—hammers, strings, pins, bridges.

Their orders for this day call for eight rims—one for a baby grand, four for "living room" grands, two for longer grands that usually go to music schools or recording studios or homes with larger-than-average rooms (and budgets), and one concert grand. Gurrado has learned to pay attention to the order list—the "load report," as the document, prepared on a front-office computer with a spreadsheet program, is known. He has learned not to assume that today's load report will be the same as yesterday's. Some days, for reasons that the schedulers in the front office do not explain, the load report calls for what business school types call a different product mix, and Gurrado's men bend more baby-grand rims and fewer long ones. But one item on the list never changes, and Gurrado's day is built around that constant. One concert-grand rim will be called for—one and only one. Gurrado's workroom has the equipment to bend rims for several small grands in a day, but only one concert grand.

Gurrado inherited the timetable, just as he inherited everything else in his domain. Once a showpiece of innovation, this room is now something of a time capsule for manufacturing methods that other industries left behind in the rush to automation. Bending a concert-grand rim at 9:45 is a long-established routine. Even the factory's one elevator is involved. Gurrado's men must carry the makings of the rim—the seventeen strips—from where the wood is cut and stored on the first floor to the basement workroom. John Miller, who operates the gray-walled behemoth of an elevator, wider and deeper than many a New York apartment, has a standing appointment with Gurrado's men. When the back-to-work bell sounds after the coffee break—actually an electronic tone, slightly more subdued than the wail of a smoke detector—Miller is waiting.

Gurrado's load report shows that the concert grand his men are to begin this morning will be known as No. K0862. Many of the steps that will follow as K0862 advances will involve small parts and the tedium of seeing that they operate smoothly—and of making small, subtle adjustments when they do not. A rim is not small or subtle. "It's a big wooden thing like an ark," Gurrado says. But it is supposed to be a very precise wooden thing. Gurrado's job is to see that it is.

In a company once legendary for its "lifers," he is a new kind of middle manager. When Steinway hired him in 2000, he had no experience in woodworking but fifteen years of manufacturing everything from leather goods to lemonade. He replaced a foreman who retired after forty-one years of making rims. Gurrado, who is in his early fifties and whose hair is going from black to steel gray, stepped into one of the factory's toughest jobs. As a foreman, he is a frontline manager. The workers have their union. Upper-level managers can insulate themselves from the day-to-day problems. The foremen cannot. The foremen are responsible when their men fall behind because someone called in sick, because a machine broke down, because someone misread a specification. They are responsible when they do not set an example by wearing safety glasses ("My eyelashes are too long" was the excuse of a foreman whom Steinway later fired) or when they take their men to lunch. Steinway frowns even more on foremen who take half their men to lunch (especially if they happen to return to work a few minutes late). All that upper-level managers will say about a foreman they have fired is something as vague as "It just didn't work out." A sentence like that hints at the camaraderie at the factory, the closeness of the workers and the foremen and the plant managers. The foremen are the ones who must "feed the next guy," as Gurrado puts it—to provide the foreman in the next department with whatever the schedule calls for. For Gurrado, that means rims ready to have their rough edges sliced off.

Gurrado is eager to show how much he has absorbed as the foreman with the least time on the payroll. It is no coincidence that among the factory's twelve foremen, he is the only one who regularly wears polo shirts with "Steinway & Sons" stitched above his heart. He is aware that he is probably still seen as a newcomer and may be resented for being on a fast track to some higher job. He has mastered the lingo and probably the details. If one of his men does not show up in the morning, he could step in and do the job without missing a beat. His we're-in-this-together attitude conveys the pressures he feels. This may not be rocket science, he seems to say, but neither is it easy. There is an art to bending these rims, to knowing just how much glue to spread on the wood, to finding the almost imperceptible dips in the surface of the maple where an extra touch is needed to force the strips into an almost-90-degree turn at the far end.

Gurrado is built like a brawler but is in fact the kind of boss who would like to be liked, not the kind whose first response to a worker's foul-up is to lose his temper. He speaks Spanish passably, which helps some of his men understand his commands. In English, he pronounces the word "length," a staple in the vocabulary of someone whose job is to give orders for measuring and trimming, without the *k* sound. The way he says it, it rhymes with "plinth."

Gurrado lives about five miles from the factory, on the block on which he grew up in Sunnyside, Queens, a working-class neighborhood with huge rail yards that funnel commuter trains toward Manhattan. His father was a machinist with the New York City Transit Authority, working on the axle-and-wheel mechanisms on subway cars. Gurrado was an assistant manager for a clothing maker in the garment district in Manhattan and then a supervisor in a sugar refinery, where a powerful union had won what it considered an important concession in a round-the-clock operation: No one worked the same shift two weeks in a row. If you had day hours this week, you would work the overnight shift next week and the 4 P.M.–to–midnight shift the week after. Gurrado found that the constant rotation wore him out. He also felt it lowered morale at the factory. He started casting about for another job.

A headhunter he knew tipped him off that Steinway was looking for someone with supervisory experience. The head-hunter figured Gurrado would jump at the short commute. "I said, 'But I don't know anything about a piano. They wouldn't hire me,' " Gurrado recalls. "He said, 'Don't be so sure.' He had more experience in placing people and he knew that quite often, they're not looking for specific knowledge in their business because they have to teach you that. They're looking for a certain background that they could utilize, develop."

Steinway hired him and assigned him to various supervisory projects that exposed him to the different parts of the factory. "They really didn't have any openings to run departments, but they knew that in the near future they would, because they had older people working there and they knew that they were going to retire," he says. After two years, when the longtime foreman in rim-bending put in his papers, Gurrado took over.

It is somehow fitting that Gurrado, the newcomer, ended up in rim-bending, a department that was once dominated by Italians. By the 1980s, Caribbean immigrants had begun taking the Italians' places. In the 1990s, the labor pool changed again. Gurrado's crew includes three Bosnians. One of them, Nazif Sutrovic, was a police official in Sarajevo during the 1984 Winter Olympics. His English is balky, so when he jokes that he used to put people in jail, the punch line falls flat. His explanation for his trouble with English is embarrassed but impeccably worded: "I don't have time to go to school." He has another job, as the superintendent of a Brooklyn apartment building. The crew chief, Eric Lall, who is Gurrado's No. 2 man, was hired in 1992 after working as a shipping supervisor in a jewelry store. And Tommy Stavrianos—at twenty-eight, the youngest man on the crew—talks proudly of the pianos he makes and of the company's traditions. But Gurrado and his men are not the concert-hall regulars that their pianos are. The radios around the factory play soft rock and jazz.

᪣

Gurrado's load report shows that K0862 will have what Steinway calls an ebonized finish, meaning that it will be lacquered black and will look like concert grands that took shape a generation ago, or before World War II, or before World War I. The guts of K0862—the strings, the hammers that strike them, the keys to which the hammers are attached—will be made according to plans and specifications that date to the 1880s and 1890s. But is a brand-new piano ready the moment it leaves the factory?

In the 1920s, a golden age for Steinway, there were probably pianists and tuners who complained that the best pianos were those made at the end of the nineteenth century. Some pianists today have a fondness for Steinways from the 1920s. But as for what comes out of the factory these days, the company's president, Bruce A. Stevens, is adamant that "older is not better, and we can prove it." Sitting behind his big desk in the factory's corner office, Stevens declares, "Where that started was with people who make their living rebuilding Steinways, and they tell their customers that. We've just about given up rebutting it." But not completely. A moment later, he is still in full rebuttal mode, spitting out words like "poppycock." His frustration continues to boil, but he seems to be reining himself in because he is talking to an outsider whose tape recorder is sitting on his desk, taking in every word.

Steinway has done some modernizing over the decades. Computer-generated bar codes now track the parts of a piano in the making. For years, starting just after World War II, that was done on paper, and when problems arose at the factory, Henry Z. Steinway, the great-grandson of the company's founder, had the final say. The rank and file respected him for more than his name, his patrician bearing, or his Harvard degree. He understood the old manufacturing methods. Since childhood, he had heard about nothing else.

Henry Z. Steinway retired in 1980, and machines now cut the wood for the lids and legs, operations that were done by hand in his day. "This is furniture making," says Andrew Horbachevsky, who, as a manufacturing director, oversees foremen like Gurrado. But Henry Z. Steinway would recognize much of

what goes on at the factory. "There are operations we can't auto-
mate," Horbachevsky says. "That would take the soul out of
Steinway." One of those operations, rim-bending, is the one that
Gurrado took over in 2002. It has gone unchanged for so long
because the piano has gone unchanged for so long.

Steinway's earliest grands did not have rigid rims. Steinway
made hundreds of pianos before it perfected the design of the rim
that will go into K0862, as well as the techniques for making it.
One of the Steinway sons, C. F. Theodore, held more than forty
patents and was friendly with the pioneering physicist Hermann
von Helmholtz. In marrying the methodology of science to the
making of pianos, they reasoned that longer and stronger strings
would produce a larger and louder sound. But it would also put
extreme pressure on the rim.

C. F. Theodore Steinway's solution is Gurrado's day-in, day-
out responsibility: the lamination of rims. Gluing thin strips of
wood together creates a better rim than one made from just one
or two thick boards, because even the glue adds strength. Such a
rim is so strong, Gurrado says, that if you karate-chop two strips
that have been glued together, the break will come in the wood;
the glue joint will hold. Another Steinway relative, Theodore
Cassebeer, the factory manager after World War I, improved on
C. F. Theodore's handiwork. Until Cassebeer tinkered with it,
rim-bending had been a two-part process involving separate inner and outer rims. Steinway built the nine boards for the inner
rim first, using less expensive poplar. The soundboard was glued
to that rim; the heavy metal plate was bolted onto it; the strings
and the keys were squeezed inside. Only later did the rim-
benders fit the eight boards of the outer rim around the piano. If
they bent both rims at once, the inner rim cracked. It turned out
that would not happen if they used maple instead of poplar on
the inner rim, the same as on the outer rim. The savings in labor
easily offset the higher cost of the maple.

Laminating the rim was one of the innovations that made
possible an instrument with a big sound, the grand piano on

which Steinway built its reputation. Still, the rim is only the structural framework for the piano. It does not contribute to a big-sounding piano's greatness, or to a lemon's disappointment. The rim is a big, inanimate backstop. The most the rim has to do with the sound is to return "airflow"—the sound waves themselves—to the sounding board for more amplification. Yet that does not give rim-benders license to be sloppy. A rim, Gurrado says, must meet close tolerances. "It has to," he says, "because the parts that are going to fit in it down the road all have to fit in exactly. I mean, being that it's mostly a handmade instrument, each part is finessed. But it's finessed to a specification. It's not just 'We'll make it fit by cutting off an inch,' no."

※

The strips that go into Joe Gurrado's rims are maple—hard-rock maple, though that is a term that you will never hear from a forester. The attributes a piano builder will mention are strength and evenness, and maybe cost. "You wouldn't build it out of walnut or cherry," Gurrado says. Walnut is almost as hard as maple, but far more expensive, and it has gnarly, swirling grain patterns that make bending difficult. Cherry has a more serious shortcoming: "gum pockets," which are exactly what the term suggests, could cause weak spots in a rim.

Maple has another advantage for a factory in the Northeast: It does not come from far away, so the cost of delivering it to the factory is fairly low. The wood that is being bent into the rim of K0862 came from old-source maple trees in New Hampshire. New York piano makers have relied on the maple forests of New Hampshire and Vermont for generations. In eleven months, when K0862 is ready to leave the factory, loggers will have moved into the Adirondacks of New York State, and Steinway will buy maple from suppliers there and in Canada.

Wherever they come from, the long logs have to be milled into boards—"remanufactured," in lumber-trade lingo. For the wood in K0862, a Connecticut mill does the work. A heavily loaded eighteen-wheeler makes the trip from there to the Steinway factory in three or four hours, unless traffic is snarled on Interstate 95 or the Triborough Bridge.

The wood is not dropped off inside the factory. Out beyond the workers' parking lot is New York City's most elite lumberyard, a temporary home to millions of dollars' worth of wood. Some of it is earmarked for sounding boards, some for lids, and some for wrestplanks, the thick chunks of laminated wood (also known as pin blocks) that hold the pins that tuners twist to bring a note up to its pitch or take it down. "We have a little bit of everything," manufacturing director Andy Horbachevsky says, walking between piles of boards twelve to fifteen feet tall as workers restack them and put spacers, called "stickers," between the layers to allow air to circulate. The spacers guard against warping. The airflow helps the boards dry out.

Gurrado's rim maple goes into a hangarlike building that Horbachevsky calls "the white elephant." It is, in fact, the grayish white of concrete, and it is tall and wide and cavernous, big enough to hold an airplane. On the rolled-up maps that the security guards check when an alarm goes off, it is Building 88.

It holds enough wood to keep the factory well supplied for months, but most of the wood in Building 88 will not end up in pianos—it is not good enough. "We buy a high grade of lumber to start with," Horbachevsky explains, and still "there are defects." In fact, Steinway scraps at least half of what comes in. A great deal of wood looks good on the outside but falls short of Steinway's standards once it is sawed or planed. As Horbachevsky puts it, "We're not Superman. We don't have X-ray vision. We think it's O.K. until we get inside."

Gurrado's maple will be machined and planed and sanded. It began as a stately, round-headed tree, with what botanists call palmate leaves, that grew to be 100 to 120 feet tall. The same numbers, in years, tell its age. From the Roaring Twenties through World War II and the Cold War, it was probably tapped for maple syrup—a couple of gallons a month in its prime. Gurrado will find out soon enough where the spigots were. He will find out, too, if it was dinged by bullets from a hunter's poorly aimed rifle.

Officially, Gurrado's boss is the man who buys Steinway's wood, Warren Albrecht. Like Gurrado, he is in his early fifties, but he favors Ralph Lauren button-down Oxford shirts and antiqued penny loafers. Unlike Gurrado, he has spent most of his career at Steinway. In 1975, when he graduated from the University of Massachusetts with a degree in wood science, he was hired as the company's wood technologist. He left after a couple of years for a job with a guitar maker that was "less stratified" than Steinway, meaning that he expected the promotions to come faster. But he missed Steinway and soon returned. He has been a regular on the streets around the factory for years: the tall guy jogging at lunchtime. His hair still glows a sunny yellow blond, but bad knees have slowed his running.

At the factory, he is part commodities trader (though, unlike Wall Street types, he wants the commodity, not the profit from selling futures), part botanist, and part shop teacher. Every month, he buys sixty thousand board feet of lumber for rims. He dreads the charts and small-print tables in *Hardwood Market Report,* a newsletter that tracks the prices of the wood he needs. "Almost every week," he says, "there's a ten- to twenty-dollar-per-thousand-board-feet increase on maple because it's so popular. In household furniture, especially kitchens, light woods are the trend."

For all his anxiousness about price fluctuations, Albrecht is competing against more than the cabinetmakers who cater to real estate developers and Home Depot habitués. Maple is in demand for schoolchildren's desks, rock bands' drumsticks, and bowling pins and lanes. It was good news for Albrecht when Japan's interest in bowling waned and the rush to build alleys slowed. Around the time he arrived at Steinway, "all the maple—the good maple—was going to Japan. The price just skyrocketed."

Soon after Albrecht bought the maple that went into K0862, the price fell, and then rebounded. He paid $2.25 for a board foot at the beginning of 2002, when he was buying the wood for K0862 and the other pianos that would be built in 2003. In the following two years the price sank to $2.03, and then in early 2005 it surged again, to $2.60. Albrecht pays the prevailing price when he needs the wood. Sometimes he manages to negotiate long-term contracts with the wholesalers he deals with, locking in prices for six or eight months. "My rationale to the suppliers is, 'Hey, listen, we've been doing this year after year, we're very steady, you know exactly what we want, you can plan for it, I can plan for it,'" he says. "To me, it's almost like a game, but I like it."

The competition for maple is not the only issue. Albrecht knows what environmentalists know: The maple for K0862 is younger than the maple that typically arrived at the factory when he started at Steinway in 1975. He also knows why that is: Loggers are cutting trees sooner than they once did. The reason is not deforestation—the forests of the Northeast still have plenty of older maples. "It's the ease of trying to get in to log the trees," he says. "For the real huge, big trees, you've got to go way deep into the forest, and the cost involved in getting there is just prohibitive." The fact that loggers are cutting down younger trees has an effect on the rims that pianists never see. The younger trees yield shorter boards, so Gurrado's men must glue boards together to create strips long enough for a rim.

Fortunately for K0862, just as Bruce Stevens believes that an older piano is not a better piano, Albrecht believes that older wood is not better wood. Think of a log as a doughnut. The oldest part of the tree, the heartwood, is the hole, and Albrecht has no interest in it. "This is the dying portion," he says, before correcting himself. "I shouldn't say it's the dying portion—it's the dead portion." Wood from close to the center of the tree is more likely to crack if bent into a rim.

Albrecht is looking for the outer ring of wood, the sapwood—the part of the tree that is just forty to eighty years old. It contains more moisture than the heartwood, making it more flexible. It also looks healthier. "You want to get that nice white color," Albrecht says. "The whiter the color, the better the tree. That's what we're after. People think we're nuts because we use all this white maple, even though you can't see it inside a rim. But you want to make sure every lamination is not just strong and doesn't have defects. *Uniformity* is very important."

Mostly, the texture of the grain in maple is exactly what Albrecht wants—smooth, tight, and uniform—compared with, say, a porous wood like oak. Maple grows rapidly, so it has fewer of the little branches that cause wavy patterns in wood. And straight-grain wood is easier to bend than wavy-grain wood. Violin makers, too, want maple for the backs of their instruments, which, like Gurrado's rims, are not supposed to vibrate. But then Stradivari and Guarneri and the other craftsmen of seventeenth-century Italy prized undulations in the grain and even knotholes. Stradivari made instrument after instrument with unusual markings—the 1701 Stradivarius known as the "Dushkin" is famous for its noticeable knot. If that piece of wood had arrived at Steinway, it would have faced an assault from saws and planers and still might have ended up in the reject bin.

Between its time in Building 88 and its arrival in Gurrado's rim-bending room, a stack of maple spends a week or two stored on the first floor of the main factory. For the first few days, the wood just sits there, adjusting to the temperature and humidity indoors. Then each board in the pile gets a makeover: It is trimmed to the size of a rim.

One of Gurrado's men, Norman Shiwprasad, is the first to lay his hands on each batch of new boards. Shiwprasad's job is like assembling a jigsaw puzzle. He combines the shorter boards into the longer lengths needed for a rim, and glues them together. "The trick is to try to get as much yield out of the lumber as we can by putting the whole puzzle together in a smart way," Gurrado explains, "because when a stack of lumber comes in, you want to be able to use as much good lumber out of it as you can, and waste as little as you have to." In this way, Shiwprasad creates the twenty-two-foot-long strips that form a "book," as the sandwich of wood that becomes a rim is known at the factory.

※

An auto factory can make several hundred cars in an eight-hour shift. Steinway, which takes nearly a year to finish one piano, can ship ten in a day. But Gurrado, more than the other foremen, feels the drumbeat of the factory, the relentless pressure to keep up the pace. Time seems to matter less in other parts of the Steinway plant than it does in the rim-bending room. In other parts of the factory, if something doesn't work right or sound good, a tuner or a tone regulator can take a few extra minutes or even a whole day to figure out the trouble.

Gurrado and his men do not have that luxury. The rim is the chassis of the piano, the one basic item the rest of the factory cannot live without. Gurrado knows that after the rim is bent, the sounding board will be glued in, the tuning pins hammered in, and the cast-iron plate bolted in. Through all this, the rim must hold its shape. Gurrado's predecessor, the rim-bending foreman from the 1960s until he retired in 2001, could count on his fingers the number of rims he had "lost"—the ones that had popped out of shape. During that man's career, Steinway made 125,000 pianos.

If Gurrado and his men do not deliver the rims that the load report demands, he cannot make excuses. He cannot fudge. He cannot stay into the night, long after his men have knocked off, and redo what they messed up. Nor can he let things slip out of control, like Mickey Mouse in the "Sorcerer's Apprentice" segment of *Fantasia*. He is careful not to communicate the pressure he feels in the words he speaks. He cannot afford to. "We're allotted twenty minutes," is all he says.

On the way to what some Steinway workers call the rim-bending "machine"—a piano-shaped vise perfected by C.F. Theodore Steinway that has no motor—Gurrado's crew picks up the "book" on the first floor and marches into John Miller's elevator. The crew trundles out with the long strips of maple after the ride to the basement. As each man passes by, Miller delivers what is perhaps best described as a medium-five, a slap on the hand at waist level. It is his contribution to the rim-bending ritual. He learned long ago that it is hard for a rim-bender to reach for a high-five with a four-hundred-pound book tucked under his other arm.

Miller's elevator fills one wall of the rim-bending room, so the men do not have far to go. The first stop is in the middle of the room, at a glue spreader that looks something like an old-fashioned washer with a wringer. The crew feeds in the book, layer by layer. Each lamination rolls out with a coating of glue, thin, shiny, and yellowish. At the far end, two of the men, Tommy Stavrianos and Jean Robert Laguerre, dip brushes in glue pots for touch-ups. "There is only one speed on the gluing operation—fast," Gurrado explains. "You don't want to waste any time. The glue starts to set up. If they took this slow and stood around and talked, the glue would dry." He is the only one in the room talking.

The big moment, the rim-bender's version of a barn raising for K0862, takes place at 9:54 A.M., nine minutes after the crew has started its work on it. Gurrado seems to hit a reset button in his head, zeroing the stopwatch he hears ticking as surely as if he were the director on *60 Minutes*. This is the count that counts.

Having aligned the eighteen laminations on a long table beside the glue spreader, the crew picks up the book again and heads across the room, to the far corner. There, the men lift it stomach-high, to the level of the press. Gurrado looks over the men's shoulders as the crew leader, Eric Lall, begins shoving the book into place along the side of the piano where the keys for the bass notes will be. Another worker, Joe Petruso, hammers the top, to see that each lamination drops into the press. Lall begins setting the clamps, called posts, each with two spindles that must be tightened, that will hold the rim in place on the press. The posts are numbered, but there are two marked No. 9. Perhaps, Gurrado says from the sidelines, the second was once a spare that had to be called into service. The odd-numbered posts are on what will be the piano's treble side, the evens on the bass.

Gurrado's face shows a hint of a smile. He knows what an outsider must think at this stage: This is nothing but a bunch of strong guys in T-shirts swarming over an oddly shaped green metal table. "It's very well choreographed, choreographed better, maybe, than it looks," he explains. "The steps they're taking are well planned. If you really watch it multiple times, you'll see that it isn't haphazard. Each guy knew he'd hand the wrench with his right hand to the next guy, and he'd take it and tighten the screw two turns and move to his left. It wasn't like one decided, 'I'll do it this way today,' different from yesterday. It's like a basketball team or a football team making a play, a specific play, where one goes to the left and one goes to the right and out thirty yards, and this one throws it and that one catches it—done. Even the tools were pre–laid out in and around the press. They didn't have to go, 'Hey, John, hand me that wrench from the other side.' "

Lall tightens spindles on the clamps while another crew member, Patrick Acosta, uses a long-handled lever to force the rest of the book toward the big curve at the end. Acosta says this is all the exercise he gets, or needs: "I build pianos. That's my workout." The lever in his hands weighs eighty pounds. The clamps are sixty-five pounds each, and bigger than tire irons.

The rim-benders use their physical strength in a way that is unusual in most modern factories, where machines do the hard work. Warren Albrecht says a first-rate rim-bender must bring more to the job than brute strength: "You've got to pay attention to detail," he says. A rim-bender must be careful, say, not to tighten the posts too much. Albrecht remembers when Steinway had a seven-foot-six-inch rim-bender, a man as tall as Yao Ming, the Chinese-born center for the Houston Rockets basketball team. "We had to take him off the job," Albrecht says; the man was so strong that he overtightened any post he touched. The risk was an uneven, almost bumpy rim. Gurrado tests rims by running his palm over the surface. He does not want to feel peaks and valleys.

Acosta struggles to bring the rim around the curve at the far end. "The hardest part of the piano is to make these turns," he says between grunts, "and you have to do it quick." He breathes heavily. He is covered in sweat, and the rim is not half done. As he makes the turn, some glue is squeezed out and lands on the cement floor. It has taken on the brownish color of peanut butter, but Horbachevsky warns that when it hardens, it will be neither creamy nor crunchy but knife-sharp. On the floor, it forms a small dome.

It is 9:59. "They should have it done in ten minutes," Gurrado says. "I'm hoping." As his men work their way around the rim, Gurrado delivers a running commentary, all but whispering the obvious, like an announcer on a golf-tournament telecast: "They're done with the tail section . . . moving on to the treble . . . the wood's resisting more." Camil Katana trails behind Lall and Acosta, tightening the spindles on the clamps with the pneumatic wrench. The tool makes quick bursts of noise, like an auto mechanic changing a tire. The pressure setting is 450 pounds per square inch—exactly, Horbachevsky says, what is called for. Gurrado continues his patter, explaining that "as it curves, the lumber's really starting to resist." He pauses. "This operation has gone unchanged since 1875," he adds. "What you see today is what you'd have seen then—except for the pneumatic wrench."

Another time check. It is 10:02. Eight minutes. "I was hoping for twelve," he says. "The faster the better."

At the twelve-minute mark—10:06—only Petruso, in his protective eyeglasses, is still standing over the rim press. The others on the crew have drifted off to prepare for the next rim. Petruso, who has taken over the pneumatic wrench, finally puts it down at 10:10 and walks away. Gurrado is happy. "Fourteen wins," he says. No one notices that he is off by two minutes: The rim for K0862 took sixteen minutes to bend.

The time allotted for bending a rim is twenty to twenty-five minutes. As Gurrado explains, "That's not company time, it's glue time. We're working against the glue." It begins to set that fast, which is why he was hoping to finish the job in only twelve minutes. "A lot of people ask me, When does a piano become a musical instrument? As far as I'm concerned, this is it." Not everyone in the factory agrees with him, but without him there would be no argument—there would be no instrument.

The rim spends its first twenty-four hours clamped in place in the rim-bending machine, because, as Gurrado puts it, "Wood has a memory." The day in the clamps is deprogramming time, so the wood will forget its past and not pop out of its new shape in a couple of months, a couple of years, or a couple of decades. "It doesn't like to move fast, it doesn't like moisture, it doesn't like moisture being taken out of it quickly or put into it quickly. It could warp, buckle, cup, split, crack. Those are the big things."

❧

Horbachevsky says that there are limits to automation, that too much mechanization would erode what makes Steinway special. But there are moments when someone watching the process has to wonder if machines would not do some jobs better. Numbering, for example. Every piano leaves with a serial number that continues a sequence that began in 1853. But every piano begins life with a different number, a case number—K0862, in this instance—that is inscribed on each of the piano's major parts, starting with the rim. In a tradition-conscious company like Steinway, numbering matters. But Gurrado gets the number wrong.

It happens just before the coffee break the next morning. Gurrado's men wrestle the rim off the press and onto a hand truck. They wheel it across the workroom floor, where they are supposed to hammer the number into the inner rim. The crew chief, Eric Lall, who does the hammering, pounds in the number Gurrado gives him: K0863. The wrong number.

Someone notices, and soon Lall is hammering in a second number, the right number. Then the crew upends the rim, and there it sits, its big curve higher than anything else in the room. Gurrado does not want to shock it by moving it out of its by-now-familiar environment too quickly.

After three days, the junior member of the crew, Tommy Stavrianos, pushes the rim into Miller's elevator. Its destination is a hot, dry room that looks a bit like a wine cellar, a room that is a temporary home to five hundred other rims that are awaiting sounding boards, cast-iron plates, and keys. "Five hundred rims sitting there doing nothing," Gurrado says.

The rim-conditioning room, as Steinway calls this place, is divided by fat structural columns like those in a parking garage, and as in a parking garage, each section has a location number. But the rim-conditioning room has a network of steam lines stretching across the ceiling, with valves that come to life with a clunk and a hiss when a sensor determines that the air is too dry. Steinway wants the moisture in the rims to evaporate, but not too fast. K0862 will spend two months in this room, standing on an iron bar that has been nailed between its two arms.

Stavrianos parks it in its assigned spot and turns out the light as he leaves. "It's going to be whatever it's going to be, good or whatever," Stavrianos says. "There's nothing you can do now but wait. It's out of our hands."

2

⸺ᨖ⸺

An Elderly Mechanic

The founder: Heinrich Engelhard Steinway, photographed by Mathew Brady

S teinway's earliest pianos were, in the words of a *New York Times* reporter, the work of "an elderly mechanic . . . and his three sons." Some of the essential elements of a modern piano like K0862 were already under the lids of the Steinways' little "squares"—rectangular instruments designed for Victorian parlors. More improvements would follow, refinements that have been passed down ever since. The mechanism that will make the keys on K0862 responsive to a pianist's touch was perfected by one of the sons, who was also responsible for the layout of the strings inside, a layout that was patented. One of his brothers worked out the mechanism for one of the piano's pedals.

The "elderly mechanic," who was all of fifty-six when Steinway & Sons was organized on a handshake, would live long enough to be photographed not once but twice in the studio of Mathew B. Brady, America's first celebrity photographer. Brady's own fame came from lugging his cumbersome camera behind Union lines in the Civil War, but he had made a fortune before the war doing portraits of the rich and famous—presidents, merchant princes, singers, everyone from Clara Barton to P. T. Barnum.

One of Brady's Steinway photographs was special; it was made a new way. Brady had built his reputation on daguerreotypes, a process that involved exposing a copper plate treated with chemicals that made it sensitive to light, but around 1856, Brady switched to glass plates. Now he could capture more detail, more nuances. He could also make his photographs larger— half the size of a newspaper page—and he hired artists to retouch the negatives and color the prints. The result was an image that looks like the work of a portrait painter—indeed, one book about the Steinways that reprinted the portrait described it as an oil by an unknown artist. And no wonder. The subject's hands were retouched so heavily that the brushstrokes show.

Brady's second photograph is smaller, less fancy, and un-retouched. Yet it caught something that the first one did not. It shows the same man holding the same walking stick. Now he is standing, not sitting in a studio chair. He has thick sideburns and wire-rimmed glasses, and this time he wears his bowler hat. He cannot have been comfortable, standing there as the minutes ticked away with a metal stand pressing against the back of his neck—"the immobilizer," Brady called it. It kept Brady's subjects still during the long exposures.

This time, Brady's subject has planted his feet on the patterned floor of Brady's studio. He has locked his hips. He looks impatient—he has better things to do than to waste his time like this. He knows who he has become, and how improbable his life has been.

❧

The man in the two photographs, Heinrich Engelhard Steinweg, would have been unusual even if he had not discovered pianos. As a child during the Napoleonic Wars, he survived a winter that killed his mother and several brothers in a cavelike mountain hideout. They were on the run because Napoleon was pushing through their stretch of northwestern Germany—territory Napoleon was assembling as Westphalia—and his father was fighting with the opposition army.

Many Westphalians had high hopes for life under Napoleonic rule, but for Heinrich, there were only more traumas. In 1812, three years after the grim winter in the mountains, lightning struck Heinrich's father, three other brothers, and a couple of workers from the family's charcoal business. Heinrich himself, who was nearby, was knocked unconscious. But he survived that catastrophe, too. A biographical sketch from 1895 says he fled barefoot and ran to a village where he knew a doctor lived. It was too late. When help arrived, his relatives and the others were all dead.

Young Heinrich Engelhard became the bugler with the Duke of Brunswick's garrison, and did more than annoy sleepy-headed army buddies with reveille. He won a medal at the Battle of Waterloo, or so family legend has it.

Honorably discharged after declining a promotion to sergeant, Heinrich Engelhard wanted to be a furniture maker when he mustered out, but he apparently balked at the idea of a long apprenticeship. At twenty-one he was too old or too impatient to put in the decade of training that would lead to admission to the furniture makers' guild. He tried building pipe organs, a specialty not controlled by a guild. He bounced from town to town. In 1825, he arrived in Seesen, population three thousand.

It was the right moment to be a newcomer there. Much of the town had been leveled by a fire, and the need to rebuild had loosened the guilds' stranglehold on craftsmen's jobs. Heinrich Engelhard caught the eye of a well-connected judge. Actually, what caught the judge's eye was a writing desk Heinrich Engelhard had built—Steinweg's "masterpiece," as the writer Elbert Hubbard described it in 1911 in an article that drew on Steinway family stories.

Soon Heinrich Engelhard had a wife to support and a son. Heinrich Engelhard married up: his bride, Julianne Theimer, was the daughter of a glove maker, and she was pregnant. The son she delivered only six months after the wedding grew up wanting the details of his parents' situation blurred. As an adult, he petitioned Seesen's municipal record keepers to change not the date of his birth, but the date of his parents' marriage.

The bridegroom's interest in musical instruments led him to combine keyboard mechanisms with elements of the guitarlike stringed instruments he had apparently taught himself to make in the army. The historian Richard K. Lieberman maintains that Heinrich Engelhard learned the basics of pianoforte building by copying an instrument that belonged to Karl Brand, the Seesen cantor's son. A biographical sketch written years later by one of

Heinrich Engelhard's sons did not mention Brand, but said that Heinrich Engelhard had been "familiar with the construction of the old English and new German pianos." It did not explain how he came by his familiarity, and Seesen was something of a backwater. Had he traveled long distances to examine pianofortes, the way Bach had walked miles to attend a performance by Vivaldi? Was Heinrich Engelhard so talented with tools that he could replicate what he had seen, the way Bach could replicate what he had heard?

Family lore has it that he worked on his first pianoforte in his spare time, in the kitchen of the family house. What happened to that instrument is a mystery. For years, the company displayed in New York what it said was the kitchen piano—a grand with a Biedermeier look, the unostentatious look of the German middle class from the mid-nineteenth century. But Henry Z. Steinway, a great-grandson of Heinrich Engelhard's, maintained that that grand could not have been the kitchen piano. (He suggested in 2005 that a cousin, Theodore Cassebeer, had discovered it while vacationing in Germany in 1933. "It was the bottom of the Depression," Henry Z. Steinway said, "and this piano was seized on for publicity.")

No one can say exactly how Heinrich Engelhard Steinweg's pianos developed—how he improved on the one he made the previous month, and how the previous month's piano incorporated all the improvements from earlier ones. He kept no known records. Unlike the inventor of the piano, Bartolomeo Cristofori, he was not immortalized in an enthusiastic write-up by an influential journalist, and unlike violin dealers, latter-day pianists do not pay much attention to the tool marks in the wood. Unlike violinists, pianists see the golden age of piano building as only a couple of generations ago, not a couple of centuries, and don't prize the earliest pianos except as historical oddities.

When Heinrich Engelhard started building the kitchen piano, he was betting on a machine that had yet to catch on. This pianoforte carrying the label "H.E. Steinweg, instrumenten-macher. Seesen" won a prize at a state fair in 1839. Steinweg had entered two squares and a grand; it was the grand that attracted attention. "Musicians came from distant cities to see and hear this wonderful musical instrument," Hubbard wrote. "The tin-kle, tinkle, tin-pan tones of the harpsichord were gone. Here was full, clear, vibrant expression." (That was probably an overstate-ment. As later and more scholarly Steinway biographers have pointed out, he is not known to have heard the 1839 piano, and if it had been everything he said it was, Heinrich Engelhard would not have had to wait nearly twenty years to become famous.) As with the kitchen piano, what happened to that piano is a mystery. One story, repeated in the German magazine *Mitteilungen* in the 1930s, is that Duke Wilhelm of Braunschweig bought it "at an unusually high price." But *Mitteilungen* later noted that the or-ganizers of the fair bought the prizewinning pianoforte them-selves and raffled it off, with the winning bid coming from a cloth maker from Braunschweig.

Exactly how many pianofortes Heinrich Engelhard fin-ished in Seesen will probably never be known. The conven-tional estimate is nearly five hundred, because the first Steinway made in America (or listed in the Steinway & Sons order book, anyway) was assigned No. 483, supposedly continuing the se-quence begun in Seesen. Heinrich Engelhard's great-grandson Henry Z. Steinway cast doubt on that idea: "I think I invented this story," he declared in 2005 as he approached his ninetieth birthday. But the evidence, such as it is, suggests that someone else came up with the explanation before Henry Z. Steinway ever set foot in the factory. Nestled in his own files on the fam-ily and the company, a yellowed clipping from the nineteenth century mentions the 482 pianos that Steinweg had made in Germany.

As for No. 483, a different number probably mattered more when it was new: the price. It sold for five hundred dollars.

The Steinwegs left Seesen in 1850—all but one of them, and that one, Heinrich Engelhard's second son, Karl, had gone the year before, when he was twenty. He was the one who had to get out. For his activism during the ill-fated revolution of 1848, he risked being imprisoned or killed as Germany tilted to the right. Hubbard, probably drawing on stories that had been handed down in the Steinway family, mentions "one accusation to the effect that a certain young man was playing 'revolutionary music.'" Without explanation, Hubbard also declares, "Government spies were on the track of the Steinways." Hubbard credits Karl with reading Benjamin Franklin and Thomas Jefferson and with using the word *liberty* "a trifle more" than Germans were suddenly comfortable with.

If that was true, Heinrich Engelhard no doubt worried that the sins of the son could be visited on the father. As an entrepreneur, he had to believe there was an easier way to make a living than under the old feudal order. For someone ambitious enough to ship his products to the next province, or the one beyond that, Germany's patchwork of states and trade regulations meant headaches.

So Karl left Seesen on a scouting expedition. His mission was to establish a beachhead in the city that dominated the piano industry in the United States—New York. He wrote enthusiastic letters home, never mentioning New York's cholera epidemic, its rampant labor turmoil, or the noise and nastiness of daily life. D. W. Fostle, a Steinway biographer, notes that it probably wouldn't have mattered if Karl had panned the place. It took so long for mail to get from New York to Seesen that Heinrich Engelhard could not have seen more than a handful of letters before he booked passage on a steamship that was making its maiden voyage from Hamburg. Hubbard's melodramatic account credits the second child, Doretta, with overcoming the

family's doubts and sending word to Karl: "We are coming."
The parents and seven children made the trip—Doretta, Heinrich Jr., Wilhelmina, Wilhelm, Albrecht, Hermann, and Anna.
The oldest son, C. F. Theodore, who was married and not a
draft risk, stayed behind, but left Seesen, moving to a different
town. Hermann, who was twelve, did not join the piano business in New York and returned to Seesen a few years later, and
little Anna died young. Steinway & Sons grew so quickly that
everyone in New York was needed, to engineer and reengineer
pianos, build them in the factory, or market and sell them to the
public.

What awaited them was a city in the making, a city in
which new industrial wealth and old-money society were jammed
side by side into the same few square miles. More important to the
Steinwegs was the German city-within-the-city, the subculture
that gave Germans their own newspapers, their own theaters,
their own beer gardens, their own political associations, and their
own trusted labor pool. Between the time Karl arrived and the
beginning of the twentieth century, the German population in
New York surged to six hundred thousand, making New York
the world's third most populous German-speaking urban center
(after Berlin and Vienna). But New York's mainstream newspapers and churches disdained the Germans, "their penchant for
radical politics," and their beer halls. The historian Peter Conolly-
Smith suggests that anti-German prejudice fueled the temperance
movement.

Karl had landed a job as a tone regulator at Bacon & Raven,
which made the pianofortes favored by Stephen Foster, the largely
self-taught composer whose disarming songs had caught the nation's fancy. Heinrich Engelhard, Heinrich Jr., and Albert joined
Karl at the Bacon & Raven factory, which made pianos for the
middle class. Fourteen-year-old Wilhelm found work at the soon-
to-be-bankrupt William Nunns & Company, which aimed at
high-paying buyers. Wilhelm later explained that the family had
spread out to "familiarize themselves with the requirements and

tastes of the American musical community." But acceptance in that community was elusive. Arthur Loesser speculates that an anti-German wage scale persisted—the very thing that had touched off a strike fourteen years before the first of the Steinwegs landed. Indeed, in 1852, Heinrich Jr. wrote that Heinrich Engelhard was earning six dollars a week making sounding boards for "a German instrument maker," adding, "If he did the same work for an American, he could earn at least seven dollars, but since he knows not a word of English and will never learn it, he will never be able to work for an American." Working for an American apparently meant working hard. Heinrich Jr., who was taking home seven dollars a week, reported he could get a better-paying job, "but I don't feel like tuning all the time."

As in Germany, Heinrich Engelhard had a workshop at home. D. W. Fostle notes that a city directory soon listed "Henry Steinweg, Piano Manufacturer, 199 Hester St.," but what Steinway manufactured at first were parts for other piano makers. *The New York Times* observed in 1855 that by doing this between "intervals of labor" for established companies, the Steinways got "their start in life."

❧

Their start as Steinway & Sons went unnoticed, or at least unreported. There was nothing much in the New York papers on the first Saturday in March 1853, just the usual wrangling among politicians and the usual accidents in far-off places. A schooner sank, slowly, in Maryland. The crew scampered up the mast and were still holding tight when rescuers arrived; the cargo—a load of cotton—was long gone, swept out to sea. March 5, 1853, was the day on which Heinrich Engelhard and his sons Heinrich Jr. and Karl went into business together. But then there was no reason that their new partnership should have attracted attention beyond the insular world of immigrant woodworkers who made the instruments with the long Italian name that New Yorkers were already shortening to "piano."

The new partners guessed that business would be better if they anglicized the family name to Steinway. The sons changed their first names, too. Heinrich Jr. became Henry Jr., Karl became Charles, Wilhelm became William, and Albrecht became Albert. The father resisted adopting a new name just as he resisted learning a new language. He remained Heinrich Engelhard, and settled in as the master designer who worked out the scale of their models—the size of the pianos and the geometry of the strings and hammers inside. William glued in the sounding boards and handed the partly finished instruments to Charles for tuning. Henry Jr. polished the cases. As customers placed orders, the Steinways' cash flow surged, and so did their profits. Fostle calculates that if the Steinways had continued to work for other piano makers as foremen, they would have taken home perhaps a thousand dollars a year. As partners, they netted that much from forty pianos. In their first six years in business, they made a million dollars—an amount that would have taken a quartet of foremen 250 years to earn.

Simply by putting the whole family to work, Steinway & Sons appeared larger and better organized than its competitors. From the beginning, it was as big as the average manufacturing firm of that era, which had a payroll of eight or nine workers. The Steinways' New York rival Albert Weber had set up shop in 1851 with a staff of only three—himself and two employees. But the Steinways had more than their size and craftsmanship to go on. Steinway & Sons boomed because the sons knew exactly how to generate the kind of buzz that would translate into sales and profits. They did not hesitate to spend money to promote their products. "First premium piano-fortes," read an advertisement they placed in the *Times*. "Prices moderate." The ad below theirs may have been more telling. Bacon & Raven seemed to be looking over its shoulder as its former employees and their young firm closed in. Bacon & Raven's ad focused on its long experience and on having "every requisite facility at our manufactories."

꧞

The Steinways made hundreds of pianos in what one writer called "the meanest of workshops," cramped rented workrooms scattered across lower Manhattan. They trimmed the wood in one place and the hammers in another and hauled the pieces to where they finally assembled them into finished pianos. They were making too many pianos to carry on like a start-up—five a day—and would soon claim sales of $1 million a year ($12 million in today's dollars). They needed to consolidate.

The Steinways moved uptown in 1860 to what *The New York Times* called "the largest and best of factories," a predecessor of the even larger factory where K0862 would be built. They bought a square block in a neighborhood on what was then the city's northern fringe, where they were surrounded by slaughterhouses and warehouses, breweries and lumberyards. "North of Fiftieth Street," the historian Adrian Cook wrote, "the island was a real estate developer's nightmare"—but north of Fiftieth Street is exactly where the Steinways went. Two blocks north, to be exact.

Fourth Avenue was more than a generation away from being renamed Park Avenue and becoming fashionable; it was still infamous for shantytowns and squatters. But to the Steinways, Fourth Avenue was the right address. The factory ran the length of the block on Fourth Avenue from Fifty-second to Fifty-third streets. Their neighbors were the city's other most prominent, prosperous factories. The Steinways did not mind that smoke-belching trains rumbled by all day. As *Frank Leslie's Illustrated Newspaper* noted after a walk-through, "The factory [formed] a standing advertisement of incalculable value." What those commuter train passengers saw was, for its day, a red-brick wonder that municipal guidebooks pictured alongside the factories that turned out everything from biscuits to bricks to bicarbonate of soda.

At the factory's official opening, several months after it began turning out pianos, the Steinways put on quite a show. An engraving in *Frank Leslie's* shows a crowd of formally dressed men in a large room with tall windows, "listening," the caption explains, "to the musical professors trying the celebrated Steinway grand pianos." In the background, waiters are setting tables for a meal with wine "of brands not to be mentioned but with respect." But the meal did not begin until after the crowd had seen everything there was to see in the factory. There was a lot to see; the reporter for *Frank Leslie's* was worn out after "an hour and a half of tramping upstairs and downstairs, to and fro [along] endless corridors of machinery, pianos and [such]."

With the meal came speeches. Charles was applauded for what the paper said was a discussion of "the lessons which America teaches" to immigrants escaping "the narrow despotisms of the Old World." *Frank Leslie's* reported that he did not credit his family's rapid success "solely to their energy, industry and unity, but to the progressive spirit of this country—to its restless striving after improvement—to its free institutions." America, Charles was quoted as saying, was a place where a newcomer could "make his mark in spite of wealthy and established opposition."

Charles's patriotism was genuine. In less than a year, Charles, the Steinway who had led the family from Germany to the United States, would go to war for the Union. After the South seceded and captured Fort Sumter, war fever swept New York's Kleindeutschland. German Americans, rushing to enlist, filled out whole units with veterans of the 1848 uprising who figured they would make short work of the Confederate insurrection. Among them was Charles Steinway.

His younger brother William apparently believed that the North should have let the South strike out on its own—William's view, as repeated by his son Theodore E. to his grandson Henry Z. Steinway, was "To hell with 'em." The eldest son, Henry Jr., opposed all "military humbug," at least at first. The youngest son, Albert, volunteered, as did their sister Wilhelmina's husband, Frederick Vogel.

Charles was too prominent and, at thirty-two, too old for rifle duty on the front lines. He signed up to be the paymaster with New York's predominantly German Fifth Regiment. Charles had his uniform fitted and his photograph taken in Brady's studio. He stood at the usual stiff, odd angle, with Brady's immobilizer clamped against his neck, his hands clamped on his sword, and his sword clamped between his boots. It is the look of a well-to-do man who expects to muster out of the army in a few months, his boots still unscuffed.

The Fifth's destination was Annapolis, Maryland, and from there, the federal capital of Washington. As other units crossed into Virginia to clear land and built small forts, the Fifth did guard duty, rousting snipers and charing spies. Ordered back into Washington, the Fifth camped out at Meridian Hill, the antebellum mansion to which John Quincy Adams had moved when he retired from the White House. The Fifth escaped Manassas; it was forty miles away, patrolling Harpers Ferry, in what was then still Virginia. Charles's time in the army ended, on schedule, a few weeks later. He let others carry on the fight. When his regiment mustered out, he returned to the factory and faced down a mob at the front door.

❧

Factories were easy targets in New York's 1863 draft riots, the Steinway factory especially so because the mobs were heavily Irish. They were angry about a new federal law requiring local lotteries to fill out the ranks as recruitment lagged and desertions rose. Where the Germans had eagerly served, New York's Irish remained resolutely opposed. As one historian wrote, "Steinway was widely known as a German—and therefore a mostly Protestant—company, and it would not be surprising that some threat might be made toward the factory." A mob arrived there in midafternoon. "It was a terrible scene," William wrote in his diary, "and we were of course all much exercised at the prospect of having the factory destroyed."

Charles defused the tension by talking to the crowd, but it took more than rhetoric to clinch the factory's safety. William wrote that Charles gave the organizers of the mob thirty to forty dollars in cash, and handed another ringleader a check for thirty dollars. The mob moved on, but Heinrich Engelhard, Charles, and William stayed in the factory until 1 A.M., keeping watch against the return of that mob or the approach of another.

They spent the following day not making pianos but worrying anew about defending the factory. Steinway & Sons was hardly alone: "All business in the upper part of the city suspended," William reported. The next day, William discovered "to [his] horror" that "knapsacks" from the Fifth Regiment had been piled in the basement of the Steinway store in lower Manhattan. Had the rioters made the same discovery, not only could they have destroyed the store, they could have taken their anger out on the factory uptown, with its large lumberyard and workroom after workroom filled with pianos in various stages of completion. As the Steinways well knew, it would all be tinder for a spectacular blaze.

Within twenty-four hours, though, William remarked that there was "comparative quiet in the city" except in a few places. "No more fires," he wrote, but Charles again stayed up until 1 A.M., "watching in the shop." The factory went back to work in the morning, and soldiers went to the store on Sunday to claim the knapsacks. William said there was a "disagreeable scene between them." He did not explain why.

At twenty-eight, William was the junior partner who arranged the details of the company's expansion—buying the land for the factory, hiring the architect, overseeing the construction work, finding and pulling in contacts beyond the usual suppliers—without actually building pianos, and his interests extended beyond music. He worked on developing a bulletproof vest early in the war. Later in life, he would work out a deal to manufacture automobiles. If his timing had been better—if the public had been ready for cars at that moment—the Steinway name might be on every Mercedes-Benz sold in this country.

As it happened, tragedy, not vision, made William the partner in charge at Steinway & Sons. Henry Jr. and Charles died within a few weeks of each other in 1865. A lung ailment, apparently tuberculosis, killed Henry Jr. The symptoms—mainly a persistent cough—had been misdiagnosed as rheumatism a couple of years earlier. Typhoid fever killed Charles while he was in Germany visiting C. F. Theodore, the brother who had remained behind when the family emigrated to the United States. For the next thirty-one years, William called the shots as Steinway & Sons became a household name and he became a celebrity.

❦

Just how much of a celebrity is clear from an item on the front page of *The New York Times* on November 13, 1896. It was only six lines long—two sentences, forty-three words. "William Steinway is confined to his bed at his home," the first sentence declared, "with a severe attack of malarial fever." The second sentence quoted his doctor as saying that Steinway was sure to recover "in a few days."

Two things make the item notable. One was that William Steinway was so well known that the *Times* did not need to identify him. No copy editor penciled in a short phrase like "piano maker" before Steinway's name, and even a longer description like "piano maker, transit commissioner, real estate developer, and automobile pioneer" would not have explained how William Steinway had eclipsed his father to become the larger-than-life embodiment of Steinway & Sons. He was not just the Steinway who presided over what his own son would call "the perfection of the instrument." He was, in the words of the historian Richard K. Lieberman, "Mr. Music in America," the impresario who "did

for classical piano music what P. T. Barnum did for the circus."
He turned famous European virtuosos into the rock stars of
his day; the latter-day promoters behind such superstars as
Vladimir Horowitz and the Three Tenors followed a playbook
he created. He let his employees build the pianos. He built the
company, its fame, and its reputation—and with all that, a
second plant, the one in which K0862 would take shape more
than a century later.

The other striking thing about the item reporting William's
illness was that his doctor was wrong. William Steinway did not
recover—he died seventeen days later. Delivering a eulogy at his
funeral, his close friend Carl Schurz—former Civil War general,
former United States senator, and former managing editor of the
New York Evening Post—choked up. "His silence [was] more
eloquent than any speech could be," the Times declared after
paying its own tribute to William as "a model man of business"
and "a model citizen." He was just sixty-one years old.

William, according to Hubbard's flowery magazine article,
had been the son who answered "Both" when Heinrich Engelhard asked him what he wanted to be when he grew up, a mechanic or a musician. "Both" does not cover everything that
William did. When Henry Jr. and Charles died suddenly in 1865
and William became the partner in charge of Steinway & Sons,
his life was barely half over. William still had time to dabble in
politics, land deals, amusement parks, subways, yachts, and eventually cars.

William was the first Steinway to live like the people who
owned Steinways, not the workingman his father had been.
William bought a town house in Gramercy Park, already a kind
of millionaires' row in his day, and hobnobbed with famous people, from President Grover Cleveland to the composer whose
name he wrote out as "Richard Wagne." His socializing had
everything to do with selling pianos. He wanted his pianos—not
Chickering's or Weber's or Knabe's—in his friends' parlors,
where, in turn, their friends would notice. The concert theater he

built in his thirties, Steinway Hall, stood behind a showroom filled with pianos that every concertgoer had to pass on the way to his or her seat. And he called attention to Steinway & Sons milestones by arranging the sale in 1872 of Steinway piano No. 25,000 to Czar Alexander of Russia and in 1883 of No. 50,000 to the European banker Baron Nathaniel de Rothschild. When, in 1987, Steinway & Sons rented Carnegie Hall and invited more than a dozen famous pianists to play piano No. 500,000, the company was merely following in William's publicity-hungry footsteps.

William's business connections overlapped with politics. The Steinway sons had been evenly divided between the two major parties. William, like Charles, voted Democratic; Albert, like Henry Jr., was a Republican. But William did not merely vote Democratic, he joined forces with the upper-class reformers who drove William "Boss" Tweed from power. Tweed had been a hero of the 1863 draft riots that had dogged the Steinways, and through the Tammany Hall political machine, he had also put a stranglehold on the local Democratic Party and the city's government. William nurtured close friendships with two leading figures in the anti-Tammany cause: the lawyer Samuel J. Tilden, who prosecuted Tweed and resented Tammany's control over ward heelers, and Oswald Ottendorfer, the editor of the influential German-language newspaper *Staats-Zeitung,* who wanted to dilute the strength of Tammany Hall's Irish base.

William, though, played both sides, forging an alliance with Tweed's protégé Richard Croker. William's grandson, Henry Z. Steinway, recalled that William's stature in the German community was such that Croker and other officials "consulted [William] and Ottendorfer when they wanted a German" for a municipal job. Democratic leaders approached William about running for mayor, but he "realized that would be too much," Henry Z. added. As William's friend Alfred Dolge explained, "He knew that his factories turned out the best pianos that could possibly be made, and he was bent not only on letting the world know it, but on making the world believe it." William's knack for marketing became irreplaceable. His heirs could still make pianos after he died, but they could not write copy to sell them. They turned to an advertising agency.

Ads and catalogs were not William's only written legacy. His diary covers thirty-four years, from shortly before his wedding until shortly before his death. "Diary of William Steinway & Wife!" he wrote, proud exclamation point and all, on the first page. He recorded the professional and the personal—including, in code, how many times they had sex and when his wife Regina's menstrual periods had occurred. That turned out to be useful data when one of his brothers relayed rumors that Regina was involved with other men. A look back through his diary told him that he could not have fathered her third child, Alfred. As William wrote before the baby was born in 1869, "Wife tells me she is ——. I tell her it cannot be."

It turned out that she had numerous other lovers—one a lieutenant who blackmailed her while courting her niece; another William's card-playing buddy Henry Reck, an architect who had decorated their Gramercy Park house; another the organist and composer Louis Dachauer, whose own wife implicated Regina when she filed for divorce. When William's brother C. F. Theodore got hold of a packet of Regina's love letters and passed them along, William wrote, "No language can describe the mental tortures I endured on reading these horribly depraved and unalterably imprudent missives." William arranged his own divorce from "the depraved creature . . . I loved so deeply" and sent her and Alfred to live in France.

He remained attached to Alfred, who used Regina's maiden name, Roos. Later, in 1890, William tracked Alfred down in Europe and helped him obtain an American passport. When William died six years later, he left $25,000 to "my nephew, Alfred Roos," who was by then a mining engineer in Deadwood, South Dakota. William's grandson, Henry Z. Steinway, said the family "sort of stiffed" Alfred—the Steinways did not pay the bequest for a couple of years, and when they finally did, Alfred came up $1,000 short.

William's diary is not all soap opera. It is a record—sometimes the only record—of the behind-the-scenes dealings that kept Steinway & Sons going when other piano makers ran out of cash. It is also the record of the life of a New Yorker in a city that put a premium on newness. He mentions a new sport, "a most interesting game of baseball," in 1894. There is one, and only one, mention of "our new aluminum soundboards." (William—along with C. F. Theodore and the other relatives on the payroll—knew when to push ahead with their experiments, and when to drop them.) And he mentions walking across the Brooklyn Bridge after it opened in 1883. He describes the new music hall that opened in 1891—Carnegie Hall; "it is glorious," he writes.

❧

Before New York had Carnegie Hall, it had Steinway Hall. Unlike later cultural centers—Carnegie Hall and Lincoln Center in New York, the John F. Kennedy Center in Washington, D.C., and similar nonprofit temples to music, opera, and dance across the country—Steinway Hall was unabashedly commercial, and William turned it into something of a laboratory for his efforts to market the company's products. On the way in, concertgoers strolled through what William called the vestibule, which was packed with Steinway instruments, and musicians who did not play Steinway pianos were not welcome on the stage, as the soloist James Wehli discovered. The Philharmonic Society, a predecessor of the New York Philharmonic that took up residence at Steinway Hall for the hall's opening 1866–67 season, canceled Wehli's appearance because he played Chickering pianos.

William was borrowing from the older European piano makers: Pleyel and Erard had rival halls in Paris that showcased the pianists who used their products. This was the kind of strategic thinking that led Steinway to assemble a fleet of concert pianos to lend out—the fleet a piano like K0862 aspires to join. If William wanted bragging rights over Chickering, he got them—until Chickering opened a New York hall of its own nine years later. In going ahead with Steinway Hall and his other efforts to promote Steinway & Sons through concerts and artists, William prevailed over his older brother, who worried about being fleeced. "The damned artists consider piano makers a cow to be milked," C. F. Theodore wrote in 1867. "I wish I could invent a piano which makes you stupid and seasick—I would donate one to each of them."

But William had the final say, and Steinway Hall was built according to specifications he himself worked out. But Steinway Hall was a Steinway project, so it was a family project. Sixty-nine-year-old Heinrich Engelhard was involved, and not just in reviewing or revising the plans in the comfort of his town house, thirty-eight blocks uptown. As Steinway Hall took shape, Heinrich Engelhard took to wandering through it, a meddlesome patriarch whom the construction crews apparently did not recognize or respect. His great-grandson Henry Z. Steinway says that Heinrich "inspected all the lumber going in, much to the annoyance of the Irish workmen. He'd tell them, 'This piece of wood is no good—get rid of it.' They'd say, 'Who's this old guy going around telling us what to do? What's he doing inspecting the beams?' And if there were too many knots, he'd say, 'Throw it away.'"

William built Steinway Hall where his customers could not miss it, in the center of the Manhattan music district, on East Fourteenth Street, next to the company's main showroom. The Academy of Music, the Philharmonic's somewhat larger home before it moved to Steinway Hall, stood a block away until May 21, 1866, when a fast-spreading fire destroyed the Academy building and the adjacent structures between Irving Place and Third Avenue. The cornerstone for Steinway Hall was laid on May 26. William made only the briefest reference to the ceremony in his diary: "Mayor Hoffman lays the stone [and] I make speeches." He did not mention the fire at all.

As the summer wore on, William worked out important last-minute details himself, including the layout of the two thousand seats. He was still drawing diagrams of the balcony seventy-two hours before the inaugural concert. Behind what he called the "elegant marble portico" leading in from Fourteenth Street, the main auditorium seated about two thousand people, and a smaller theater held several hundred more seats behind a partition that could be removed to join the two spaces. But while Steinway Hall was finished in time for the Philharmonic's celebration of its twenty-fifth season that fall, the Philharmonic itself was not on the bill for the hall's opening concert. William had made arrangements with the rival Theodore Thomas Orchestra, whose pioneering leader was on his way to becoming the nation's symphonic tastemaker. Thomas also played in the violin section of the Philharmonic, but "it was [Thomas's own] well-disciplined band . . . that imparted the first genuine . . . impetus to the establishment of sound symphonic standards," the orchestral historian John H. Mueller points out. Thomas's programs—subsidized by William, among others—"attained European celebrity," and William would later press for Thomas's appointment as conductor of the Philharmonic.

For the opening concert at Steinway Hall, Thomas and his musicians accompanied the English pianist Sebastian Bach Mills, the Scottish soprano Euphrosyne Parepa, and her husband-to-be, the German violinist Carlo Rosa. William was exuberant. "Everybody is delighted with the acoustic qualities," he wrote in the diary. "House filled to overflowing. Great Success." George Odell, in his *Annals of the New York Stage,* said the opening night program was "the best concert then possible in the city" during what he lauded as "a season of sensations."

Thomas's orchestra continued to appear at Steinway Hall regularly, as did well-known European performers. The Swedish violinist Ole Bull played a recital there in 1868. He "enchants all with his play," declared William's teenage niece Lizzie Ziegler, who attended the concert. But William also began booking nonmusical events, mainly speeches by well-known literary and political figures. Charles Dickens read from his works in December 1867 and January 1868, and returned in April 1868. Always aware of the box office, William's diary merely notes, "great crowd." The *New York Tribune* said that Dickens was "not only an excellent reader but a greatly-gifted actor" with a "mellow and musical voice." Dickens's performance charmed Lizzie Ziegler, too, who echoed the *Tribune* critic by confiding in her diary, "I think him splendid."

Before long, the Philharmonic was gone—it needed the higher ticket revenues from the larger, rebuilt Academy of Music hall—and there were rumblings that Steinway Hall's appearance was not all it should be. The *Times* noted that the interior had been "somewhat hastily concluded" when the Steinways apparently rushed the opening to take in several bookings displaced by the fire at the Academy of Music. The hall was "plain in all its appointments, almost to poverty—austere as a country church." And so, after only two seasons, Steinway Hall was given a makeover. William's unadorned look was replaced by what the *Times* described, with a straight face, as "the elaborate yet chaste style of ornamentation known as that of Louis Quatorze." It was the handiwork not of a Parisian but a Viennese. On a trip to Europe, William had hired the architect Heinrich Beck, whose claims to fame included numerous theaters and a railroad car for the empress of Austria. William paid $50,000 ($660,000 in today's dollars) for the renovation—twice what he had budgeted.

Beck, who had arrived in New York even before William returned, was to "beautify the place." He installed a proscenium that blocked the audience's view of the organ console. He placed busts of Beethoven and Mozart on either side of the stage; he frescoed the walls and the ceiling in the main hall; he put up cornices "of exquisite design." William boasted that Steinway Hall was so fancy that it "creates the impression that it is an opera hall." (It was not. There was no room above the stage to raise and lower scenery.)

The big-name star one night in 1870 was the legendary actor Edwin Booth, whose brother had assassinated President Abraham Lincoln not quite five years before. He had been hired to read a poem as an introduction to a brand-new (and since forgotten) symphony. There were other big names: The Reverend Henry Ward Beecher, who had campaigned against slavery before the Civil War, campaigned on the Steinway stage for women's suffrage. Sojourner Truth and Julia Ward Howe (who wrote the words to "The Battle Hymn of the Republic") also filled Steinway Hall.

But the great marketing idea behind Steinway Hall was concerts. William's son, Theodore E., said that William merely carried out an idea that had occurred to William's brother, Henry Jr., in 1859: bringing virtuosos to perform on Steinway pianos at a great concert hall. The Steinways tried to arrange an American tour for the German pianist Hans von Bülow in 1864, but Theodore E. reported that "nothing came of it." Eight years later, with Steinway Hall open and well liked after its makeover, William masterminded the American debut of two stars. William was uncharacteristically breathless in the advertisement he wrote for the performance: "First appearance in America of Anton Rubinstein, the greatest living pianist, together with an ensemble of eminent artists never before heard in this country, chief among whom is Henri Wieniawski, the world-renowned violin virtuoso, and regarded as the only rival to the memory of Paganini." The critic who reviewed the concert for the *Times* was even more enthusiastic. "More remarkable piano-playing than Mr. Rubinstein's cannot be imagined," the reviewer declared. "The marvelous combination of force and delicacy is particularly noticeable." So were Rubinstein's looks. His wild, flopping mane prompted comparisons to Beethoven—the musicologist R. Allen Lott points out that Liszt called him "Van II"—and Samson. Rubinstein was the equivalent of a twentieth-century rock-and-roll sensation, and like any temperamental star, he had his demands. He would not play in beer gardens, and his contract stipulated that he was "not obliged . . . to play in establishments devoted to purposes other than artistic ones."

William had guaranteed Rubinstein $20,000 for a nation-wide tour. He played 215 concerts, every one a promotional op-portunity for Steinway. He appeared in Poughkeepsie and in Portland, Maine, in "opera houses" in Hartford and Newark, and in the courthouse in Harrisburg, Pennsylvania. He played fifteen concerts in Boston, eleven in Philadelphia, nine in New Orleans, four in Cincinnati. Wieniawski missed only one concert along the way, a near-perfect record that Henry Z. Steinway credits to William, who outsmarted Wieniawski in drawing up the contract for the tour. Wieniawski had a reputation for not showing up at curtain time, and with Rubinstein on the bill, Wieniawski had nothing to worry about: the show would go on—not the show that had been advertised, but if Rubinstein simply played a longer program, Wieniawski figured the audience would proba-bly not demand its money back. William, though, took no chances. The contract said Wieniawski would not be paid if he did not appear. By tour's end, Rubinstein called the pressure-cooker schedules and long performances "nothing more than slavery" and would not take his payment in U.S. currency—he wanted gold. As with the no-beer-garden clause, Steinway hu-mored Rubinstein. The bag containing his pay weighed 140 pounds.

In 1870, William looked across the East River to a remote stretch of Queens that he could develop as he pleased. Henry Z. Stein-way maintains that the "real reason" was vertical integration, so Steinway & Sons could "make our own plates and cut our own lumber." But the isolated location was William's revenge on labor agitators—"anarchists and socialists," he called them, sputter-ing in anger. They had repeatedly slowed production at the Fourth Avenue factory in the 1860s and had organized a full-fledged strike in 1869. In its infancy, Steinway & Sons had lived by a Machine Age belief in centralized institutions—one factory, with the owners living just down the block. Now William decided that the institution would be best served if he decentralized its operations; separating the workers would create a new obstacle in the way of labor organizing. No longer could his nemeses— "who were," in William's words, "continually breeding discontent among our workmen and inciting them to strike"—address all the workers at once, in the street outside the factory or in union halls in Manhattan. They would have to waste the better part of a day on a trip to Queens, first crossing the river, then hiring a coach to negotiate three miles of frontierlike dirt roads leading to William's factory. That factory was where K0862 would take shape.

William committed himself to moving a number of essential elements of the company's manufacturing operation out of the Fourth Avenue plant, the plant that he and his father and Charles had defended during the draft riots. "We felt," William declared, "that if we could withdraw our workmen from contact with these people"—the organizers—"and the other temptations of city life in the tenement districts, they would be more content and their lot would be a happier one."

More was at stake than simply outwitting labor. Opening a second plant promised other dividends that mattered a great deal in the hotly competitive piano-making industry of the 1870s. Anyone who wanted to do what the Steinways themselves had done when they arrived from Germany—learn the piano business from top to bottom—could not do so in a far-flung manufacturing operation. No one could know everything the Steinways had known about how to organize a factory and make a piano. William was also frustrated with the location of the Fourth Avenue plant, squarely in the middle of Manhattan, too far from the Hudson and East rivers. "We needed shipping facilities near the water," he wrote, "and a basin in which logs could be stored in water to keep them mo[i]st and prevent them from cracking."

William bought several parcels of land that he probably heard about from his connections in New York's German community. He probably also heard, from his connections in New York's political establishment, that the taxes were among the lowest in the city. His first purchase included what became the Steinways' country house, a short stroll from what William described in his diary as "Over 14 Acres of Waterfront." Always concerned about getting a good buy, he noted that the stone mansion alone had cost $80,000 to build—more than twice what he spent on it and the land.

The day after William agreed to the purchase, he loaded his parents and his brother Albert into a carriage for an inspection. It went well. William reported, "All are delighted with the magnificent house." As was often the case, he committed no emotion to paper. His matter-of-fact account of the trip does not say whether he had to convince them that he had found a bargain. He does not tell whether they were enthusiastic or reluctant—he does not waste time on such details. He is thinking ahead, hinting at the next land purchase. "Returning," he wrote, "we drive through the German Cabinetmakers reservation." He was trying to whet the family's appetite to buy ninety acres that the cabinetmakers' group had bought for a "cooperative community," a commune in everything but name. The reservation had not caught on for the same reason that William had his eye on it: The location was too remote. "At that time, it was a beautiful garden spot," William recalled in the 1890s, "surrounded by waste lands and vacant lots [and] partly wooded." The purchase gave Steinway & Sons what it did not have in Manhattan, a stretch of shoreline along the East River where barges could unload raw lumber.

The first factory buildings went up within two years. Among them were a steam-powered sawmill and foundries to make the cast-iron plates that help the curved wood hold its shape. Little by little, William filled the new compound, putting up a case-making building, kilns for drying the wood, and a foundry for casting the iron plates. Outside were waterfront "shipping facilities": a dock and bulkhead created a basin for the logs, with a crane to lift the logs off the barges that delivered them. The workers he transferred there rented rooms in Long Island City hotels or commuted from Manhattan on what everyone soon called the Piano Ferry. William moved the key-making operation there without telling C. F. Theodore, who fumed that the damp air on the waterfront would wreak havoc with the wood. But William was the Steinway in charge. The key makers did not move back to Manhattan.

William wanted the original plant in Manhattan to concentrate on finishing the pianos—assembling the parts made in Queens and polishing the completed instruments. He had something else in mind for the rest of the land in Queens: a company town. He commissioned plans for workers' houses and went to see another one-owner town, "A. T. Stewart's new improvement," as he called it in his diary—Garden City, New York. Stewart, who was New York's first department-store tycoon, had created a four-square-mile enclave in the flat center of Long Island. Stewart had spent lavishly—he offered one-third more than other prospective buyers for the land alone, and then built large Victorian houses at a cost of $17,000 apiece. He rented them to his workers for $100 a month.

Like Stewart, William built houses and sold lots, at least in the beginning. But the Panic of 1873 devastated the New York economy and precipitated Steinway & Sons' first annual loss, all but wiping out the cash that William might have spent on his company town. This was, after all, a side venture, and suddenly the family's main business—Steinway & Sons—was not generating the profits he had come to expect. The company town languished. By 1881 only 130 houses had gone up.

Still, the Steinway village was a company town like no other. The church William built had a "cathedral organ," a hand-me-down from the Steinway concert hall in Manhattan, and

William saw to it that the town's private police force was ready for crowd-control emergencies, even if he had to intervene himself. On the Fourth of July in 1886, when revelers descended on the beach below his mansion, William sent them running. As he explained in his diary: "I drive them off with my revolver."

3

Anti-Manufacturing

May 19: Joseph Klimas sprays the "ebonized" lacquer finish onto the case of K0862.

C. F. Theodore Steinway, who would become the family's patent-generating genius, hated America so much that he moved back to Germany in 1884 and opened a factory in Hamburg. He never returned to "that land of iniquity," as he described the nation of unbearable weather and uncouth concertgoers that he found so unpleasant, but he kept in close touch with his relatives by transatlantic mail. He crammed his long letters to New York with illustrations and instructions for improvements to the instruments manufactured there, and for generations the two factories turned out the same lineup of models, made to the same standards.

Somehow, though, the pianos made in Hamburg have always been just a bit different from their American cousins. Many pianists maintain that Steinways from Hamburg tend to sound warmer, mellower, and more even—whatever that means—than Steinways from New York. But one very real difference between a New York Steinway and a Hamburg Steinway is easily recognizable: the shape of the arms, the part of the piano case that frames the ends of the keyboard.

On nearly all New York Steinways, the curve of the arms ends in a sharp corner—a Sheraton arm, named for Thomas Sheraton, the eighteenth-century furniture designer who was famous for his lightness of form and grace of proportion. On a Hamburg Steinway, the edge of the arm is rounded.

Once, New York Steinways had rounded arms, too. Frank Mazurco, Steinway's executive vice president, says the New York factory switched to the Sheraton arms around 1910 to stay current. "Obviously, somebody said, 'Guys, furniture styles have changed; we need to adapt,'" he explains. "New York adapted. In Hamburg, they said, 'That's not happening in Europe.' They kept the design the way it was. And later, when the Japanese entered the market, they started with rounded arms, like Europe. So now it's New York that's standing unique in the architecture."

Not that it must. Andy Horbachevsky, the manufacturing director to whom the arm cutters and their factory floor bosses answer,
says the New York factory could change to a different-shaped
arm in no time. "I tell the marketing guys"—meaning Mazurco,
who is Steinway's head marketer—" 'You want a round arm
shape, I'll make it.' The point is what happens at the end." That
is, when somebody actually plays that fine piece of furniture that
Horbachevsky's people at the factory have created.

Cutting the arms gives the piano an unmistakable identity.
The laminated rim of K0862 gets its New York look on Monday,
May 19, 2003, a couple of weeks after rim-bender Tommy Stavrianos wheels it out of the hot and dry rim-conditioning room
where it has spent much of March, all of April, and the first weeks
of May. It stood with its tail in the air and an iron bar between its
arms for support. Now Stavrianos whacks at K0862 with a
wooden paddle. The blows land on the bar, which must be removed, and Horbachevsky figures out the timetable for K0862.
In the fall it will become a musical instrument. First it will become a piece of furniture.

Describing the steps from furniture to musical instrument
is like explaining the answers on the public-radio program *Car
Talk*. You don't need to know that stuff to drive a car, and you
don't need to know this stuff to play a piano, but if someone
hadn't paid attention to mechanical arcana, the car wouldn't start
and the piano wouldn't play. The wooden parts that are the next
stage in K0862's creation are the guts, the things that perhaps
only a piano technician, a shop teacher, or a weekend woodworker would care about. Workers are about to drill holes in
places a pianist will never see. They are about to spread glue—
odorless this time—and hammer in tight-fitting dowels. They are
about to tackle K0862 with a colorful array of clamps and blades
and drills.

As all this goes on, the constant in the life of K0862 will be
Andy Horbachevsky. K0862 will move through the sections of the
factory that he oversees, and he will hover over the workers'

shoulders, explaining to an outsider why these minuscule tasks (make a tiny notch here, glue in an eraser-sized piece of wood there) are anything but trivial.

Horbachevsky is five feet nine inches tall. In a how-are-we-going-to-fix-this huddle with workers and foremen, he might well be the short guy. On a normal day, he wakes up as early as the early-morning television stars—he pulls into the factory parking lot in the darkness before dawn, at least ninety minutes before the workers are due at 7:30 A.M., sometimes earlier. Unlike Matt Lauer or Diane Sawyer, he is still at work at evening news time, eleven or twelve hours later. He once ran the New York marathon and sometimes bicycles to the factory from his home in Westchester County, a ride of nineteen miles. For safety, he figured out a route that skirted the expressways he takes in his minivan. Taking the less-traveled local streets adds to the distance. Still, he can make the trip in ninety minutes, door to desk.

At the factory, his dark blue coat and his walk set him apart from the workers—and from his bosses up the corporate ladder. The coat is not the blazer he peels off in the morning and pulls on when he leaves for home at the end of the day—this one is thinner, unlined, reaching nearly to his knees. It adds authority. It marks him the way a white coat marks a doctor on rounds in a hospital.

His walk, too, is about projecting the right image. There is a noticeable change in his stride, a sudden swagger, when he goes from management row to the factory floor. It is a don't-mess-with-me power walk. It has a bit of the "pimp roll" that Tom Wolfe made famous in *Bonfire of the Vanities*—but only a bit—and it is not completely convincing. It is the walk of a middle-aged man who, after becoming a boss, looked in the mirror and saw a boyish face.

Like C. F. Theodore, Horbachevsky has spent much of his adult life rethinking the way Steinway does things. C. F. Theodore had an advantage: He was mostly doing what someone like Horbachevsky would call clean-sheet engineering. Because he was family, because the piano business was hotly competitive in those days, C. F. Theodore could invent something new. If Horbachevsky wants to move a few workbenches across the room for efficiency's sake, he must convince everyone involved—the workers as well as his own bosses—that tampering with Steinway's ways really will improve the pianos.

So changes come slowly to the factory. Horbachevsky says the factory moves to a drumbeat of just ten pianos a day, or about twenty-five hundred a year. (The total for K0862's class of 2003 will be fewer than that. Concerned about a sputtering economy and sluggish sales before the war in Iraq, Steinway shut the factory for two weeks, in addition to its usual three-week summer vacation.) Once a showpiece of innovation, the factory is now something of a time capsule for manufacturing methods that other industries left behind in the rush to automation—so much so that manufacturing director Horbachevsky describes what goes on at the factory as "anti-manufacturing." He means, among other things, that Steinway never embraced, and now consciously rejects, most of the automated assembly-line techniques that boosted productivity in the nineteenth and twentieth centuries.

Horbachevsky, who is in his mid-forties, knows all about assembly lines and high-volume manufacturing and modern plants. His first job after college was in a General Electric management training program that focused on how to run a factory. He spent two years in G.E. factories that made lawn mowers, irons, electric skillets, and toasters. He worked by turns as a foreman and a quality control specialist. Later he worked at a Clairol factory that made what Madison Avenue calls hair-care products. He quit after his boss was fired. "He had outstanding reviews. I said, does this make sense?"

A help-wanted ad led him to Steinway, where he had an Oz-like behind-the-curtain experience different from a pianist's. A pianist visiting the factory sees the pianos, hundreds of pianos in various states of undress—this one's keyboard has been pulled out, that one's pedals don't work—and the workers, hundreds of workers with the know-how to tweak the dream piano. What fascinated Horbachevsky were tools, processes, and manufacturing methods of which he had no knowledge. "It was almost like walking back in time, seeing wooden floors in some sections of the plant and looking at all these operations that I'd never before seen. You know, there are still some leather-belt-driven pieces of equipment. But I guess the thing that really appealed to me was, I could make a home here." He had recently married, and his wife was expecting—"I always know how old my daughter is by how many years I've been at Steinway, or the reverse." He delighted in the rhythms of the factory, the notion that what went on there was important, the idea that he had finally landed a job that would let him contribute to something that mattered in the world. It was all so engrossing, and seductive. "This company kind of sucks you in," he says. "I've had a dream where my wife turned into a piano."

At that time, in 1987, Steinway was at an in-between stage. Some of its most experienced workers had quit, and the word around the factory was that it had seen better days. The message from management had a traditionalist ring. As Horbachevsky remembers it, "We wanted to go back to the recipe." But the front office had an updated recipe in mind. Just as newer editions of *The Joy of Cooking* call for less butter and less sugar, Steinway was emphasizing standardization of materials and manufacturing methods. The hope was that uniformity would quiet pianists who had complained about Steinways made—depending on the age of the complainant—since World War II, or since the 1970s, when the Steinway family sold the company.

When Horbachevsky answered the want ad in 1987, the world around Steinway was changing, too. Baldwin—Steinway's main rival after World War II, the *Newsweek* to Steinway's *Time*—hired an executive from Procter & Gamble to be its president. She compared Baldwin to the mass-market brands she had worked with, like Crest toothpaste and Dial soap. But by 2003, Baldwin had flirted with bankruptcy, closed plants, and sold what was left to a guitar maker, and Horbachevsky was presiding over what he happily called "the flip side of modern manufacturing." Above all, that means not straying from the way Steinway has always done things. Steinway bends rims using the methods and clamps C. F. Theodore developed in the 1870s and 1880s. It makes sounding boards according to designs patented in the nineteenth century, in a factory that opened more than thirty years before Henry Ford invented his assembly line. Horbachevsky likes to talk about "the Zen of wood" and how the material that makes up four-fifths of a piano differs from batch to batch, unlike the steel or glass or plastic that goes into cars or television sets. And how men, not machines that can be calibrated and controlled, shape the wood. "There are nuances in anyone's approach to anything—every craftsman has a particular approach to the wood," he says.

Indeed, what goes on day after day at Steinway borders on being custom work. Competitors like Yamaha use machines where Steinway uses hand-operated tools (though Yamaha says it takes as long as Steinway does to turn out a grand the size of K0862—about nine months). Kawai sells a concert grand that costs more than $150,000—or nearly $60,000 more than Steinway's price for K0862—and has plastic parts in places where Steinway uses wood; a team of twelve people Kawai calls "master piano artisans" assembles it by hand. Brian Chung, the senior vice president of Kawai America, maintains that what differentiates one piano from another is the skill of the people who make it. "To say something's handmade," Chung says, "does not describe the skill of the person. I could say something is handmade by a kindergartner."

Which is why Horbachevsky's "anti-manufacturing" is a more useful term. It covers the fact that Steinway largely shuns the efficient "just-in-time" production system that was widely adopted by American factories in the 1980s and 1990s. Besides giving Japanese automobile companies high-quality results and low production costs, just-in-time production saved them from keeping large inventories of parts and raw materials on hand to tie up money and space.

Steinway, by contrast, has its lumberyard, and is proud of it. "Certainly if you're talking about manufacturing in the twenty-first century, you're talking about efficiency, optimizing every little thing," Horbachevsky explains. "For us, that doesn't really work. We are so tied into our craftsmen and our workforce here, and really New York in other aspects, that I don't think we'd succeed if we were to take everything here and plop it down somewhere else." A Sun Belt factory would not have the architectural limitations that Steinway copes with every day. It could be spread out on one level, and rim-benders would not have to schedule their elevator rides. True. Horbachevsky notes it is also true that Sohmer, another venerable New York piano maker, did not survive its move to Connecticut.

But if Steinway has not embraced production methods that have benefited higher-volume manufacturers, it has been willing to depart from the prevailing practice of the woodworking industry. In 1989, it changed the way some of its workers had been paid since the day the factory opened. Rather than paying them for how many pieces—legs, lids, sounding boards—they finished during a seven-hour shift, they began paying for hours worked. The piecework system had put pressure on workers to rush, and that was not a good thing; quality could—and did—suffer. "This is not about speed necessarily," Horbachevsky says. "We're dealing with wood. If you rush things through, things are going to end up with wood twisting and warping in sixty days, and then you're going to say, 'Why did we do that?'" It is a question that a foreman would have put to a worker after rejecting an imperfect piece—and, under the old system, ordering the worker to redo it on his own time. Now Steinway's 425 manufacturing workers are paid an average of $15.50 an hour.

Steinway departs from other companies in the woodworking industry on tolerances. It trims some parts to plus or minus three-thousandths of an inch, narrower than a lowercase *l* in a sentence like this. "When I go to woodworking shows and tell them that, a lot of people say, 'You can't do that. You can't get that kind of tolerance with wood,'" says Horbachevsky. "With cabinetmakers, plus or minus a sixty-fourth, you're looking good. Carpenters, a sixteenth."

Another manufacturing trend that Steinway shunned is subcontracting—hiring outside suppliers to do work that had been done in the factory. Steinway, in fact, has gone the other way, buying the subcontractors that made the keys and the cast-iron plates. Both made parts for other piano companies, and still do. "We've got this controlling nature," Horbachevsky says.

Horbachevsky's definition of anti-manufacturing encompasses Steinway's reliance on time-tested processes. Consider the lacquer that Steinway applies to the rims, lids, legs, and keyboard covers, the "coating," in front-office jargon. Steinway developed the coatings in the 1980s. They come from a company that also makes the paint for Major League Baseball players' helmets—blue and white for the New York Yankees, a brighter blue and orange for the New York Mets. Newer coatings contain more toxic materials, and Steinway has not switched to them because the older ones are safer. In terms of appearance, it's a toss-up: the new coatings do not make pianos look better than the older ones. The man who runs the lacquer company knew about the look of Steinways before he added Steinway & Sons to his list of customers in 1989. "In their scheme of things," Bill Wurdack, Jr., says, "we're still neophytes." But he grew up in a household with three pianos, all Steinways. His father, who retired in 1992, is a serious amateur pianist who practiced two hours a day, from 5 to 7 A.M. "I woke up to Brahms or Chopin," recalls Bill Jr. He landed the Steinway account after the Steinway dealer in St. Louis sent flyers to everyone in his neighborhood. He was the young guy on the block—he had been out of college for less than a year, was living in a rented house, and had not bothered with much furniture. Nor was he a likely Steinway buyer: He plays the piano, but "not very well." He took the flyer to work to show to his father. Bill Wurdack, Sr., picked up the telephone and called the Steinway factory. "The next thing I know," says Bill Jr., "I'm making a sales call. They had environmental issues. We helped them with that, and we reduced their labor cost by twenty percent." He has definite ideas about New York Steinways and Hamburg Steinways. The finish on the ones from Germany is "like what you'd see on a bar top." And he says the different coatings affect the sound of the piano. The hard, shiny Hamburg look contributes to what he says is a "hard, tinny" Hamburg sound.

Anti-manufacturing, in Horbachevsky's mind, also means dealing with government regulations that would not come into play if the factory were in a less densely populated area. On smaller pianos, though not on concert grands like K0862, Steinway uses electrical generators to help lock newly bent rims. The generators arrived around World War II, when Steinway stopped making pianos and converted itself briefly into a military subcontractor turning out parts for wooden gliders; the equipment transmits high-frequency radio waves that accelerate the curing of the wood. In this case, Steinway decided the faster way was the better way. But for years, the generators added to the burden of operating the factory. Because the factory is less than half a mile from La Guardia Airport, federal regulators were concerned that the generators would interfere with communications between pilots and the control tower. Steinway was required to obtain a license for the generators, just as if it were operating a little radio station.

To Horbachevsky, Steinway also differs in its history of working without a written manual. In the old days, the factory bosses did not keep comprehensive patterns or recipe-style instructions. Unlike most other manufacturing companies, for generations Steinway depended on the memories of its workers, who often held the same jobs for twenty or thirty years and had learned what they knew from the workers who had been on that job for twenty or thirty years before them. Each worker learned the job by watching the person who had done it before.

Fears of corporate espionage may have been the driving force behind the policy in the years before World War I, when New York was a piano boomtown and the Steinways worried that a worker who knew all of their secrets could tip off their competitors. Steinway has long since written down the whys and hows of each worker's job, but one of the factory's many traditions is an oral one: Instructions are handed down in a variety of languages, with English often second to German, Italian, Spanish, or, lately, Serbian. That is because Steinway's workforce changes along with New York.

For generations, Steinway hired German, Austrian, Irish, and Italian immigrants. By the 1980s, job applications reflected the influx of immigrants from Haiti and the Dominican Republic. Haitians now account for the largest single group of immigrants at the factory, 17 percent of the workforce. Dominicans make up 4 percent. New York City's immigration patterns changed again in the 1990s, and so did Steinway's. The company hired refugees from the war in Yugoslavia—Serbian, Bosnian, and Croatian immigrants, like Nazif Sutrovic, the former policeman on Joe Gurrado's rim-bending crew—who now make up about 7 percent of the workforce. Serbs worked in some parts of the factory and Croats in others. "At the height of the conflict, we had fundraising going on on one floor and clothing and food collections going on on another floor for the opposite sides," recalls Michael A. Anesta, the personnel director, "and still made pianos every day." There were arguments at lunchtime, but no blows.

Silvio Dodos immigrated from Romania when he was eight. Steinway hired him in 1998 when he was twenty, after he graduated from the State University of New York at Morrisville with a degree in wood products technology. After five years at the factory, he finally feels comfortable there. He was self-conscious at first, working for a company that had traditions to uphold, a reputation to live up to, and, for a newcomer, a hierarchy to live with.

"It was a little hard," he says. "I was the youngest on this floor."
No one was hostile, but as a brand-new apprentice, he worried
about learning the processes, the tools, the tolerances. He worried about making mistakes, about having to do things over to get
them right. Those worries no longer run through his mind. "I'd
say I'm good," he said. "Everything is hard when you first start."

He is one of the few craftsmen to work on K0862 who has a
piano at home—not a Steinway but a Kawai upright. His sister
plays, and he has tried to learn. So the question was inevitable:
What does he think of the Kawai, a mass-produced piano from a
company whose production for a week almost equals Steinway's
for a year?

The answer, too, was inevitable. "It's well made," he said,
"but I don't think it's the same quality as a Steinway is. The sound
pretty much tells it. I've tried a lot of pianos in the factory. I'm
not really a musician, but you can tell."

Dodos's work on K0862 begins after the top and bottom of
the rim are trimmed off by Louis Nozil, a Haitian, working alongside Jorge Roca, an Ecuadorian. When the rim arrives at Nozil's
big table saw, it has rough edges. Though the rim-benders had
been careful in matching and marrying the strips of maple to each
other, each of the eight strips that formed the outer rim of K0862
is a different height from the one next to it. One towers over another by a sixteenth of an inch; yet another is short by almost as
much. There is a run of mountains on the top and bottom of the
rim—the peaks of the laminations alternate with the ski runs of
now-dried glue that the rim press squeezed out. The strips on the
inner rim, too, are uneven. Nozil's task is to steer the entire rim
around a fast-spinning cutting head that makes the floor shake
beneath his feet and sends a cloud of sawdust floating toward the
ceiling. Nozil does not worry about breathing in a lungful. He is
careful to cover his nose and mouth with the white mask that lolls
around his neck when the machine is off.

The saw functions like a slicer. It lops off about three-
eighths of an inch, top and bottom, leaving a rim with flat

surfaces all around and sharp corners. This creates two souvenirs, a pair of thin pieces of wood the shape of the outer rim, each with one side that has been machined smooth and one side that remains mountainous. Make one more cut, as Nozil does—a quick slice that turns two pieces into four—and they look like hockey sticks, size extra-extra-long.

The rim itself sits on the table saw. Nozil sets the height of the inner rim so it perfectly hugs the plate and the sounding board when they are fitted into the case. He looks down the rim from the end. He makes some adjustments to the saw, and makes one cut. He lifts a ruler off a nail on the wall and measures. Too high. He readjusts the saw and runs the rim around the blade— four times. He shakes his head. One more cut. A sigh of relief.

Now it is Dodos's turn. Gino Romano, the foreman in his department, does not worry about catching Dodos napping at his workbench. Even though Dodos works in the middle of an open area, far from the windows, the aroma of fresh coffee is strong— some days, like this one, French roast, but often vanilla-flavored. It comes not from a hidden coffeepot but from the restaurant supply company across the street from the factory, which grinds coffee beans all day long. It is so much a part of Dodos's day that he no longer notices it. Nor does he bother to answer when someone asks, jokingly, if he works slower when the coffee being ground is decaf.

Dodos uses a power saw to make a rough cut at the end of the rim, forming the sharp-elbowed arms that will bracket the keyboard. In the piano business, this kind of cutting is called "fraising." Most dictionaries trace that term to a French word meaning "to ream out." But Andy Horbachevsky knows Steinway's roots. He says the word "came to *us* from German." He has learned to listen for it when executives at Steinway's other factory, in Hamburg, Germany, launch into a complicated explanation in German, forgetting that he never studied their language. Wherever it originated, the term, also used in watchmaking, worked its way into English in the last third of the nineteenth century, a heyday for piano makers, and the essential elements of Steinway's manufacturing process have not changed much since then. Steinway workers hired in the 1960s, for example, say they learned to use handsaws to cut the ends of rims, the way Steinway workers had done a hundred years before. "It took two men, like you were cutting a log," Romano recalls. Behind his gold-rimmed glasses are the seen-it-all eyes of someone who remembers when he was a young man struggling at one end of the saw. Romano, who is in his late fifties, is the foreman with the longest time on the payroll. Steinway hired him in 1964, when he was just out of high school.

These days, a machine does what elbow grease and teamwork once did. But first, Dodos has to finish the preparations. After cutting the arms from the ends of the rim, he drops the two blocks of wood into a barrel behind his workbench. To avoid wasting expensive wood, Steinway sends such blocks to another woodworker at the factory; they are trimmed into smaller pieces, with a 45-degree angle at one end, known as cheek blocks, which will be glued back onto the rim to strengthen it. So Dodos's next move is to cut a 45-degree notch into the rim of K0862 and reach into another barrel that is loaded with completed cheek blocks.

Next he rubs soap into the rim at the point just beyond where the cheek blocks will go. Soap repels the glue; if Dodos applies too much glue, the soap will prevent it from seeping into the wood before he scrapes it away. But first he must prepare the wood to take the glue. With a small-bladed tool, Dodos scrapes his way around the top of the rim. The sound is not pleasant. "Like nails on a chalkboard," as Andy Horbachevsky describes it.

Dodos keeps working, scraping and gluing and scraping and gluing, screwing clamps into place and later removing them. His foreman, Romano, tells stories about the things he has seen around the factory in his long career: a piano tuner who was known for hitting his tuning fork against his head (apparently he thought he could hear the note better that way); a case maker who followed the just-add-water recipe for glue so carefully he looked like "a master chef making a whipped cream pie." Over his forty years at Steinway, Romano has developed his own theories about the making and aging of pianos. "The pianos we made when I came here, those are the old pianos now. Let the new ones mellow out, age. The strings stretch out, the wood acclimates to the surroundings it's in, the tone starts to get a little better," he says. "You get a new car, they don't tell you to go out there and go ninety miles an hour. They tell you to break it in. Same with a piano."

A few days later, after the cheek blocks have set, another worker in Steinway's case department, Louis Auguste, loads K0862 onto the machine that completes the shaping of the piano's Sheraton arms. Auguste, who arrived in New York from the Dominican Republic in 1970, went to work at Steinway five years later. Unlike a lot of new employees, he had experience in woodworking. "My father was a cabinetmaker. My grandfather was a cabinetmaker. My girlfriend is a cabinetmaker. I've been doing this since I was seven. In my head, I can do anything."

It is up to Auguste to plane the curves the machine creates, but only after he has taped his fingers with the kind of white adhesive tape found in a medicine kit; Auguste's eyes tell of the pain of too many fingertips scraped raw by the file. He works rapidly, and there are no complications with K0862.

The case department is behind schedule when K0862 rolls in, partly because a worker has been hurt in a car accident and has missed several weeks of work. Romano cannot simply assign a substitute because it takes almost a year to train a case maker. "When you lose someone for a long period of time," he says, "it has a serious effect on our output." (Four months later, Romano will hire an experienced case maker from Florida, a relative of another Steinway worker.) But the case department is also one of the funnels through which every piano must pass. "There are a lot of things we stop in here because they're not up to our standards," Romano says. But not K0862.

To make the point, Romano resurrects his analogy between cars and pianos. "All right, let's do a little comparison: cars of old versus cars of today," he begins. "Old cars were made of steel, so if you hit a pole in a 1955 Plymouth—and I did, learning how to drive—I bent the parking meter and did not scratch the bumper. I would not do that with the car I have now." His Nissan Altima gets better mileage, but he bought it for its reputation as a well-made, trouble-free compact. "The same with our product. It lives up to what we say. That's the test."

A few days later, when Dodos and Auguste finish their cutting and gluing, Auguste stamps a date on the wrestplank. "The dating game," Auguste announces with the smile of someone who enjoys a play on words.

Auguste also writes the case number—K0862—and the date in a little notebook that he stashes in a drawer with his tools. Like most of the workers, he keeps a record of the pianos he works on, by number. Pocket-size notebooks are popular, though a few keep full-fledged ledgers in a drawer. They pull them out before they send the piano on to the next guy. The notebooks are unofficial. The foremen know who worked on each piano, and the official record, the record the front office can always check, is a quality control ticket. One is prepared for each piano, and it rides along as the piano moves from workbench to workbench. The notebooks provide a personal record, a scorecard, a career total, an answer to the question "How many pianos did you work on this week?"—or this month, or this year, or over a career. Notebooks can be flung on the desk of a foreman if a worker is accused of being slow, though in such cases, closer scrutiny will probably come from the union's shop stewards as they build a defense. A notation—the sparsest marginalia, like a star or an arrow—can remind a worker of a piano that was a special headache, and what he did to improve it.

※

In May 2003, K0862 is "still pretty much a carcass," Andy Horbachevsky says when the piano arrives at Senad Beharovic's workbench in a back corner of the factory. Beharovic is a Mace-

donian who goes by the nickname Dragan, a square-shouldered
man in his mid-thirties who has been on the Steinway payroll
since 1995. He will spend more time with K0862 than any other
worker so far—about seven hours, with time out for lunch and
coffee breaks. His job is to put in wooden parts you won't see
unless you lie on your back and wriggle under the piano. You
could not stand at the keyboard and see Beharovic's contribu-
tions to K0862. They will be blocked from view by more famous
parts—the sounding board, the cast-iron plate, the strings. If
the rim is the foundation of the piano, he is responsible for the
trusses, the thick support pieces that help hold the curved
shape of the rim and resist the tremendous pressure of the
strings.

Beharovic begins by laying out a red trellislike pattern for
the four thick braces that he will add to the inside of the case. On
the inner rim, he makes sharp marks with a pencil. Soon he is
sanding, nailing, clamping, and planing four bars of maple that
spread out from the keyboard end of the rim like long fingers.
Andy Horbachevsky explains that the machine-made braces are
intentionally cut a bit too big so they can be hand trimmed, by
Beharovic, for a precise fit before they are glued in for good.
"We're dealing with wood here," Horbachevsky says as Beharovic lifts the braces to chest height and lugs them to a band
saw, where he trims them down. "Every rim is a slightly different
shape. This one could be off one-sixteenth from that one. We're
not talking very different, but enough to contribute to the personality of the piano."

Other piano makers use more than wood for the Atlas-like
job of the braces. Mason & Hamlin runs a metal truss rod it calls
the "tension resonator" from one side of the inner rim to the
other. The company maintains that its rod is better than Steinway's wooden braces because metal does not expand and contract the way wood does. Mason & Hamlin argues that its rim is
thus locked into shape, while Steinway's will change by tiny

fractions of an inch as the seasons change, as the piano is moved from place to place, as the wood ages.

Because Steinway uses no truss rod, Beharovic works only with wood—which means that he also works with glue. Two kinds are within his reach: white glue, the industrial-strength cousin of the kindergarten art-class mainstay, and hide glue. As he prepares to glue in a piece called the nose-bolt block, he turns off a big fan behind his workbench. The nose-bolt block is attached with white glue, and Beharovic switches off the fan, not to keep the fumes out of his face, but to keep the glue from drying too fast. White glue does not bond instantly—as every former kindergartner knows, the adhesive comes without those warnings about what to do if your fingers get stuck to the thing you are gluing—and Beharovic needs ample time to wrestle with the clamps that will hold the nose-bolt block in place. The time he spends positioning and attaching it is warm-up time for the braces. He has stowed them in a "hot box," a warming oven for wood and glue that maintains a temperature of about 200 degrees Fahrenheit. For the braces, Beharovic uses hide glue, which Horbachevsky says is the old-fashioned kind, a throwback to the days of horses, buggies, and slaughterhouses. The braces must be heated because, Horbachevsky explains later, "if you didn't heat the surface, the glue wouldn't penetrate the wood."

Watching Beharovic is like watching a gymnast perform a solo routine, turning and reaching and leaping—his moves have a confident rhythm. He picks up a hand plane and slides it along the braces in long, easy strokes. Long, smooth strands of wood, barely thicker than a sheet of paper, ribbon out. "It's how you stand; it's not in your arms, it's in your legs, getting that nice curl," Horbachevsky says with the admiration of someone who has rehearsed those same moves.

Beharovic puts a wide rectangle of wood, the keybed, in last. Yet another wide rectangle, the one that will support the eighty-eight keys, will float on it someday. Like the braces, the keybed helps hold the rim's shape, but it is fitted with expansion joints designed to deal with changes in humidity. Horbachevsky says there is a reason to let it to spread or shrink a few millimeters. "We don't want the keys sitting on a foundation that twists," he explains, as Beharovic measures and glues and fits it into K0862.

This is solitary work. Horbachevsky is called to a meeting in the front office, and Beharovic works for an hour without speaking. Only when another worker walks by and tells him that it is time for the midmorning break does he say anything: "I'll be back." It is sunny outside, and he heads to the factory courtyard for a snack—peaches he brought from home.

❧

By the manufacturing director's timetable, K0862 needs a three-week R & R to become accustomed to Beharovic's additions before the final step in the furniture-making part of its creation. Beharovic's keybeds are covered with cardboard, held in place not with ordinary masking tape but with a low-tack variety. "Otherwise, you'll pull up that spruce," the foreman in the coating department, Michael Senia, explains.

Beharovic's braces are not taped up, nor is the innermost layer of the outer rim. The wood under the lid of the piano will be the same color as the wood on the outside. Like the shape of the arms, that is a clue as to whether a Steinway was made in New York or in Hamburg. At the Hamburg factory, the inside layer of the rim is covered with tape and brown paper that absorb the lacquer. When a stagehand raises the top of a piano from Germany, the audience sees natural wood, a six-inch band of reddish brown. When a stagehand raises the top on a New York Steinway, the audience sees black lacquer. Unless it is a white piano, of course.

A worker in the coating department, Jeremy Shepherd, sponges linseed oil on the rim. Senia explains, "You've got to fill the pores, that's important, so the lacquer doesn't go in and damage the wood. This way, you know you'll have a smooth finish." Then K0862, riding on a metal trolley, is wheeled into Joseph

Klimas's booth, a small, battered stage of sorts, with an actual waterfall at the back. The booth is framed by a contemporary proscenium arch, for Klimas's booth is a modular unit, a three-sided box inside the larger workroom. Klimas works next to the windows, though one wall of the booth blocks the view. Klimas, whose previous job was to paint cars in an auto body shop, will spray five to six gallons of lacquer onto K0862, the older-formula lacquer that Andy Horbachevsky cited in his notion of anti-manufacturing. The waterfall is designed to catch droplets of the lacquer that miss their target and which could raise health issues if they drifted into the factory.

Like the shape of the arms at either end of the keyboard and the coating of the inside case, the lacquer itself will give away that K0862 was made in New York, not Hamburg. The lacquer on Hamburg pianos gives them a shinier finish. The formulations are different, and no one at Steinway can say how New York decided to use one and Hamburg the other—they just did. The New York look is less like a mirror, and the color does not have to be black. Working its way through the factory ahead of K0862 is a piano with an electric-green case, a copy of a Steinway that the Seattle glassblower and sculptor Dale Chihuly designed for the 2002 Winter Olympics. In the ballrooms at the Plaza in Manhattan are several white Steinways from the days when Donald and Ivana Trump made the decorating decisions there. Horbachevsky remembers an order for a pink piano—not just any shade but "Pepto-Bismol pink," to match a fabric sample the buyer had brought in and proudly handed over. Going from workbench to workbench in a factory where most pianos wear basic black, that piano was almost distracting. "All I could think," Horbachevsky says, "was, if this is the piano, what does the interior, the room, look like that it's going into?" Hamburg has filled orders for pianos that most eyes would see as fire engine red and school bus yellow. The man who bought the yellow one was not thinking of school buses, though. He wanted a piano to match his Porsche and told Steinway, "Bet you can't do this."

Klimas has been lacquering pianos since Steinway hired him seven years ago—he knew the coating foreman's brother-in-law, who knew there was an opening. "There's less trouble with these than with cars," says Klimas, who starts on the long, straight side of the rim and works back and forth like an oscillating fan. "Not as many colors to match. There's less aggravation." And, he says, "This has better benefits." The rim rotates before him.

Klimas has hooked K0862's trolley onto a spindle on the floor of his booth that turns the piano clockwise, as if it were on a turntable. He holds a high-pressure hose in one hand and aims. Horbachevsky, watching from a distance, says the lacquer has been warmed to 140 degrees Fahrenheit, to thin it out. Klimas's strategy is to do the rim as if he were doing a crossword puzzle: first across, then down. He is done in twenty minutes.

Of the two dozen steps in building concert grand K0862—the steps listed on the quality control ticket that will carry Klimas's signature below Gurrado's and Beharovic's—this is the most dramatic. But it is no big deal to someone who paints pianos all day long. A question came to mind: Are the housepainters on an important job—painting the White House, say—as nonchalant as Klimas? There is a difference, of course. A painter at the White House knows how important the White House is. K0862 is still an unknown.

Klimas will spray five coats on K0862 between May and Labor Day. K0862 spends the time between each coat in an aisle not far from Klimas's booth. In contrast to the hot, dry weeks in the rim-conditioning room, this waiting period goes by at normal temperature. But between the first and second coats, K0862 is in the hands of Tomasz Kawalko.

Kawalko's job is to give K0862 the Steinway name. He rubs the decal that spells out "Steinway & Sons" in inch-high gold letters onto the side of K0862, where the name and the company's lyre-and-treble-clef symbol will be seen even from the back of an auditorium. Kawalko also rubs a smaller Steinway decal inside the fallboard, the cover that hides the keyboard when the piano is closed. The decals would not look right if Kawalko affixed them to bare wood, or if he waited to apply them until after the last of Klimas's spray dates. The gold on the decal—actually gold leaf—repels Klimas's lacquer.

Kawalko, who is twenty-six and was a parking attendant before Steinway hired him five years ago, likes being the man who puts the "Steinway" on Steinways. "It's fun to watch MTV and show my wife, 'Look, this is what I do,'" he says, rubbing the decal.

4

Part No. 81

Paul Verasammy wedges glued strips of wood onto a press to make a sounding board.

Steinway pays Paul Verasammy, a lanky Guyanan in his mid-thirties, to load and unload a steel-gray machine that looks like a slow-moving Ferris wheel. There is no job description for his ten passengers, which, like so many things at Steinway, are named with a number. Each one is a Part No. 81 on the company's glossy chart titled "Grand Piano—Cross Section," which is the size of a wall map, with a piano spread across the middle instead of the United States. The piano is shown from its long, straight side, with the keyboard taking North Carolina's place on the right side and the tail of the case sliding into northern California's territory on the left.

On the chart, the piano's side is sliced away, exposing the parts inside, from tiny ones such as the trapwork pivot pin, the spoon, and the fly to big ones like No. 81, a line that runs nearly the whole length of the piano from the imagined Kentucky to the Pacific Ocean. The qualities of Part No. 81 could make a pianist love K0862—or hate it. But Part No. 81 won't get the credit. It will also elude blame if pianists, critics, or sharp-eared impresarios are not captivated by K0862. They will mumble something about the action: It's too stiff or too shallow, or it's too mushy. They will complain about the acoustics of the hall: It's too dry, they will say, or it's too boomy. Someone with an over-the-shoulder understanding of what a piano technician does might grumble that the hammers need voicing, and maybe they do. Someone who is catty will put down the pianist for having a bad night. That, too, could be true.

Part No. 81 is so essential to the piano's being that no one will think to mention it. Yet it will give K0862 its recognizable tonal signature. More than any of the several thousand parts in K0862, Part No. 81 will determine whether the piano is voluble and strong-willed (which would be wonderful for, say, Rachmaninoff or Tchaikovsky or Ginastera) or warmer and mellower, almost meek (which could be better for Haydn or Mozart or

Schubert). Either is acceptable, though modern audiences have been conditioned to listen for a growling bass and a shimmering but not glassy treble. They expect sound that is physical, visceral, throbbing. Not all Steinways pack that kind of punch, and for that reason, not all Steinways will satisfy everyone.

There is no better way to explain how a piano differs from other almost-mass-produced products than the variations that come with Part No. 81. In contrast, the companies that manufacture heart pacemakers, for example, emphasize sameness. They promise that the pacemaker they ship tomorrow will operate just like the ones they shipped last week, and all of them will function exactly like the prototype that was approved by federal regulators. In a world in which one Airbus A300 performs about the same as another, Steinway acknowledges that there could be conspicuous differences between pianos shipped on the same day. But then airline pilots are not given their choice of planes, the way concert artists are given their choice of pianos.

Pianists who maintain that Steinway is not what it once was mention factors like employee turnover at the factory, which they say has cost Steinway experienced hands. Steinway counters that the number of employees who have quit, retired, or been fired has not changed over the years. But the turnover argument pinpoints something basic: Pacemakers and airplanes are made of metal and glass and plastic, which can be forged and cast to create perfect, or near-perfect, clones. Part No. 81 is a sheet of glued-together wood thinner than the ubiquitous four-by-eight sheets of plywood that weekend woodworkers jam into their sport utility vehicles on Saturday mornings. And Part No. 81 isn't just any part in the piano; it is the sounding board.

Once the sounding board (or, more formally, soundboard) is fitted into place beneath K0862's strings, it is the largest single piece of wood in the piano, a five-by-eight-foot slab of planks that is rounded off at one end. It will function as the piano's amplification system, a preelectronic triumph of physics. Without help from a single audio cable or input jack, it will transform relatively weak vibrations of the strings into sounds powerful enough to fill a concert hall. The more accurately it passes along the vibrations that the strings send its way, the better K0862 will be judged to be.

The fitting will come later. For now, the latest batch of sounding boards is on its ride with Verasammy. He occupies a dim corner across an aisle from where his co-worker, Pompeo Arena, aims a spotlight—actually three automobile headlights wired together—on soundboards that have just been assembled. Arena looks for imperfections in the grain, or gaps between the glued-together pieces, that have escaped notice. Mostly, the headlights—which double as heat lamps, to dry the glue—are unnecessary. Arena, an excitable man who has just turned sixty, has spent his adult life making sounding boards. His first employer, a piano company whose own nineteenth-century factory was less than a mile away, went out of business before he was forty. By the time K0862 receives his inspection, he has twenty years' experience at Steinway. Only rarely do the headlights reveal anything he has not already noticed.

Verasammy's wheel treats the soundboards that pass the headlight test to a leisurely whirl around a hub outfitted with a heating element to harden the glue and dry the wood. At the top, fifteen feet above the cluttered workbenches and dilapidated-looking storage bins, Verasammy's machine offers an unobstructed view of some of the oldest workrooms in the factory. But his passengers have been in higher places, for they are Sitka spruce, from some of the world's largest and longest-lived trees—trees that survived in the forest for two hundred to five hundred years. The expected life span of a soundboard is about fifty.

❧

The spruce trees being felled these days are found in British Columbia and Alaska. At the factory, there is no way to know where a batch of wood originated, so the most important part of this most American of pianos could be foreign. Its exact age, too, is something of a question mark. The wood in K0862 could date to the era of Columbus and Magellan. But most spruce these days comes from newer trees, trees that did not poke through the green canopy of the forest until sometime in the eighteenth century. Before too long, the wood going into pianos will come from trees that were saplings in Heinrich Engelhard Steinweg's day.

Steinway depends on the forests of the Pacific Northwest not because the wood from there is cheaper, and not because the men on management row invoke trendy terms like "the global economy," but because they cannot find enough of the wood they want anywhere else. The forests of New England, which were packed with usable spruce after World War I, were eventually cleared by loggers who reached their prey by wading through icy streams and inching their way up steep, mossy banks.

The Sitka spruce for K0862 was brought down the modern way. The loggers did not trudge to an out-of-the-way camp; they flew there in a helicopter and slithered down a rope ladder as the chopper hovered over them. They did not float their day's work down a river to a mill; they radioed for the same helicopter to lift the fallen tree to a waiting eighteen-wheeler, which hauled it to a dock and a southbound barge. Still, they have the most dangerous jobs in the Pacific Northwest, these men whose paychecks classify them as chokermen, chasers, hooktenders, and riggers. They are, in the words of a Steinway supplier who hires them, "the prima donnas of the forest."

One person at Steinway sees the Pacific Northwest regularly at the company's expense, but the company's wood technologist, Warren Albrecht, has not met the prima donnas of the forest. More often than not, Albrecht's trips to the Pacific Northwest are passionless, adventureless, and punishing. No doubt there are characters in the forest—Bunyanesque he-men with the hard-won confidence to do things their way or not at all—but he does not usually venture beyond a medium-sized mill in Tacoma, Washington. Out front, where Albrecht parks his rental car, is a small, almost shacklike office. It is surrounded by acres of long boards and the machinery to slice them into more manageable sizes. Albrecht is in his usual outfit, loafers, khaki pants, and a button-down shirt. Everyone else wears work boots and flannel shirts and dodges forklifts whose jaws are stuffed with wood that will not be here long, because this noisy, dusty place is only a pit stop.

The lumber industry calls this operation a remanufacturing plant. The wood here has already been through another mill, which shaved off the tree's bark and divided each round log into dozens of rough, mostly rectangular boards. A layman would work a word like "middleman" into the description, because the owners of this mill buy their wood in Canada and Alaska and sell it to far-flung buyers like Albrecht. In 2003, they brokered deals on fourteen million board feet of Sitka spruce. That earned them bragging rights as the largest commercial supplier of Sitka spruce in the United States.

Like Steinway, theirs is a company with an ampersand and the word "sons" in its name. Unlike Steinway & Sons, a public company with shares traded on the New York Stock Exchange, Fred Tebb & Sons is still family-owned and privately held. Like Steinway, the Tebbs' operation is several miles from downtown, on low-lying land near water—Puget Sound and a harbor where giant cranes loom over container ships anxious to be rid of their cargoes. In the distance is a freeway that curves by the Tacoma Dome, a 152-foot-tall structure that opened in the 1980s and has been home to hockey teams and the Seattle Super Sonics basketball team. It looks like an environmentally correct version of an R. Buckminster Fuller sketch. The Tebbs had a hand in it, for the Tacoma Dome is made entirely of wood—1.6 million board feet, to be precise.

The first few minutes of a conversation with Tom Tebb, a grandson of Fred, could be about Steinway: He describes a company that is less automated than it might be. This is not a place where a computer calculates which cuts will yield the most wood from a board—the board has to be looked at, by someone with the understanding to know how a customer like Albrecht wants it sliced. This is not a place where a laser dances across the rough grain of each board, tracing the narrow line a big whirling saw will follow. Here the process requires thought, and thought requires manpower—and experience. Like the managers at Steinway, when it comes to automation, Tom Tebb says, "We haven't found a way to do that."

Like Heinrich Engelhard Steinway, Fred Tebb learned the business somewhere else. He was the son of T. W. Tebb, a lumberman who had worked his way across the South, trading in yellow pine, before moving to Tacoma in 1910. T.W. was a newcomer in an industry that began with oxen, horses, and big-shouldered men who muscled their way through the forests with axes and crosscut saws. A dozen years later, Fred Tebb bought a plant that made silos and assemble-them-yourself houses. He turned it into what it is today: a "concentration yard" making shorter-length lumber.

Now Tebb & Sons is also a relic in a declining industry that is worried about being overmatched by foreign competitors. In the 1960s, timber-related jobs accounted for nearly 15 percent of Washington's employment. As late as 1979, the lumber business employed 160,000 people in the Northwest. But while log exports soared from 210 million board feet a year in 1960 to 4.2 billion in 1988, employment dropped 20 percent because technology reduced the need for manpower in the mills.

Tom Tebb, who is seventy-one, began selling wood to Steinway when Warren Albrecht was in grade school. By the 1990s, Tebb was also selling to such Steinway competitors as Baldwin and Young Chang. Albrecht often stewed about that when he visited the Tebbs. "I used to watch the different grades of soundboard come out to make sure I wasn't getting gypped," he remembers.

That seems to describe Albrecht's relationship with the Tebbs. They can share comfortable banter during the day and easygoing dinners in the evening, but there is always a dark undercurrent, a deep-seated suspicion. The Tebbs have been dealing with Albrecht long enough to have a sense of the pressure he feels. If he cannot bring back good wood, the foremen complain. "This batch of wood stinks. How come you don't get us anything we can work with anymore?" they will say. So Albrecht is finicky—sometimes, they believe, simply to remind them who's who. As Tom Tebb's older son, John, a beefy man who could have doubled for the comedian John Goodman, puts it, "We think Warren always finds some defect on purpose."

The Tebbs have other customers who are easier to read. Some are airplane restorers who work on sleek wings that are older than they are. During the Cold War, the Tebbs sold Sitka spruce for the nose cones of missiles. Nose cones must withstand heat and, sometimes, water, and "nothing is lighter and cheaper" than spruce, Tom Tebb observes. The Tebbs have also done business with NASA, which buys spruce for wind tunnel blades because it does not expand much in the heat. Before ski manufacturers discovered lamination, the Tebbs sold wood to them. They once sold wood for surfboards, too. No longer: "Surfboards have gone to China."

Albrecht takes a seat in the Tebbs' office. John Tebb, across the room, says, "China's going to make sixty, seventy percent of pianos."

"I guess," Albrecht says in a monotone.

"We're trying to sell wood there," John Tebb says.

"We're trying to sell pianos there," Albrecht says with a snort.

John Tebb cannot resist needling Albrecht. He mentions that the Japanese have an appetite for spruce in their homes. "They drove Warren's prices up," he says.

Already Albrecht has had a long day, and it is only eleven o'clock in the morning in Tacoma. To catch a seven o'clock flight from La Guardia Airport in New York, he had set his alarm clock for 3:30 A.M. and promised himself that he would sleep on the plane—all to look at wood. So the question is inevitable: Why spruce?

"I don't know," Albrecht says. "I just walked in, and that's the way it was being done."

The way it was being done when he walked into Steinway in the 1970s was the way it had been done for a couple of generations, but not the way it was done under Heinrich Engelhard. And Heinrich Engelhard had walked into piano making just in time to take advantage of the lucky convergence that spurred the industrial age: Factories' insatiable appetite for raw materials was matched by a seemingly inexhaustible supply. Steinway's first wood was a tiny fraction of the billions of board feet from Vermont and Maine that jammed the rivers of New England on the way to mills in Connecticut and, later, New Hampshire. Steinway made its soundboards with eastern white spruce until the 1920s.

Today the remaining spruce trees in the East cannot provide boards long enough, or wide enough, for pianos. "That's all logged out," Albrecht says flatly. And, while Steinway can glue boards together vertically (with the grain), as it does for the rims, it cannot do so horizontally (against the grain). So, long before Albrecht came on the job, Steinway had gone west and found the Tebbs. Steinway adopted the northwestern spruce from twenty-five hundred miles away, where gnarly roots serve as an anchor in soil so wet that logging is often an amphibious proposition.

This wood is not what Heinrich Engelhard used, and if there is a difference between the wood from the Pacific Northwest and the wood from back east in the old days, maybe that is why pianists grumble that pianos made before the Depression sound better than the newer ones. But making soundboards from a wood other than spruce is not an option. Nothing else flexes as easily or vibrates as freely. "Cheap manufacturers use lauan," Albrecht says with disdain. (The word "lauan" has become a generic term in the United States for imported tropical plywood; red lauan and white lauan came first from the rain forests of the

Philippines, and later from the Amazon.) Lauan, like most varieties of spruce, does not bond readily with glue and does not come long enough. For a concert grand like K0862, Albrecht needs a clear piece of wood 103 inches long. Fortunately for him and the Tebbs, concert grands account for less than 10 percent of Steinway's production these days.

Albrecht spends about $2 million a year buying spruce, but only about half of what the Tebbs send him is good enough for pianos. The rest ends up in a stack behind the factory—the priciest reject pile in New York. Sometimes, when the stack is tall, word circulates, and foremen drive off at the end of the day with as much as they can cram into their cars. If a state trooper pulls them over on the way home, would the trooper believe the explanation?

❧

There is a predictability to Albrecht's visits. He tends to spend time on the Tebbs' lot, doing what he trusts them to do when he is back in New York: grade the wood and earmark the best for Steinway. He wants to see what he is getting for Steinway's money. As he and John Tebb head out the back door and across the lot, Tebb points to a stack of lumber in a shed and says, "Got one for you, Warren: What's that species?"

"It's too obvious. It's walnut."

"Black walnut. My brother's building a house. This is the floor. He got it back east, bought a whole container. He's trying to sell some of it to pay the freight."

Albrecht is not interested; Steinway needs no walnut. They walk a few more steps, stopping at boards that will go into the Tebbs' next shipment. He seems pleased. "It just looks so nice. See how clear it is?" he asks.

"This is better than I've seen out of B.C.," John Tebb says.

Albrecht counters that it is still very wet—80 percent moisture by weight. "When you grade it when it's dry," he says, "it takes on a different appearance, and you see defects."

But he sees plenty that has promise for Part No. 81 as he works his way through the stack, which holds fifty-seven boards. On the first he finds and marks a pitch pocket, a void between growth rings where sap collected. The Tebbs will cut the board below the pitch pocket and send the clear piece to Steinway.

Albrecht rejects the second board with a quick look. "The grain's not straight," he says. The grain, the board-size snapshot of growth rings, matters because it affects a soundboard's ability to vibrate. He wants straight grain lines running the length of each board, with no little twists or turns that could slow the vibrations and blur the sound.

In his twenties, Albrecht spent eighteen months in Philadelphia working for an entrepreneur who had worked for a large guitar maker and had a doctorate in mathematics. They spent hours discussing the way spruce transmits sound, the way it behaves after being shaped and glued. "He wrote this paper that said that to get the best dampening properties, you want a ninety-degree angle at the end of the board," Albrecht recalls. "I don't know why that is. Maybe it's the way cells line up. When a board starts to turn from flat to vertical, it's winter growth." That is a tipoff that it is not a board he will accept as is. The order follows: Trim it.

On to the third board. He marks pitch pockets and a knot. The fourth is out, for small defects; the fifth is also out. "See that heart grain? That's what they call brown streak." Grading is a mind-numbing chore that requires good vision. Photographs of Steinway executives from the late 1970s show Albrecht with thick glasses. "I was 20/600," he says. He had laser eye surgery in 1999 and is now 20/15 in one eye and 20/20 in the other.

He glances at the tenth board. To John Tebb, he says, "That's a good one." Under his breath, he says, "Pretty good, except for the end."

The eleventh—out. He sees deficiencies in color and consistency. The twelfth, a knot. Once it is cut away, a section only about four feet long will be left—too short for a concert grand.

The thirteenth, fourteenth, and fifteenth, all out: bad grain. The seventeenth, finally: "O.K."

On the eighteenth, Albrecht notices a mark: bear claws. But that is not a rejection. "I don't mind them," he says, and the color and grain are fine. On the twenty-first, John Tebb points to a wavy patch of grain. "Does this bother you?" he asks. Albrecht says it does, explaining that the wood's inconsistency is a worry. Tebb cannot resist teasing. "Your German counterparts seem not to mind." Albrecht replies, "Give it to *them,* then. Out."

He sees coarse grain at one end of the twenty-seventh board and fine grain at the other, a mixture he does not want. The board, unsurprisingly, is rejected. Half of the fortieth board is marked to be trimmed away for blemishes. He inspects the forty-seventh board. He shakes his head, marking a section where the grain is wavy. He walks the length of the board "to see if I could get anything out of it." He marks a five-foot section in the middle as O.K. The rest will have to go. A knothole ruins the chances of board number fifty. A dark section on board fifty-one catches his eye, and he marks an X. He also marks the end, where the grain changes, becoming coarse. Then the last board: O.K.

The wood Albrecht does not reject goes inside the mill, where it will be trimmed on a circular saw later in the day. Albrecht walks across the yard to watch boards that were graded before he arrived glide out on a conveyor belt. They have been marked for specific uses by the saw's operator as he guided the blade through them: *SB,* for soundboard; *7,* for aircraft; and *K* or *AAA,* for guitars.

Albrecht expects to see some *SB*s. So does John Tebb, standing beside him. But the conveyor rolls out *7* after *7*. After a couple of minutes and a dozen *7*s, Tebb steps inside to tell the operator, in effect, "Adjust the mix." Perhaps he says that Steinway is outside, watching; perhaps not. But his message is clear: Find some soundboard.

Outside, *7*s continue to roll by, followed by a board with *AAA* crossed out and *SB* written in. Three *SB*s zip by. For the first time all day, Albrecht sounds testy. Of the first *SB,* he says, "This one ought to go into aircraft"; of the second, "Get that pitch pocket out of there."

Later, Albrecht says of John Tebb, "He hates it when I come out and inspect."

❧

The distance from Albrecht's office on management row to where the wood originates—those twenty-five hundred or so miles—is a measure of how the piano business has changed. When Heinrich Engelhard Steinweg started the business, wood did not travel thousands of miles from forest to factory. He used wood that was available locally. That was the way of the nineteenth century. If Steinway & Sons makes it to the twenty-second century, it is not clear where it will find wood. Will Sitka spruce still be available, and at what price?

These are not questions that Albrecht, tall and taciturn as always, mentions. What he excels at is looking at boards. He does not have X-ray vision. He cannot see problems that lie below the surface. His involvement with the wood he buys usually starts at Fred Tebb & Sons. But the wood starts its journey hundreds of miles from Tacoma, Washington, on the Queen Charlotte Islands, a lush cluster that is the far western edge of British Columbia, and the Tebbs have arranged a quick trip to the Queen Charlottes.

At first, Albrecht appears to be a reluctant traveler. The trip is a detour that will take him far from the familiar territory of the Tebbs' lot. He has never been to the Queen Charlottes. He has been to Alaska—the other source of spruce—only once, with a film crew that harbored the romanticized, Hollywoodish notion that the soul of a piano starts with a particular tree. He does not need to see what forest a board came from any more than a chef needs to see what herd a steak came from.

So the Queen Charlottes were as unknown to Albrecht as they were to the explorers who discovered them. At least they wanted to go there. In Vancouver, his body language was stiffer than it had been on the Tebbs' lot. The word that came to mind, watching him check in to a hotel and confirm the next morning's flight to the Queen Charlottes, was "dutiful." Enthusiastic he was not.

By coincidence, the Queen Charlottes were discovered at about the same time that the modern piano was evolving; they first appeared on maps at around Heinrich Engelhard Steinweg's day. In the lingo of geologists, the Queen Charlottes escaped glaciation, meaning that they survived the Ice Age unscathed. They also escaped the later age of European explorers, until the Spaniard Juan Perez sailed by in 1774. They were surveyed thirteen years later, making them, as John Vaillant noted in his lyrical book *The Golden Spruce,* "the last significant feature to be added to the earth's portrait"—except, of course, for the North and South Poles.

The Queen Charlottes are also known by the Indian name Haida Gwaii. The native population was devastated by a smallpox epidemic in the last half of the nineteenth century that killed all but two thousand or so people—about as many as live there now. The surviving descendants are, in the words of a thirtyish lumber broker in Vancouver, "the toughest, meanest natives on the coast." It is a predictable description, for he is a bit player in the long-running battle between the Haida and the government over who controls the ancient timber there. Land is also an issue; the Haide have never come to terms on a treaty with Canada. To preserve their "Misty Isles," they want more say over the management of the forests and more oversight of timber companies.

Their cause has been joined by environmentalists who want the loggers to change the way they harvest old-growth trees. For much of the twentieth century, the most desirable forests of the Queen Charlottes were stripped, leaving a barren landscape pocked by dead and undesirable trees. After a year or two, as old root systems loosened, landslides jammed stumps and topsoil into the islands' waterways.

Loggers have a different worry: Forests like those in the Queen Charlottes are proving uneconomical in a changing world. The problem, according to *The New York Times*, is that "the industry wastes up to half of each tree that is cut, and thousands of acres of old-growth forests have never been replanted." For that reason, some forest ecologists refer to British Columbia as "the Brazil of the north." As in Brazil, they worry that the forests that once seemed endless and self-regenerating may be gone in less than a century. Others are more alarmist, and predict depletion in another generation or two.

Albrecht, who wanted to be a forestry major at the University of Massachusetts but switched to wood technology when his professors told him forestry would lead to a job as a park ranger and not much else, has heard the environmentalists' arguments. "My contribution to the environmental thing," he says in a weary voice, "is to get as much out of the wood as possible." Efficiency, economy, no waste.

But he says that more trees are growing today than at any time, just not necessarily the right trees. "On the East Coast," he explains, "if you take down a cherry, they'll replace it with a pine. But you don't want pine, you want cherry." Sitka spruce presents the same problem. It grows well with hemlock, and only one in a dozen trees will be a Sitka spruce. The rest will be hemlocks, and when they are taller, they crowd out new Sitkas.

From their place on the green crescent that rims the West Coast from Alaska to Northern California, the Queen Charlottes are a rain forest more pleasant than the Amazon's. Everything that grows there grows tall, or so the early Europeans reported, and that, historians say, is why Jonathan Swift probably had the Queen Charlottes in mind when he dreamed up Brobdingnag, his land of giants. As Vaillant observes, the Queen Charlottes are "perfectly suited to support life on a grand scale, including the biggest freestanding creatures on earth."

One reason is that they comprise some of the wettest territory in the Western Hemisphere. Rainfall in the Queen

Charlottes averages about six feet a year, but has been known to exceed eighteen feet. Vaillant postulates another reason, one with which Albrecht easily concurs: Conifers will grow continuously unless the temperature drops below 38 degrees Fahrenheit. The canopy on the Queen Charlottes is so thick that the forest floor is protected from dips in temperature. That often keeps winter rain from turning to snow, and it leaves the wood too wet for Albrecht. At a sawmill near Vancouver that is stripping timber from the Queen Charlottes that is bound for the Tebbs, Albrecht stops midway across the lot to make note of a log that he puts at 80 percent moisture by weight. He does not like what he sees: rings that are not uniform, a sign that the tree grew in spurts. "If that tree grew at a steady rate for twenty years, you'd have even rings," he says. "That's what I want. What I don't want are gyrations."

Uneven texture can lead to problems when a sounding board is glued into place, and that, Albrecht says, could lead to problems with the sound the piano produces. To explain why, he must rely on supposition more than on science. "Acoustics in wood, there's not a lot of research," he says. "Why is a Stradivarius so good? I think it's the varnish. But Stradivari put it in brine for seven years, fourteen years, something like that. And then, no two Stradivariuses sound alike. It's the same with Steinways. If you put ten Steinways together, all the sounding boards are basically the same, but they won't sound anything like each other."

In the lumber business, the middlemen have middlemen. The Tebbs buy their wood from a wholesale firm near Vancouver, Husby Forest Products. On this trip, the Tebbs arranged for Albrecht to meet Glenn Fox, the wholesale broker at the firm with whom the Tebbs deal on behalf of Albrecht and Steinway. Fox is a romantic, and something of a gambler. He has calculated the odds: Less than 5 percent of the Sitka spruce from the Queen Charlottes will be of soundboard quality. It is a high-risk venture. Fox pays for the sawmilling, the early work on the logs to remove the bark and cut rough boards, betting that his profit will cover the mill's fees—and then some. "You can make a hundred thousand dollars, or you can lose a hundred thousand dollars," his partner, another broker, John Okamoto, says.

Fox agrees.

"In a single day," Okamoto adds for clarification.

Fox's goal is no different from a hedge fund manager's: to make 10 to 15 percent clear. "If you do that twelve times a year, you're doing O.K.," Okamoto explains. Another broker, Rolf Komlos, recently purchased wood somewhere in the supermarket of lumber that is Vancouver. There is, of course, no public-address system, no nicely modulated announcer's voice murmuring, "Attention, shoppers, today's special on Douglas fir . . ." Word of bargains circulates by telephone and e-mail, and brokers like Fox can, in effect, roam the aisles by boat if they have time to browse. There is a lot to see: The Fraser River is a fifty-mile-long channel where shipments of lashed-together logs—called booms— are parked in pockets along the shoreline. The red cedar, pine, and spruce can float there for as long as six months; the fresh water does not damage the wood. That gives brokers time to call prospective buyers, including Rick Tebb at Tebb & Sons, to negotiate terms and arrange for the boom to be towed to a local mill and stripped of its bark. As in Tacoma, the timber industry is consolidating. Vancouver had more than sixty mills in the 1920s, but has only twenty now. In the last ten years, one mill has closed down every year.

The boom holding Komlos's logs, the logs destined for Steinway, is a twenty-minute ride away in a chartered fishing boat that is waiting at a marina near his office. Albrecht climbs in as Komlos talks about the details of what he says is "a pretty good boom." It took six weeks for the logs to reach Vancouver from the Queen Charlottes, and Komlos expects them to yield plenty of soundboard-quality wood.

The boat accelerates, its bow slapping at the water as it zips by boom after boom. To untrained eyes, they look alike. A central computer keeps track of where each shipment has been parked. The captain has the coordinates, and Komlos has the binoculars.

When the boat slows, Komlos looks for the tag number. The shipment is at the front of the boom, next to where Komlos and Albrecht climb out. Komlos brought along a pair of golf shoes so a novice could walk with them. The golf shoes are lighter than a logger's spiky boots, but they serve the same purpose: traction on the wet wood. They hold fast as Okamoto jumps out of the boat and the boom rocks from side to side. There is a cartoonish moment when the logs seem to be spinning and some Road Runner footwork is the only way to remain upright, but Komlos never loses his balance—or his salesman's enthusiasm. This is, he announces yet again, "a pretty good boom." But the logs are smaller than usual, only thirty inches in diameter (forty to fifty inches is normal). Still, Komlos gestures to one small section that he says will be clear enough for soundboards.

From the river, the wood will go to an automated mill, where the bark will be stripped away in less than a minute as each log whirls around on a spindle. Then the log will slide toward a saw, untouched by the hands of the few men in the plant. A computer figures out the cuts that will yield the most wood, and laser beams trace the shapes with thin red lines. An operator gives the go-ahead by pushing a button on what looks like a computer-game joystick.

The operator sits in a cab like one on a tractor, barely big enough for three people to stand inside, looking through the windshield. The cab reduces the noise level, but even so, the operators wear headphone-like ear protectors. Shouting above the noise, Komlos says the mill can turn out 120,000 board feet in an eight-hour shift, enough for thirty thousand houses.

Fox has scheduled the trip deep into the Queen Charlottes for the next morning. As those first few European explorers learned—among them Captain Cook—the Queen Charlottes are a territory of fast-moving squalls. At the Vancouver airport on the morning Albrecht is set to fly there, the words "weather advisory" flash on the departure board next to the gate number of his flight. He asks an agent at the gate what "weather advisory" means.

"Oh, he'll get through it," the agent responds. "It'll just be a landing you'll tell your grandchildren about."

That is too much for one of Albrecht's traveling companions, who calls off the trip—there is no reason to fly through rough weather only to board a smaller plane for a short flight to a logging camp. Albrecht is clearly relieved. The memory of flying over Alaska with the film crew had been on his mind. It was not a level flight. The pilot had humored the cameraman by keeping one wing down the whole time and sliding back the cabin door as they skimmed the forest. The cameraman had braced himself in the opening, all but dangling over the trees below. He got the footage he wanted. Albrecht remembers nausea setting in.

He still has not seen where his wood comes from. He has not seen any logging, and he is not unhappy.

❧

A shipment from the Tebbs takes a couple of weeks to reach Steinway. The boards spend the winter in the lumberyard beyond the factory parking lot, and several days in the kilns that bake the moisture out of them. Then woodworkers like Jagdesh Sukhu do all over again what Albrecht did in the Tebbs' yard: He sorts them. Then he sorts them again. Sukhu has fourteen years of experience in deciding what wood is right for Part No. 81 and what is not. On the day he chooses the wood for the sounding board for K0862, he rejects more than half of the presorted wood in the stack for blemishes, knots, wormholes, and other imperfections almost too small to see. Never mind that spruce costs about seven dollars a running foot.

"How much we reject depends on the bundle," Sukhu says as he marks the rejects with a blue crayon. "Sometimes we reject one-quarter, sometimes three-quarters, sometimes more than three-quarters. When you do it every day, you know exactly what you want and what you don't want."

After so many years, his eyes, like Albrecht's, can see flaws that ordinary eyes cannot. But he claims no special connection to the wood, no special talent that makes him better at this than someone else; like Albrecht, he is just doing what was being done when he walked in. "They showed us a finished soundboard, what they accept, what they don't accept," Sukhu says, explaining how he learned the job. "I took over from there."

But he cannot tell what the raw wood of a sounding board will do for a piano. He cannot tap a sounding board and say whether it will deliver a bigger, more resonant tone than the one next to it. Neither can Albrecht. So he assumes all soundboards to be equal, and leaves one of the most important decisions in K0862's young life to the luck of the draw. Which sounding board goes into K0862 will be determined almost at random, when a worker on a different floor in the factory picks one from a rack of seemingly identical pieces—whichever one happens to be on hand at the moment a sounding board is needed.

The marriage of the rim and the sounding board is a crucial moment in defining what K0862 will become. The randomness of it only deepens the question of how good K0862 will turn out to be. The moment when the instrument can finally be played, and listened to, is still months away.

For now, what counts is what can be seen. Sukhu and the other workers in his part of the factory have grain counters, clear plastic rulers they can use to measure whatever comes before them. The standard is straightforward: If there are fewer than ten grain lines to an inch, the wood is not good enough. The wider the grain—in other words, the fewer the lines per inch—the faster a tree grew in the forest, and piano makers do not want wood from trees that grew too fast; it is weaker. Nor does Steinway want trees that had many branches, because branches cause knotholes. Wood that is even helps the piano's sound.

Like a jigsaw puzzle player, Sukhu assembles the boards into the size and shape of a soundboard. Each puzzle he finishes goes under Pompeo Arena's headlights and then onto Paul Verasammy's drying wheel.

"There's nothing very high tech here," Andy Horbachevsky, the manufacturing director, explains.

Then there is another layover. Each soundboard spends a few days in a small, hot room. There is only one reason to be there. "We're trying to get it bone-dry," Horbachevsky says. Dryness matters because the next step is to glue a handful of narrow sugar-pine ribs across the bottom of the soundboard, running against the grain. The ribs will hold the soundboard's crown, the slight semicircular bulge that will improve the way it transmits vibrations. "If we didn't get it bone-dry, you wouldn't get any crown, and it wouldn't be any good," Horbachevsky says as a worker, Antoine Hilaire, puts the ribs in place and settles the soundboard into a press, essentially a large clamp that will hold it in place overnight, long enough to fix its shape for good.

It moves across the aisle to Byron Bhairo, who will scrape off the excess glue in the morning. Appearance counts. "We want it to look uniform," Horbachevsky explains. "You're paying ninety grand, you don't want a zebra stripe."

5

Descendant

The birth of the piano-forte: a Cristofori pianoforte dating from 1720

For all its newness, K0862 is a descendant of a long black instrument in the Metropolitan Museum of Art in New York City that sits behind a velvet rope and a sign that says it is the world's oldest piano. It is more than 280 years old and is, for the record, two years older than the world's first fire extinguisher and four years older than the world's first mercury thermometer.

Like K0862, it is an ingenious assembly of levers and hammers. Like K0862, it is somewhat plain looking—the painters who lined the lids of so many eighteenth-century keyboard instruments with marshy hunting scenes did not get their brushes on this one. It is ninety inches long, seventeen inches shorter than K0862. Unlike K0862, with its curves and bends and dips, the world's oldest piano has a surprisingly rectangular shape, almost like a coffin.

It was made by Bartolomeo Cristofori, who worked for a Medici (though, as the pianist and historian Arthur Loesser has pointed out, a backwater Medici, Prince Ferdinand of Tuscany, not Lorenzo the Magnificent). For someone who did something so important, Cristofori was casual about his name; historians note that it turns up as Cristofali, Cristofani, and Christofani. Before he made the first of his twenty pianos—and before he apparently became disillusioned and gave up on them—he was known for his harpsichords. He also turned out other instruments, notably cellos and double basses. But he did not revolutionize things for the likes of Pablo Casals and Yo-Yo Ma.

Cristofori lived in a world of frustrated keyboard players. Harpsichords could be played only one way; they did not respond to changes in touch. If a harpsichordist slammed or smacked or whacked a key—in other words, if he hit it with more than the usual force—the sound did not become louder. If he used less force, the key might not swing into action at all. Some performers resorted to what the instrument historian

Richard Burnett calls "subtlety or guile," to generate more sound, or clumsy add-on attachments.

Cristofori invented more than an instrument: He invented a name for it. His "invention" was described in the Medici "Inventory of Diverse Musical Instruments" of 1700 as an *"arpicembalo che fa il piano e il forte"* ("large keyboard instrument that produces soft and loud"). By the time the Steinways came along, that mouthful had been shortened, at least in conversation, to "piano."

The world knows about Cristofori from two documents written in 1711. One was a diary entry that dated Cristofori's work on his new instrument to 1698. The other was an article by Scipione Maffei, whom the historian Eric W. Cochrane Jr. has called the "noisiest gadfly" in Italy at the time. Like so many others, Maffei misspelled Cristofori's name, and the sketches he drew for his article are problematic. Maffei reports that Cristofori used an inverted wrestplank to hold the tuning pins, but the wrestplank in the instrument at the Metropolitan Museum is not fitted that way. Historians suggest two possibilities: Maffei drew from memory, and his memory was no better than his spelling; or Cristofori had reworked the design by the time he built the pianoforte that ended up at the Met, as well as the two other Cristofori pianos that survive.

Still, Maffei got the basic facts right, and Cristofori's "pianoforte" was an engineering marvel. Instead of using the customary quills to pluck the strings, this instrument had leather-covered hammers, each as small as the eraser on the end of a pencil, to strike them head-on. Cristofori's piano also had the beginnings of an escapement mechanism that let the hammers fall away quickly. Among other things, that let the person at the keyboard play soft (piano) or loud (forte). Cristofori also installed a hammer catcher called a backcheck.

The keys on Cristofori's piano are wooden levers that pivot on a balance rail, like seesaws. The player's end of the seesaw travels less than half an inch. Within that short distance is everything: the control of the speed at which the key descends, and thus the control of the speed with which the hammer flies up against the string. Pressure, too, makes a difference. How hard the key is pressed determines how hard the hammer attacks the string—the greater the force, the louder the sound. It all seems so basic, but in a world of harpsichords that were not responsive to changes in touch, it was an accomplishment that changed the rules of music. Johann Sebastian Bach endorsed the products of a copycat pianoforte builder (who, to please the one and only Bach, softened the instrument's heavy touch and did something about its watery treble). In the 1760s, six-year-old Wolfgang Amadeus Mozart learned his first piano piece. Being Mozart, he did it in only half an hour. One of Bach's sons played in what is widely considered the world's first public piano recital, in London. A few years after that, Thomas Jefferson, always a trendsetter, arranged to have a piano delivered, rather than the clavichord he had originally ordered for his fiancée.

The basic principles that govern the inner workings of Cristofori's piano will also guide K0862—though refined and extended to cover a larger range and generate a bigger sound. Cristofori's piano has just fifty-four keys—four and a half octaves—compared to K0862's eighty-eight; K0862 will have nineteen keys above the Cristofori's highest note, and fifteen below its lowest. K0862's cast-iron plate will weigh about 340 pounds, heavier than the entire Cristofori piano. The longest string on K0862 will span six feet seven and a half inches, five inches longer than the longest string on the Cristofori; the shortest string on K0862 will be only a couple of inches long, a bit less than half the length of the shortest string on the Cristofori. The thickest string on the Cristofori is smaller in diameter than the thinnest string on K0862. The musicologist Henry Edward Krehbiel, who worked out these comparisons nearly a century ago, estimated that the top note on the Cristofori exerts a strain of 170 pounds on the frame. The pressure of the top note on K0862 is enough to crush the Cristofori's entire frame, just as Krehbiel calculated would happen. Steinway's design—the design of K0862—has not changed much. The Cristofori has not changed at all.

❧

K0862 is also a descendant of later European pianos— Broadwoods like the one in Daniel Mason's novel *The Piano Tuner* and Erards like the one in Thad Carhart's memoir *The Piano Shop on the Left Bank*. John Broadwood, a Scot who married the boss's daughter and took over his father-in-law's London firm, invented the world's first grand piano. It was really nothing more than a pianoforte built to fit in a long harpsichord case. It stood out because his German competitors, who had converged on London after the Seven Years' War, favored squares.

Like K0862, the shape of the world's first grand was determined by the long strings in the bass. Some piano makers eventually pushed their grands past the ten-foot mark, thirteen inches beyond K0862. The nineteenth-century virtuoso Louis Moreau Gottschalk bragged of having not one but two ten-footers that he called "cowardly mastodons." But Broadwood's first grand was only about half that length and carried a keyboard of six octaves, or seventy-eight keys, enlarged from his earlier design of sixty-five. He had also teased out a few technical refinements that would be passed down to K0862. It was Broadwood who devised the bridgework—risers that sit on the sounding board and point the strings on their way like the stanchions that guide the cables on a ski lift. The bridges created a noticeably more resonant bass register. Broadwood also developed the right pedal to sustain notes, replacing a knee lever that had been used by performers to lift and hold the dampers above the strings.

Broadwood attracted the attention of big-name customers, including Beethoven. Liszt later owned Beethoven's Broadwood, and he remained loyal to the Broadwood brand, playing one on his last visit to London, in 1886. The pianist Melvyn Tan, who recorded a good deal of Beethoven's piano music on the Beethoven-Liszt Broadwood in the 1990s, said that it is "much closer to the modern piano" than to Viennese forte-pianos of its day. "The texture and sound is much denser, almost 'fruitier,' " but the action does not feel as crisp, he explained. "This probably explains why it feels much closer to a Steinway, particularly an old Steinway." Of course, Liszt was a when-in-London-do-as-the-Londoners-do type; he had also endorsed Steinway. And he would have known that Broadwood's pianos were not just something to listen to: A Broadwood made for the queen of Spain had a case with Wedgwood medallions by Thomas Sheraton, whose designs inspired the cut of the arms on K0862 and other American Steinways.

But there is also something French in K0862: the hammers and the action. In the first third of the nineteenth century the Parisian piano maker Henri Pape substituted felt for leather on the hammers, and his rival Sébastian Erard developed a double-escapement mechanism that at last made the keys sensitive to the pianist's touch. It was that mechanism that Heinrich Engelhard Steinweg and Henry Steinway, Jr., adapted for No. 483, their first piano in America. When they graduated to making grand pianos, "Erard was the ideal" that Henry Jr. had in his sights, the music historian Cynthia Adams Hoover writes. "He sought a quick repetition 'as in the Erard action.' The Steinway grand at that time was not strikingly different from the Chickering or the Erard." Within a year, though, the Steinways made a grand that was equipped with something that was different from the Erard: a one-piece metal plate, which would become the standard for Steinway concert grands. The Erard carried a weaker two-piece frame.

A number of early Erards are still playable. In 1997, when Emanuel Ax recorded a Chopin concerto on an 1851 Erard, he worried about how hard he could attack a piano that old, but soon realized it could take a pounding. He found the action "slightly shallower" than on a modern grand, but Ax and the Erard came to terms without "a radical rethinking or adjustment" in the way he played. He reported that the Erard was mellower in the bass than a modern piano and more brilliant but less sustained in the treble.

If the Steinways had not come along, that shallower touch and mellower sound might be the antecedent of a modern concert grand like K0862.

❧

What the Steinways came up with was an ancestor of K0862, one of a handful of instruments that marked the turning points in the development of the modern concert grand in the last half of the nineteenth century. This particular ancestor had a surprising "elasticity of touch," in the words of a *New York Times* writer who tried one at a nineteenth-century forerunner of a world's fair. The judges, too, found that entry captivating, awarded it a gold medal, and put Steinway & Sons on the map. It was as simple as that.

The scene was New York's answer to London's Crystal Palace, a giant display case for everything that was new in the mid-nineteenth century. New York's Crystal Palace was a colossal iron-and-glass greenhouse a block from where Times Square now pulses and blinks, on what were then the outskirts of the city. It was a far-off destination in a city that was packed into the southern end of Manhattan. But what a destination the Crystal Palace was: Morse's telegraphs, Colt's revolvers, Tiffany's lamps—the household names were all there. Wandering by, staring at the biggest in this category and the best in that, were everyone from the local dignitaries who had built the place to a teenage tourist from Missouri named Samuel Clemens, who called it the "perfect fairy palace—beautiful beyond description."

Expositions, the forerunners of world's fairs, were a parade of entrepreneurs and hucksters and potential customers, part circus and part see-and-be-seen fashion show. To fledglings like the Steinways, in business for only two years, fairs offered exposure—huge crowds would jam their booth. But fairs also offered recognition—big-name judges would hand out prizes. And those prizes were the Steinways' best hope of toppling the piano establishment. William probably picked up on the importance of fairs from the moment he went to work in New York. As the historian Arthur Loesser points out, the original Nunns firm had collected a prize at the Mechanics' Institute show in 1830.

Steinway biographers presume that the Steinways heard about the 1851 exposition in London and visited the 1853 fair in New York as spectators who paid the five-cent admission. The Steinways did not become exhibitors until 1855, when one of their pianos won a prize for "superior workmanship" at the Metropolitan Mechanics' Institute Fair in Washington, D.C. The setting was as new as the items on display. The institute moved from the hall it had rented in previous years—described in the institute's superlative-laden brochure as "one of the longest and most magnificent rooms in the United States"—to the Smithsonian Institution's "new and splendid" building. The Smithsonian's first secretary, the pioneering physicist Joseph Henry, doubled as president of the Mechanics' Institute and scheduled the fair as the first event in the Smithsonian's barely finished fortress on the Mall. *The New York Times* called the musical instrument area "large and interesting" and, playing up the local angle, said that New York "contributes the gems of the exhibition," the pianos from Steinway & Sons. The *Times* reporter mentioned that the tone of the two Steinways was "incomparably superior to anything ever before presented" for inspection—"full, round, rich, even, sweet and brilliant."

It was the only out-of-town tryout with which the Steinways bothered. They were ready for the big time, for the Crystal Palace in New York. That first time, at least, the judges acted honest. There were no allegations that bagmen paid them to favor this entry or that, no talk of behind-the-scenes skullduggery.

Henry Jr. had figured out a solution to something that had bedeviled piano makers since Cristofori: how to put longer strings under the lid without lengthening the case. It may not seem like much, except to a tuner or a physicist. But Henry Jr. realized that longer strings would deliver the kind of room-filling sound that earlier pianos lacked. He devised a new, two-level layout under the lid, with the treble strings on the bottom level and the bass strings crossing over them in a fan-shaped pattern. This design allowed the Steinways to install longer bass strings than those on their earlier square models or—and this probably mattered more to the Steinways—than those on their competitors' pianos.

The New York Times reported that the Crystal Palace judges noticed the difference and reached a consensus almost as soon as they heard the Steinway's first note. "One by one the jurors gathered round," the *Times* told its readers, "and without a word being spoken, everyone knew that it was the best piano in the exhibition. . . . There was no argument, no discussion."

The pianos the Steinways had sent to Washington were "semi-grands"; the ones at the Crystal Palace were squares, which accounted for four out of five pianos made in the United States at the time. The design was popular with the emerging middle class because, among other things, a square did not occupy too much space in a parlor. A grand's ungainly shape made it harder to fit, and American manufacturers had concentrated on the consumer market. When professional pianists—that is, European stars whom Americans would pay to hear, the way they paid to see circus acts or famous actors—crisscrossed the country, they hauled along their monster-sized European grands. As William later wrote, "The sale of grand pianos were [*sic*] about as scarce as angels' visits."

The Steinways made their first grands in 1856 for that year's Crystal Palace fair. The design posed a number of risks, and the pianos did not do as well as in 1855—the Steinway grand won only the silver medal. Chickering took home the gold. There was talk of unfairness, of judges who were in the Chickerings' pocket. But Steinway's incremental design changes and refinements soon added up to something revolutionary: a piano whose voice would carry all the way to the back of the two- and three-thousand-seat concert halls that were going up. The sound was clear, not shrill, not tinny. And the touch was both rapid and delicate: The keys could rebound fast enough to keep up with any virtuoso or composition.

The Steinways tinkered and tweaked and tinkered some more, and in 1857 finished a piano to which they assigned the serial number 1199. This piano, like the Crystal Palace piano an important ancestor of K0862, had almost all the elements of the modern grand: felt-covered hammers, a cast-iron frame, a double-escapement action like the French piano maker Erard's repetition action. The strings ran straight out; Henry Jr. had not yet adapted the fan-shaped layout to the grand's case. But this piano had more power than its predecessors. "No longer could Beethoven have complained . . . that the piano sounded too much like a harp," Professor Edwin M. Good wrote. "That small, quickly decaying tone was a thing of the past, except on the most shoddy of instruments made for the most modest parlors."

Had the Steinways stopped with 1199, they would not have become a household name, and their company would not have lasted to make K0862. They realized that the logical next step was to combine ideas from harpsichord and piano making: overstringing and nineteenth-century advances in metalworking—specifically, metal frames that could be positioned over the sounding boards. In 1860, Henry Jr. patented the scale, or design, of the "overstrung grand." Its debut with the New York Philharmonic attracted as much attention as the performance itself. *The New York Times* loved the sound. "It impressed us as being one of the most majestic instruments we have ever heard in the concert-room," the *Times* declared. In 1862, Steinway's overstrung grand astounded Europe by taking first prize at the London World's Fair. But the Steinways still had work to do. That piano was not the modern grand. Not yet.

※

The Paris exposition of 1867 was about newness and showiness—the sudden supremacy of industrialists, the demise of Beaux-Arts academicians, the splendor (and the cluelessness) of soon-to-be-overthrown royals. It was a gathering of big names—Victor Hugo himself wrote a guidebook—and the entire spectacle took place under one roof, a huge iron-and-glass installation that was the work of the future tower-builder Gustave Eiffel. Steinway & Sons sent one son and five pianos—three grands and two uprights. The son, C. F. Theodore, brought home two gold medals, a special "grand testimonial" medal (in this instance "grand" referred to greatness, not to the size of the piano), and bragging rights of the most valuable kind, for America still looked to Europe for cultural validation.

The company spent months preparing for Paris. William reported in his diary that he tested the pianos for the fair in Steinway Hall in January, then sent them on their way. By the time the exposition opened in May—on a day that was either bright or rainy, depending on which newspaper account one believes—Theodore had spent $80,000 ($1 million in today's dollars) on advertisements and on entertaining well-connected people who could put in a word when the judges began making the rounds. Theodore's heart was set on capturing "a medal and a cross"—not just the first-place prize in the piano division, but a best-in-show medallion.

If Steinway was preoccupied with winning, so was Chickering & Sons, and everyone knew it. Ernest Closson, in his *History of the Piano,* quotes a nineteenth-century account that says Chickering had matched Steinway's heavy spending. A French columnist cast the Steinways as the Montagues and the Chickerings as the Capulets in a Shakespearean feud. The dispatches in the New York newspapers contained no such grandiloquence. In *The New York Times,* a reporter identified as "Monadnock" dutifully noted that the American instruments were "more talked about than all the rest," though he said that "the French pianos are beautiful, brilliant in tone and exquisite in form and finish." Another writer, "C.B.S."—apparently the *Times* music critic, Charles Bailey Seymour—yielded nothing to the French. He was convinced that the piano industry's center of gravity had already crossed the Atlantic. "More good pianos may be heard in a single American street of Boston and New York than can be heard in any salon of Europe," he declared.

The showdown between Steinway and Chickering had its comical moments. "In the morning, Messrs. Chickering & Sons have a few first-class artists to play upon their instruments," Seymour wrote. "In the afternoon, Messrs. Steinway & Sons have a few first-class artists to play upon *their* instruments." "Monadnock" concurred, describing times when both companies had pianists poised at the keyboard. "Monadnock" did not go so far as to say that the pianists sat there with their hands in the air, their fingers spread in the shape of their opening chord. But each was waiting for the tiniest break in the other's melody. "At the first pause, if only a two-bar rest, the other fellow would cut in."

Pianos not being played were vulnerable to what would now be called industrial espionage. Tuners and rival piano makers pried open the locked cases. The guts, the *Times* said, were "whipped out . . . and examined."

Theodore sent William a telegram in May saying that Steinway had won the first gold medal. That was all the telegram said—it contained no details, leaving William to wonder and worry. It took weeks for a rundown of the medals to reach New York in the mail. "We head the list," he was finally able to write in his diary. But that rundown was not enough for William. The order in which the awards were presented did not necessarily follow the published list. Again William worried from afar. And eventually, as he noted in his diary, Steinway "got gold medal before Chickering." In reporting the news, the *Times* seemed to be rooting for the home team. It never mentioned Chickering's name, referring to Chickering only as the "firm exhibiting from Boston." Noting that the third-place medal went to Broadwood, the *Times* commented, "It is certainly most humiliating . . . that even the most celebrated piano-forte makers of Paris, Vienna, Berlin and Leipzig take only silver medals, ranking as second-class instruments."

As K0862 was moving through the factory, another ancestor, a rosewood piano with elaborately carved legs, languished in a classroom at California State University at Fresno. The budget is too tight to tune it regularly or pay for new hammers and strings, and No. 33610 is played only when a second piano is needed to rehearse a duet—an ignominious retirement. Its beginning was illustrious, for No. 33610 was one of two Steinways that C. F. Theodore built for the Centennial Exposition in Philadelphia in 1876. C. F. Theodore was closing in on the direct predecessor of K0862. William referred to the centennial piano as "the new extra large concert grand," and at eight feet nine inches, it was larger than Steinway's grands of the time, and less than three inches shorter than K0862.

William tempted the virtuoso Hans von Bülow long before he sent it to Philadelphia. William set it up on the stage at Steinway Hall at the end of 1875, and sneaked in von Bülow—who was in the midst of an American tour arranged by Chickering, Steinway's longtime rival—for a private tryout. Von Bülow was probably as famous for having married Liszt's daughter as he was for having studied with Liszt, and the gossips who whispered about him had kept tabs on Cosima Liszt von Bülow's affair with Richard Wagner, the two children she had by Wagner while married to von Bülow, and their eventual divorce. William, always the promoter, knew that people were fascinated by von Bülow, that people talked about him wherever he went, and that if they talked about him, they would talk about the pianos he played. No doubt William hoped that von Bülow would defect to Steinway.

The pianist was "very friendly," William wrote in his diary, and—more important—was "very pleased with the tone and action." Indeed, William and C. F. Theodore had high hopes for the touch of No. 33610. Steinway had received a patent for a new mechanism, the "regulation action pilot"—better known as the capstan screw, which lifts the parts that drive the hammer toward the string. The Steinways' device was adjustable, an advance that would simplify the chore of modifying a piano's action to a pianist's liking. Henry Z. Steinway calls that patent the birth of the moden grand-piano action.

But his grandfather's salesmanship failed to win over von Bülow. He remained on Chickering's roster, and No. 33610 went off to Philadelphia, where, as in Paris, Steinway and Chickering tried to outdo each other alongside typewriters, air brakes, and telegraphs that could transmit two messages simultaneously over the same wire. The historian Bruno Giberti says the crowds were mesmerized by "the fragrance of exotic goods … and the nearly continuous sound of music emanating from various stations—the bandstand in the center of the building, the displays of instruments in the American section, the organs in the north and east galleries." Richard Wagner was commissioned to write the "Centennial Inauguration March," and judges included the distinguished Joseph Henry of the Smithsonian Institution, who had figured in a small way in the Steinways' 1855 triumph in Washington. Not everything that the Crystal Palace crowds saw was brand-new. The Steinway biographer D. W. Fostle points out that Chickering displayed a piano it had made in 1823. Some fairgoers probably saw it as evidence that the piano industry had come a long way since the days of James Monroe and John Quincy Adams. But that piano was also a not-so-subtle reminder—to the Steinways, anyway—that Chickering was the brand with experience. Not even Heinrich Engelhard's "kitchen piano" was that old.

In their corner of the main building, the rival piano makers settled in for eighteen months of scandals and squabbles; William was still fighting for preeminence a year after the last visitor had trudged through. It did not help that William's younger brother, Albert, called Frank Chickering "a loony fool," or that some of the judges were corruptible. One was said to be close to the Chickering family; another had endorsed Weber pianos; a third, Julius Schiedmayer, was an acquaintance of C. F. Theodore's who had been on the jury at the Paris exposition in 1867. There was talk that the fourth had taken bribes at past expositions. Fostle says the consensus was that there was "a Chickering judge, a Steinway judge, a Weber judge and a judge for rent"—

and the Steinways set out to rent him. The plan, apparently dreamed up in a closed-door session with Schiedmayer, was to have Frederic Boscovitz, the pianist they had hired to serenade fairgoers, function as the Steinways' bagman. They would pay Boscovitz an extra thousand dollars. Boscovitz would pay off the judge. They would see nothing, and would say they knew nothing.

But that was not all. William and C. F. Theodore actually wrote Schiedmayer's report, to leave nothing to chance. They even prepared a second version during the deliberations in Philadelphia. William said he "worked like a beaver" with Schiedmayer. The rewrite incorporated changes to which Schiedmayer tipped them off—changes intended to make Schiedmayer's report acceptable to all four judges. How this was accomplished sounds laughable. There were rumors that someone passed Schiedmayer's report out a window, and that it was taken to the Steinways, rewritten, taken back to the same window, and returned to Schiedmayer. Other piano makers waited out the deliberations inside, by the judges' room. Frank Chickering could not have liked what he overheard. The judges seemed to agree that his pianos had a smallish tone. The consensus was that the bigger Steinway sound was better.

Chickering, as Fostle puts it, "appeared to be honest" even in what looked like defeat. But Schiedmayer's connection to the Steinways soon became known, and the Steinways found themselves accused of trying to influence the judges. The *Times* summarized the developments in three words: "The piano war." The paper published an article by a writer identified as "Sphinx"—as in 1867, when it printed dispatches from "Monadnock" in Paris, The *Times* had yet to forbid catchy pseudonyms. "Sphinx" promised to provide "the inside history of the piano awards which are causing so much stir in the papers." He was playing catch-up. The hubbub had begun when a headline in *The New York Herald* asked: "What's the Price of Awards and Medals?" The long article that followed reported talk of "maneuverings" for the piano prizes, just as there had been "murmurings" that in other departments the fixes were in. The article mentioned bribery and collusion by other piano makers, but zeroed in on Schiedmayer and Steinway. William prepared a rebuttal defending Schiedmayer, which the *Herald* published. Later he sent an official of the fair "a positive statement that we never paid any money to any of the judges." Of course, he made no mention of Boscovitz, and the historian Richard K. Lieberman writes that William used a lunch date to remind Schiedmayer "to stick to the official story—that they had done no wrong."

Somehow, William carried the day; when the Centennial commission's report finally came out, Steinway & Sons was listed as winning two awards. One recognized the "highest degree of excellence." The *Herald* announced: "Steinway & Sons proclaimed the standard pianos of the world."

That should have been the end of it. But William, it seems, had not been alone in cruising the shadows of exposition, where results could be influenced. A second "judge's report," now believed to have been written by Steinways' rival, Albert Weber, surfaced. It praised the Weber piano as superior to the Steinway. The secretary to the judges called it a "bare-faced fraud." Publicity-conscious William could not have been pleased when *Frank Leslie's Illustrated Newspaper* published a 324-page book describing the Centennial Exposition in relentless detail. The one engraving of a piano manufacturer's display booth showed Weber's booth with a sign on the wall that said: "A. Weber received the medal." The write-up in *Frank Leslie's* mentioned only one manufacturer, and it was not Steinway: Weber's "magnificently inlaid concert grand" impressed the reporter. Perhaps No. 33610 was too plain-looking to attract the attention of a reporter who seems not to have played the pianos, but something else in the article in *Frank Leslie's* was more troubling for Steinway. The article quoted an unidentified judge as saying that the Webers were "unquestionably the best pianos on exhibition. Weber's grand piano was the most wonderful piano I ever touched or heard." William rounded up ten "examining judges," including Scheidmayer and Joseph Henry, and had them sign an extraordinary document that he reprinted in company catalogs as late as 1888. The first two words were in large letters, and the rest of the opening line was in smaller, boldface type: "Official confirmation of Steinway & Sons' complete victory at the Centennial Exhibition." It went on to note that Steinway's entries had received an average of 95½ points "out of a possible 96." The headline in the *Times* read "The Truth at Last."

William had had enough of fairs. He declared that Steinway would never again be an exhibitor "because of the payoffs." A few years later, when a foreign dealer entered a Steinway in a minor fair, he sent the dealer a reprimand, even though the piano had won a prize. What happened in Philadelphia rankled the Steinways long after the fair. "I've always been in denial about the 1876 thing, where we know they handed Boscovitz a thousand dollars," William's grandson Henry Z. Steinway said more than a century later. With a chuckle, he added, "We don't know what he did with it."

❧

C. F. Theodore, for his part, went back to the drawing board, sketching out technical refinements at the Fourth Avenue factory and building models in the basement of his home nearby. He continued reworking the innermost details of the company's products after he moved back to Germany in 1880. He sent complicated illustrations and explanations to New York; Henry Ziegler, his sister Doretta's son, was responsible for making the necessary patterns at the factory. Steinway & Sons incorporated C. F. Theodore's improvements as he developed them, so while the "Centennial" grands that Steinway manufactured looked like No. 33610, they had refinements that No. 33610 lacked.

Steinway finally discontinued the Centennial grand in 1884, replacing it with a larger piano that was marketed as the Model

D. No. K0862 is its direct descendant. It was a Model D that the virtuoso Ignace Jan Paderewski played on a pair of grueling tours arranged by William Steinway and the concert-booking department he had set up. Paderewski was the kind of phenomenon William longed to send around the country playing Steinway pianos. Paderewski was talented; he was, at thirty-two, younger than Hans von Bülow or Anton Rubinstein; and he captivated the crowds. One cartoon shows him playing inside an iron fence labeled "female kiss-fender." But Paderewski was not happy as he barnstormed the country on the first tour, in 1891. He whined about the "dangerous action" on the piano Steinway had provided. He had taken to calling it "my enemy" even before his recital in Rochester, New York. There, as he played the opening chords of Beethoven's *Appassionata* sonata, pain shot through his hand and up his arm. A less determined musician would have stopped. Paderewski not only finished the concert, he finished the tour, relearning his repertoire using only four fingers. He treated the injury the way a gymnast would treat a pulled muscle, bathing his arm in ice-cold water and undergoing electrical shocks to try to stimulate the nerves. None of it helped. Paderwski played hurt for the rest of his life.

Paderewski's unusually stiff Steinway was the latest Model D. The first Model D, No. 51257, has a music rack with elaborate fretwork instead of the solid one on K0862. It has barrel-shaped legs instead of the plainer, tapered ones on K0862. It has rounded arms because Steinway did not switch to the angular Sheraton arms of K0862 until later. Under the lid of No. 51257, though, "is our piano of today," explains Tali Mahanor, a sharp-eyed private piano technician who recognized No. 51257 when it turned up on the showroom floor at Steinway Hall in 2004. (Steinway will not say who traded it in.) No. 51257 is essentially the same size as K0862—it gained nearly three inches over the Centennial grands—but, more important, the cast-iron plate that sits above the sounding board of K0862 would fit comfortably inside the case of this ancestor, and every concert grand Steinway has made ever since. Some of C. F. Theodore's modifications matter only to a technician. He expanded the seventeen-note bass register of the Centennial grands to twenty notes in No. 51257, the same as on K0862. No. 51257 has agraffes on the notes in the bass—specifically, below the G-sharp below middle C; it has a capo d'astro bar above. Agraffes are brass lugs whose heads have holes through which the piano strings can be threaded. The agraffes are screwed into the plate at the tuning-pin end of the piano. Erard invented them; the Steinways used them as a point of demarcation between the part of a string that was supposed to generate the tones and overtones of a note—the so-called speaking length of the string—and the part that was not. The capo d'astro bar, or "V-bar," is part of the plate and serves the same purpose by pressing down on each string at a particular point.

No. 51257 was not the perfect Model D. "It obviously had some design flaws," said Lee Morton, a technician who restored No. 52340, a Model D made by the Steinways a few months later. "You hit a note in a quiet room, and you can hear high overtones that are not wanted." Morton explained that because "the angles are not quite right," early Model Ds were prone to "after-ringing," which is caused by the not-quite-perfect geometry in the layout of the strings. Ziegler eliminated the problem on later Model Ds by installing agraffes all the way up the scale, to the C-sharp above high C, and relegating the V-bar to the top thirty-five notes in the treble. Morton says that such small technical refinements forced Ziegler to work long and hard. One photograph of Ziegler shows him in his workroom with full-size plate patterns hanging on the wall behind him. Ziegler took down those patterns and laid them on his drawing tables whenever he was ready to incorporate a new idea into the pianos being manufactured. "Every change probably required dozens if not hundreds of changes" in the production line, Morton says, and every change affected the cast-iron plate in some way, however small.

Steinway is surprisingly unsentimental about pianos from its past—at the beginning of the twentieth century, it destroyed

one of its original 1856 grands for firewood. So the company
knows surprisingly little about what happened to No. 51527 over
the years. A faded entry in Steinway's ledger shows that No.
51257 was sold in June 1884 to a customer in New York. It was
apparently sent back to Steinway three years later and sold to a
man in Connecticut. Steinway's records tell nothing of the piano's
next sixty-six years—it returned to New York in 1944, to the
showroom of a dealer who handled used pianos Steinway did not
want—or of the sixty years after that. Steinway bought it in 2004,
reconditioned it, and would have sold it immediately if not for
Ms. Mahanor, who alerted Steinway officials when she noticed it
at Steinway Hall.

Steinway realized that No. 51257 was an artifact, but while
Steinway Hall may look like a piano museum, it is not: it is a
showroom, and its purpose is to sell pianos. Several Steinway executives who had heard about No. 51257 met and decided that it
should be taken off the sales floor. The problem was deciding
where it belonged. One possibility was to add it to the company's
fleet of loaners—pianos that performers can borrow for concerts.
It was moved to the factory, where tuners "pushed it as far as they
could" to see how good it was, recalls Frank Mazurco, Steinway's
executive vice president: "We didn't know what we were going to
get out of it." The verdict was that No. 51257 was not suitable for
the concert fleet after all, and Mazurco began looking for a buyer.
Peter B. Goodrich, the vice president responsible for artist relations, had wanted the piano added to the concert fleet and admit-
ted to "mixed feelings" about letting it go. "We probably shouldn't
be selling that piano," Goodrich said, "but we're in the business of
selling pianos."

Mazurco, like Goodrich, sees No. 51257 as a piece of the
company's history that might hold technical secrets—"small little
construction things that you see when you tear a piano apart."
Steinway, he explains, "was serious about trial and error," and
some ideas were tried on only one or two pianos before they were
abandoned. These failed experiments, however small, are not re-

ported in Steinway's records, and Mazurco hears about them from Steinway's restorers. They call him after going to work on an old piano "and say, 'Look at this, it's unique.' I'll think, let's keep that piano. Then, two weeks later, they'll call with something else. It would be nice if we had a museum, but we'd need a museum as big as the Met."

Mazurco led the way to a drafty room—a corridor, really, between the first-floor offices and the factory workrooms where pianos are parked before they are shipped. There, its keyboard toward the wall, was No. 51257. Mazurco, the only high-ranking Steinway executive who was trained as a musician (but as an organist, not a pianist), played No. 51257 standing up—there was no bench nearby. He is not a tall man, but he has a surprisingly strong touch. He ran through the wide bass intervals in the opening bars of Ernesto Nazareth's *Odeon,* a tango by a Brazilian who made a living improvising in cafés and accompanying silent movies. "The tone at the bottom is too tubby" for a concert piano, he announced when he finished.

He zipped through a scale and shook his head. "There's a nice solid sound," he declared, "but then it falls apart"—exactly where Henry Ziegler changed his uncle's design so the notes around middle C would have agraffes, as they do in K0862.

6

~~~

Bellying

September 9: Bellyman Ante Glavan pares away wood as he installs the piano's sounding board and bridges.

In the cascade of small print that rolls by at the end of a television documentary is the name of someone whose title is "executive producer"—the person who supervises things, who keeps tabs on the correspondents with the famous faces and the unseen producers and editors who piece everything together, and who reports back to the executive in charge. The executive producer, in other words, is a boss, powerful but not all-powerful, a boss with a boss. There is a similar hierarchy at a piano factory. Steinway's executive in charge is Ron Penatzer, the vice president of manufacturing, and the executive producer who has been supervising K0862 so far has been Andy Horbachevsky. As a manufacturing director, he oversees what he calls "the furniture-making part" of building pianos—cutting and shaping the wood. On Tuesday, September 9, 2003, K0862 moves out of Horbachevsky's jurisdiction and into that of Michael Mohr, Steinway's other manufacturing director. Mohr has the day-to-day responsibility for the departments that turn Horbachevsky's furniture into musical instruments.

Mohr, who is in his early forties but looks younger, carries a name that is famous in the piano world. His father, Franz Mohr, is a tuner to the stars. He was Steinway's chief concert technician from the mid-1960s until he retired in 1992. Franz Mohr's workbench was not at the factory but at Steinway Hall, on Fifty-seventh Street in Manhattan, but if someone telephoned for him, chances were that a secretary would answer and say that he was out, which he was. As he once explained: "I play more in Carnegie Hall than anybody else, but I have no audience." Seeing him alone on the stage hours before a concert, you could mistake him for a virtuoso rehearsing.

For thirty years, he shadowed the real virtuosos of his generation: Vladimir Horowitz, Arthur Rubinstein, Rudolf Serkin, Claudio Arrau. He logged more miles than the main character in

Daniel Mason's novel *The Piano Tuner,* but he, too, worried about sticky keys and broken strings. It turns out that the first strings Franz Mohr loved were on a violin, but he gave up playing when he realized he would never be another Heifetz. He could not give up music, so he became an apprentice with the piano manufacturer Ibach & Sons in Germany in 1950, when he was twenty-three. Twelve years later, shortly after Michael Mohr was born, Franz decided to move to New York. A devout churchgoer, he had contacted a minister in Queens, who in turn had called Steinway. When the Mohrs arrived, a job was waiting and, thanks to the church, so were temporary quarters in an apartment usually reserved for missionaries visiting New York.

Over the years, Franz Mohr endeared himself to Steinway's most famous customers—and, when the pressure was off, had a good laugh about the close calls. The first time he tuned Arthur Rubinstein's piano, for a concert at Yale, Franz Mohr did what anyone would do: He cleaned the keys. "Young man," Rubinstein said as he stood in the wings with the audience already in its seats, "you didn't know, but nobody ever cleans the keys for me. It makes them too slippery." The stickiest thing Mohr could find backstage was hair spray. Mohr opened the stage door and headed toward the piano. "I went *pssst* up, *pssst* down," he recalled years later. "The audience laughed. But he loved it."

Franz Mohr took Michael along when Rubinstein was appearing in Washington in the 1970s, when Michael was nine or ten. The day before the concert, when Rubinstein tried out the piano, Franz Mohr mentioned that Michael had started piano lessons. Rubinstein's face lit up. "Play something for me," Rubinstein told Michael Mohr, and he did: "The Wild Horseman," a short piece by Schumann that, for a beginning pianist, is a page-long test of staccato technique.

By the time Michael Mohr was a teenager, he preferred taking pianos apart to playing them. Over the objections of his father, who wanted him to go to college, he applied to Steinway when he

graduated from high school (and went to college at night). He
started as a stringer, threading the fat strings for the bass notes and
the razor-wire-taut ones for the treble notes, and then spent his
twenties and thirties at workbenches in the factory, drilling and
sanding and gluing. He worked alongside some of the men who
are old-timers now, men who taught him the jobs of the belly
department—how to fit a plate and glue a sounding board and
pound the pins that hold the strings. That department fills an upper floor of the factory where compressed-air hoses hiss and plate-
grinders zing, and where someone always seems to be pounding
something.

"Belly's always a loud department," Mohr says, standing beside K0862. "You think this is loud—years ago when I was working here, we had little jackhammers to push the pins in." But
Mohr is getting ahead of K0862. Before the piano can be strung,
it needs a cast-iron plate. The tuning pins, which will be anchored in Senad Beharovic's thick wooden wrestplank, will stick
through the plate.

Plates are one of the handful of parts that Steinway does not
make itself. In keeping with Andy Horbachevky's notion of "anti-
manufacturing," Steinway farms out surprisingly little—but more
than it once did. Until the 1940s, Steinway made its own plates.
In 1999, it bought its main plate supplier, O.S. Kelly and Company. Springfield, Ohio, where Kelly is located, is the piano-plate
capital of the world. Kelly once had several competitors, including its main rival, the Wickham Plate Company, also in Springfield. Ron Penatzer, Mohr's boss, can name a dozen companies
that supplied Steinway with plates—"local ones, too," Penatzer
points out. For years, Steinway avoided Kelly plates because, Penatzer says, there always seemed to be problems with the measurements. Then Wickham failed. Kelly, which made plates for
Baldwin, was the only company in the United States that could
deliver the number of plates Steinway needed in a year. One
thing led to another, and Steinway bought Kelly.

Kelly made the plate for K0862 even before Joe Gurrado's crew had bent the piano's rim. The plate was cast using what Kelly calls its no-bake process, the slower of its two casting methods. No-bake casting yields only one or two plates per batch; plates for smaller grands are made the other way, in batches of forty or fifty. One shift of workers at Kelly's plant starts at 2 A.M. so it can cast two batches by sundown. "It's a real dirty operation," Penatzer says. "Pouring the stuff, running the line and everything, they work hard. There's heat, it's dark, and there's sand all over the place."

There are piano makers who call a plate a "harp." No doubt they are romantics who see some resemblance to the instrument Hermes created for Apollo. That suggests something presentable. What emerges from the casting is the color of the sky in a midsummer thunderstorm, angry and dark and wild. It does not stay that way long. Kelly has a paint shop stocked with plenty of "Steinway gold," which is a different shade than the gold it uses for the plates it sends to Charles Walter, a small Indiana piano maker. Kelly sprays the plate for K0862 with the right gold and ships it to New York in a rack with other freshly cast plates, their curved tails in the air, their wide, flat bottoms a couple of inches from the floor. They look presentable.

The design of the plate has been more or less the same since the 1880s, but the plate for K0862 carries a modification Steinway has only recently instituted: having Kelly put the word "Steinway" on one of the gold bars near the dampers, where a photographer cannot miss it. Another change pleases Penatzer more. Having a wholly owned foundry in the corporate portfolio meant that Steinway could order Kelly to put two words in little raised letters elsewhere on every plate—"Steinway casting." To a piano man like Penatzer, the two words are a reminder of the days when every plate was in fact made by Steinway itself—in William Steinway's first building in Queens, a building Penatzer can see from his office—and carried the words "Steinway foundry casting."

〜

To Michael Mohr and the men in the belly department, *fine* does not mean *finished*.

The first worker to get his hands on the plate for K0862 is Eddy Salvodon, not to be confused with his brother, Paul, who also works at Steinway, and will shape the hammers on K0862. Eddy, though not shy, is the less talkative of the two. Before they emigrated from Haiti, it was Paul who was a reporter for a radio station.

Eddy Salvodon's first assignment on a piano is to join the plate to the case—one of a complicated series of custom fitting operations that, among other things, govern the exact placement of the strings, the soundboard, and the keys. Those are the parts of a piano that make music, so in a sense, the music starts with Eddy. Yet so much of his job is incomprehensible to outsiders. Salvodon has watched Mohr explain what Salvodon does to tour groups and seen their eyes go blank with a lost look, as if they are puzzling over a geometry problem they don't get. There is some geometry in Salvodon's job, and some visualization—and a lot of measuring. After twelve years at Steinway, Salvodon sometimes smiles as Mohr leads the tour groups on to their next stop. It is a grin they do not see, and it is knowing and impertinent. It says, "I get it, and I know you don't." (Some do, though. Manufacturing director Andy Horbachevsky remembers a skateboard designer—"a Gen X grunge sort of guy"—who was so impressed that he told Salvodon, "Man, you are it." The grin that Salvodon flashed in *his* wake was softer and wider, and lasted longer.)

Salvodon begins, at 9:45 A.M., by hooking an octopus-like rope around the plate for K0862. He ties some of the rope's arms through the circular openings—called rosettes—that are spaced along the right side of the plate as precisely as portholes on an ocean liner. He hooks other tentacles of the rope around the long bars on the left side of the plate. The rope is connected to an electric winch that can lift the plate's 350 pounds. Up it goes, in less

than ten seconds, to hang about three feet above the piano—
around the level of Salvodon's forehead. As he kicks away the
sawhorses the plate has been resting on and wheels in K0862's
case, he mentions the danger of working under the plate. "Once,
I walked into one when I wasn't paying attention," he says.

He sets a coffee can on the keybed that fills the space between the rim's Sheraton arms. The can is filled with a black powder that he sprinkles on the wooden wrestplank. "This is where I
get to play like I'm an artist," he jokes, dribbling the powder in
adventurous arcs. Jackson Pollock could not have done it better.
Salvodon pushes the "down" button on the winch. The plate descends into the case. He gives the plate a tug and turns the winch
on again. Up goes the plate. The wide, rectangular wrestplank is
nearly clean. Most of the powder is stuck to the bottom of the
plate, and the handful of smudges that remain on the wrestplank
tell Salvodon where the plate and the wrestplank are not fitting
snugly—where he has to smooth things out.

He pulls on a face mask, a plastic shield that keeps chips of
wood and sparks and burrs from hitting his skin and eyes, and
makes a few quick passes with a jigsaw. A cloud of sawdust rises
and is caught in the light behind him—a low-lying, tightly centered cloud, like the one around Pigpen in the comic strip
"Peanuts." Salvodon unwinds a compressed-air hose and blows
the shavings out of K0862. He checks some measurements. He
lowers the plate again, then pushes the "up" button and looks at
the black spots that have been left behind. "It's too deep inside,"
he says. "I'll use the machines to take it down."

Tiny sparks fly as he shaves away fractions of an inch with a
grinder. He planes the wrestplank. He spreads more powder
around. He raises and lowers the plate fourteen times, checking
for black dots that become tinier as the morning goes on. Finally,
the last of the smudges disappears.

It is time for more geometry. Salvodon must align the bass
side of the plate to K0862's case. He must also slim down the
rounded curve of the tail. He marks Xs in white chalk in places

where he could grind away a few millimeters. "This is like a dentist saying, 'Go tap-tap-tap' and grinding a filling or a crown to fit," explains Horbachevsky, who has stopped by to watch.

But a dentist does not use belly bars. The belly bars, the long wooden ribs that are wedged between the piano and the ceiling, hold a plate in place while Salvodon works, but when he needs to raise the plate, they are easy to remove. Salvodon will jam in three before he checks the position of the plate in the horizontal plane—more geometry. "It's nine feet long," Horbachevsky says. "If you're off a few degrees, it makes a difference." Specifically, the strings will be all wrong—again, it's the geometry.

The plate goes in and out three times before Salvodon is satisfied. After every up there is an inspection and a sprinkling of powder. On the downs there is the *tap-tap-tap*. Salvodon is concerned that the plate is "riding up" on the bass end—that it is not level there. He pulls a small sander from a drawer. His striped shirt is working its way out of his slacks.

The crowd around his workbench changes as the morning goes on. Mohr and Horbachevsky have left for a meeting on management row, and Gus Christophorou, the lead man in the belly department, has taken their place as a kind of sidewalk superintendent, watching and talking. Trained as an airline mechanic, Christophorou, who is in his forties, is unusual at the factory. For years he worked at New York's airports, far from the crowded passenger terminals, repairing engines and hydraulic systems. As deregulation hit the airline industry, "all the airlines were going bankrupt," he says. He decided to change careers but did not want to leave New York. He knew the president of the union at Steinway. "He said, 'Why don't you come on over?,' so now I'm a mechanic to this." He pats the curved end of K0862. "It's starting to look like a piano," he says.

Salvodon slips a shim, a piece of wood thirteen-thousandths of an inch thick, under the plate. If there is too much wiggle room, Salvodon will have to do more grinding. "We want this tight," Christophorou explains. "Once the pins are drilled in, nothing should force the wrestplank back." Salvodon tries to wiggle the shim. It stays put.

It is 11:54 A.M. Salvodon is ready to drill the registry holes, which will position around the rim the twenty screws that hold the plate in place. But the electricity has gone out in his corner of the factory. Someone anticipating lunch has put a sandwich in a microwave oven, and a circuit breaker has tripped. Workers' power-draining appliances, hidden in cabinets or drawers near their "stations," tax the parts of the plant that have not been rewired in years. From time to time, the plant managers—manufacturing director Michael Mohr or Andy Horbachevsky, or the vice president who handles personnel issues, Michael Anesta—look for devices brought in by workers that could pose safety hazards. That is not the only reason the managers want to root out such things, of course. They do not want distractions that could slow what Horbachevsky calls the drumbeat of the factory, the day-in, day-out rhythm of making ten pianos a shift. Anesta says they have found, and confiscated, such high-voltage hazards as toaster ovens and popcorn poppers, and—in the category of distractions—televisions and videocassette recorders.

The lights have come back on, but not the wall outlets for Salvodon's tools. He spends the minutes before lunch changing his shirt—he is not one to walk around in a shroud of leftover sawdust. After lunch, the electricity is back on. Salvodon drills the registry holes and sends K0862 on its way. At its next stop, a couple of stations down the belly department's aisle, Eric Anderson will trim the inside of the rim in preparation for perhaps its most important addition: the sounding board, the sheet of slightly curved wood that serves as the piano's amplification system. "One size does not fit all," says Mohr. "Once this is done, that soundboard will not fit any other piano."

Mohr could just as easily say that K0862 is now deep into what, by almost any definition, counts as custom work. No.

K0862's encounter with Anderson begins unceremoniously. He unscrews the twenty screws that Salvodon installed minutes earlier and hooks his own winch to the plate. He punches a button, and the plate rises from the case, just as it did so many times for Salvodon. But Anderson's assignment involves lifting the plate out once and only once, and guiding a piece of machinery the size of a cash register toward the dangling plate. When the machine, which rides on a track in the ceiling, touches the edge of the plate, Anderson steps back and switches it on.

The machine is battered from use but represents one of the newest changes in the belly department. What the machine does as it slithers around the edge of the plate, memorizing the shape, was once done by hand. For Anderson, this is like the "record" function on a tape recorder, though what Anderson's machine records are measurements and coordinates, not noises or music. In "playback" mode, a companion machine trims the wooden soundboard according to the measurements from the first pass.

Mohr says the process is exact, more exact than if Anderson were to trace the shape by hand and transfer it to the soundboard, the way Mohr himself did in the 1980s when he was a bellyman doing Anderson's job. "The requirement is that the soundboard fit snugly into the case," Mohr explains. "You don't want to have a lot of gaps in between. Years ago, it was never as precise." The machine arrived in the 1990s, after Mohr had been promoted; no one—not Mohr or Horbachevsky or Anderson—remembers exactly when.

There is an easier way to fit the plate and the soundboard into the case. "A lot of manufacturers leave space between the soundboard and the rim," Mohr says, adding, "real cheap ones." They use rope—Mohr compares it to "the rope on your soap in the shower"—to fill the gaps. He says there is good reason not to do that. "We want a precisely fitted soundboard, because once the strings are in there, there is a tendency for the soundboard to flatten," to lose the crown that improves the piano's amplification. "If it relaxes," Mohr explains, "it won't be eager to vibrate."

❧

Eddy Salvodon and Eric Anderson are the belly department's warm-up acts. They get K0862 ready for the main event, on Friday, September 12, 2003, in Ante Glavan's bright corner of the room. There is a row of windows behind Glavan's station that face south. Once, if the sky was not too hazy, he could see the World Trade Center. On September 11, 2001, he watched the sky fill with smoke after airplanes slammed into the twin towers. "Every morning, I look out," he says. "I cannot forget."

Glavan has one of the factory's most demanding jobs: belly-man. It is a job that figures in the company's storied tradition: William Steinway was a bellyman for a while in the nineteenth century. A bellyman glues in the sounding board—the part, more than any of the thousands of other parts under the lid, that will determine how K0862 will sound. Glavan will also glue on the bridges that support the piano's strings, and he will carve notches for the metal pieces, called bridge pins, that hold the strings in place.

Glavan's job earned its name long ago because the only way to do it is for the bellyman to lie on his stomach on top of the sounding board, with the plate hanging three or four feet overhead. Glavan, who is fifty-seven, has a belly to lie on, but he is not rotund. He is on the short side in a factory where many workers are taller and have longer arms, the better to reach into the pianos. But their longer legs would hang over the edge of a piano like K0862. When Glavan climbs on top of the soundboard, he looks casual. He does not worry that he could crush the painstakingly crafted piece of wood, less than three-eighths of an inch thick, that lies beneath him, or that he could be crushed by the 350-pound slab of cast iron that is dangling over his head. But he is relaxed only from the waist down. His torso is tense; his neck is at an uncomfortable angle; his hands are busy with his tools. "All part of the job," he says.

Glavan arrived from Yugoslavia by way of Italy. He had

been in Tito's army. "I was a traffic policeman," he says, "and there's no money in that." In New York, he landed a woodworking job, only to lose it in a round of layoffs. He remembers having seen something on television about Steinway & Sons—exactly *what* is lost in his memory and his English, which has a way of running off track halfway through an anecdote. The point is that he called Steinway and applied. "And here I am," he says, thirty-five years later, his face fleshier and his hair grayer. He wears half-frame glasses now, and blasts himself with compressed air from a hose to blow away sawdust. He looks forward to working on Saturday, making soundboards at time-and-a-half wages. "It pays for the house," he explains. "I've got to pay the mortgage."

His immediate boss—who is also his brother-in-law, a wiry, silver-haired foreman named Lou Begonja—watches as Glavan planes yet another sliver of wood from just inside the rim. Begonja does not put it this way, but this is the first of many moments when Glavan will have to demonstrate an understanding of geometry and a talent for visualization. "We want to make sure the inner rim follows the same pitch as the board," Begonja explains, describing how the slight crown at the center of the soundboard gives its thin edge a downward angle that must be matched by the rim. "That's basically the secret of the Steinway. That's basically the whole idea. The beautiful sound the Steinway has comes from that."

Bellying involves complicated, repeated steps, but Glavan never seems to stop to think about what comes next. He has laid the tools he needs in the "mouth" of the piano, where the keys will eventually go. He has placed them in the order he will use them, left to right: hammers, wrenches, planes, clamps. That saves him time—not that he is rushing. "It's going to be a long day," he says as he goes to work on K0862. "Pull up a chair."

Almost as soon as he says it, though, Glavan walks away from K0862. He trudges down the aisle to help another bellyman glue a soundboard into a smaller grand. Favor swapping is a custom among bellymen.

Next he must find K0862's sounding board. Eric Anderson stored it in "the five-point-two room." Glavan calls it simply "the hot room." It is another of the rooms around the factory where the temperature is kept high and the humidity is kept low to dry the wood. The moisture content in soundboards is supposed to be just above 5 percent—specifically, the number Anderson mentioned, 5.2 percent.

After retrieving the soundboard, Glavan marks guides with chalk that tell him where on the bottom of the soundboard to place the braces, the long bars that are visible to someone sitting in the front row in a concert hall. He flips the soundboard over, lays it inside the case of K0862, and jams his own belly bars in place. He pounds the edges. He lowers the plate, checks, makes marks. "That's only a guesstimate," he says.

Glavan has been a bellyman long enough for his guesses to be on the mark, and before long he is lining up the assortment of clamps that he will need to tighten after he has glued in the soundboard. He signals two co-workers from down the aisle, including the bellyman on the smaller grand, and the three of them dip brushes in a glue pot. Then, quietly, they work their way around the inner rim, painting on a thin layer of glue, before pressing the soundboard into place. It is another milestone in the life of K0862; but Glavan still has work to do.

As his co-workers saunter off to their stations, Glavan lowers the plate into the case and prepares to attack the bridge, the ear-shaped curve of wood that sits on the soundboard and supports the strings. Piano technicians call this step "taking the bearing," and it is crucial because it creates the path that the strings will follow on their way from the wrestplank, with the tuning pins, to the tail of the piano.

Glavan scurries around K0862, marking the soundboard with his pencil. "On a violin," Mohr explains from a few feet away, "the strings run up to the bridge and down to the neck. It's almost the same on a piano: up to the bridge and down to the plate. Since you have that upward angle, it puts a load on the soundboard. If the angle is too much, it could cause the soundboard to be choked and not free to vibrate. So half a millimeter matters."

Glavan stretches what looks like a handful of silver shoe-strings over the bridge, laying out the path for the strings. He does not bother to check the measurements with a ruler. "I know how to do this without the tool," he says. "I'm here too many years."

What follows is a tour de force. Glavan carves eighty-eight little notches into the top of the bridge, each at the right spot, each at the right angle. He could have used a ruler to see that each was spaced just right, but that would have taken the fun—and the daring—out of this performance. Lying on the sound-board, his feet over where the keyboard will go, he starts at the treble end and creeps toward the bass, leaving behind indentations about the width of a thumbnail, and not much deeper. Only after he has carved the last one does he measure. He does not say the words "I told you so."

He gives a quick smile, and he steadies the plate, which has begun to revolve slowly over his head. "I don't want this coming down," he says.

On the following Monday, Glavan cannot see the Manhattan sky-line from his window. Dense clouds hang over New York, and the weather forecast is mostly about humidity and the chance of rain. There is also a mention of a hurricane that could hit North Car-olina or Virginia. It is not the kind of forecast a woodworker likes to hear, but Glavan looks more relaxed than he did on Friday. He got a haircut over the weekend—"to be cooler," he says. His brother-in-law and foreman, Begonja, walks by and says he does not like hot weather. He went fishing over the weekend and did not catch much. K0862 spent the weekend with the plate hanging in the air, exactly where it was when Glavan knocked off on Friday.

Again he hammers. He planes. He glues. Again he checks that the notches—the ones he cut without measuring—are the correct depth. He aims a tiny mirror, the kind a dentist uses to see out-of-the-way molars, in a couple of places. Then he pounds the bridge with his fist—one hard blow. "This," he says as the echo reverberates loud and long, "is good sound."

Glavan worked on K0862 the way bellymen have always worked on pianos, with hand tools. But the next steps in building the piano involve machines Steinway began using only a few years ago—one to drill the holes in the wrestplank at a four-and-a-half-degree angle for the pins, the other to twist the strings around the pins once they are in place. Steinway stopped having workers do these jobs by hand not because the machines are faster, but because the machines are more accurate, manufacturing director Michael Mohr says.

The man operating the drill, Chris Mammarelli, has another job on his mind. He is No. 6,081 on the list of applicants who have passed the city's firefighter test. The city will call more than two thousand applicants before his number comes up, so he expects to be at Steinway a while longer.

At the stringing machine is Anous Vertus, who wraps adhesive tape around his fingers each day to guard against cuts—steel strings can shred flesh, he says. By the time he finishes with K0862, it has 243 strings. Seventy-five of its eighty-eight notes have three strings. Five bass notes have two strings, and the eight lowest bass notes have only one. The same as every Model D for 110 years.

"What's changed is the consistency of the job," says Mohr. "Each pin is fed in at the right angle. When it's done by hand, one guy could hit the pin in four shots. Another guy would need seven or eight shots, and the angle might not be perfect."

Mohr slaps the strings with the palm of his hand. K0862 rumbles. "You get that? That thunder?" he asks. "It's alive now."

7

~~~~~

The Company That Was

The fourth generation: Henry Z. Steinway at Steinway Hall.

William Steinway had flirted with making automobiles and speedboats in the 1890s, but Steinway & Sons was a one-product company when Henry Z. Steinway graduated from Harvard with what he remembers as only vague career plans. "I thought maybe I could try this piano thing," he recalled more than sixty years later. "My father"—Theodore E. Steinway, the younger of William's two sons and by then the company's president—"said, 'Fine.'"

It was 1937, eleven years after Steinway's biggest year ever. In those eleven years, Steinway & Sons had gone on the real-world equivalent of a roller-coaster ride at William Steinway's amusement park: A stomach-churning plunge had followed the dizzying climb. But even the climb had been illusory, because the handsome sales figures and handsomer profits of the twenties had masked a deeper problem, one that the Steinways did not seem to grasp—pianos were no longer an essential element of every living room. Their place at the center of America's social life was fading. Consumers' changing tastes and buying habits were marginalizing the piano industry.

Technology was the culprit—technology that brought excitement, worldliness, status, all things that owning a piano had once promised. In 1896, the year William Steinway died, an Italian college student named Guglielmo Marconi perfected a wireless transmitter. In 1915, the year Henry Z. Steinway was born, the ambitious young commercial manager of the American Marconi Company wrote a memo that suggested selling radios as "music boxes" for homes. David Sarnoff was aiming squarely for the spot that Steinway and other piano makers held in the popular imagination. He said that radio could become a "household utility in the same sense as the piano or the phonograph."

The American Marconi Company did not see the possibilities, and Sarnoff had to change jobs to find bosses who did.

RCA marketed the nation's number one brand of radios, and Sarnoff understood what they could provide: entertainment at the twist of a knob—no lessons, or talent, were necessary, and radios were cheaper than pianos, particularly Steinway's. Steinway had survived the phonograph stampede during World War I—piano sales totaled $56 million in 1914, more than double the sales of phonographs, but in 1919, sales of record players hit $158 million. Radio soon eclipsed that. Two-thirds of the households in the United States had radios by 1933.

Worse, from a strategic perspective, Steinway & Sons had not even tried to market a less expensive brand. Most Steinways, like cars, were sold by locally owned dealers. The salesmen's paychecks came not from Steinway & Sons but from the dealers, and unlike car dealers in those days, piano dealers usually sold more than one brand. Most piano dealers had long since made arrangements with other manufacturers to sell the pianos that Steinway did not make except as something of an afterthought— uprights. Steinway had concentrated on its grands, and in doing so, had become a stuffy throwback to high culture at a time when America was going low. Ignace Jan Paderewski, who favored Steinways, returned to the concert repertoire after a quarter-century hiatus—time he spent composing, framing Poland's constitution, and serving as prime minister. But Chopin was not what Americans wanted to hear anymore, not in the Jazz Age, when George Gershwin was writing hit songs and concert pieces like *Rhapsody in Blue*.

Even the customers who wanted grands in the twenties did not want big ones. Apartment buildings were replacing block after block of town houses in New York. Henry Z. Steinway was born in an apartment building that took the place of Steinway's original factory on Fourth Avenue, now Park Avenue. What sustained Steinway & Sons as people squeezed into quarters smaller than their parents' town houses was its Model M, a grand piano introduced in 1912 that was three and a half feet shorter than a concert grand like K0862.

Steinway's decision to go ahead with the Model M—to expand the product lineup, as a business school type would put it—came as new inventions were changing the way Americans spent their leisure time as surely as Henry Ford had changed the way they got around. Corporate hierarchies were now dominated by executives who seemed more comfortable making deals than making products. But Steinway & Sons soldiered on, making its one thing as the world left it behind. Before too long, when Henry Z. Steinway was introduced at a cocktail party, "People would say: 'You're in the piano business? That doesn't exist anymore.'"

They had a point. Piano making in the United States had peaked in 1905 at 400,000. A decade of slow annual declines ended in 1914; production rose modestly through World War I. After a sharp drop between 1919 and 1921—and an equally sharp rebound between 1921 and 1923—the numbers fell off again, more each year. By the time Theodore E. Steinway took charge in 1927, piano sales nationally had slipped to 200,000. Fortunately for him, Steinway & Sons concentrated on high-end grands, not mass-produced uprights for buyers on a budget, and sales of grands nationwide had doubled since World War I. Steinway had tried lowering itself to the new mass market by making player pianos in a deal with Aeolian, which marketed piano rolls by famous pianists like Josef Hofmann—Steinway built the pianos, Aeolian installed the player mechanism. It turned out that player pianos had peaked in 1924. Yet the Steinways seemed blinded to the larger cultural shifts by its own sales figures, which continued to rise. Steinway & Sons made and sold more than 8,300 pianos in the United States and Europe in 1926, and almost that many in 1927.

Those figures capped a remarkable run. Steinway did so well in the first few years of the twentieth century that it built a second plant in Queens, a few blocks from the one William had started in the 1870s. The new plant looked like an old-fashioned factory, with its red-brick walls and closely spaced windows lining two long wings. It was about a mile from William's plant and a few blocks from the school and the church that William had underwritten. It became more than an annex when Steinway closed the Park Avenue factory and moved everyone there but its executives, its salespeople, and the technicians needed to tune the pianos at the Manhattan store—and, of course, the workers who cast the plates and bent the rims at the plant William had built. To accommodate the crowd from Manhattan—including Henry L. Ziegler, the cousin who had inherited C. F. Theodore's job as the principal designer and technical expert—Steinway added three floors to the new factory. Ziegler's workroom bridged the two wings and had a view of the Steinway mansion and William's plant.

Profits continued during the easy-money years of the twenties, and Steinway built a third plant in the shadow of the second. This newest building was boxy and modern looking; its loading dock was built for gasoline-powered trucks instead of horse-drawn wagons, and it had room to grow. Its extra-large support columns could hold several more floors and thousands of square feet of manufacturing space if sales continued to climb.

The company also built a new Steinway Hall, a palatial showroom at the base of a stately office building on West Fifty-seventh Street, just steps from Carnegie Hall. It could be argued that the new Steinway Hall was a monument to Steinway & Sons' marginalization, a sign of Steinway's grudging acceptance of the new ways of the world. The original Steinway Hall had been the city's preeminent concert theater. But the Steinways shut it down in 1890 rather than compete with Andrew Carnegie's music hall, a monument to an industrialist whose fortune was newer—and larger—than theirs.

The new Steinway Hall was also a sign that Steinway had become part of the establishment. Where William Steinway had boasted of designing the old Steinway Hall without an architect, the new Steinway Hall was the work of Warren & Wetmore, the prestigious firm responsible for the look of such New York landmarks as Grand Central Terminal. The new Steinway Hall's "impressive dignity is most fitting," *The New Yorker* declared. "It seems to embody everything we expect Steinway to stand for." Inside was an octagonal room the Steinways called the rotunda, a thirty-five-foot-high space, with lavish paintings by N.C. Wyeth and Rockwell Kent. Thirty-five musicians from the New York Philharmonic and the pianist Josef Hofmann played at the opening. In the audience were Rachmaninoff and a crowd of society figures that included a Rockefeller, a Harriman, and a Guggenheim.

Steinway filled the first four floors and rented out the rest, at first to music-business figures like the impresario Arthur Judson and *Music Trades* magazine, which covered Steinway. The New York Philharmonic's offices were on the sixteenth floor; the Symphony Society of New York, which ran a rival orchestra, leased an identical suite on the tenth floor. But the new Steinway Hall was not the center of New York's classical-music world the way the old Steinway Hall had been. Steinway was now an important name in a business in decline.

The 1920s, in the words of "Recent Social Trends," the academic study of "the next phase in the nation's development" that was commissioned by Herbert Hoover a month before the stock market crash, had "hurried us dizzily away from the days of the frontier into a whirl of modernisms." At the dawn of the Jazz Age, Woodrow Wilson was president of the United States and New York was caught up in a giddy celebration of flappers and philosophers, a celebration of new wealth and new ways that were personified by Gershwin and by F. Scott Fitzgerald. Fitzgerald's generation was in a hurry—in a hurry to make money; in a hurry to spend it; in a hurry to be famous. The 1920s brought what Sally Bedell Smith, the biographer of William S. Paley, who masterminded the success of CBS, called "the new vanguard of business," led by advertising executives who were the "principal agents for the prosperity" signaled by one of Wilson's successors, Calvin Coolidge. By 1927, businesses were spending $1.5 billion on advertising nationwide.

The piano industry had been overtaken by what the historian David M. Kennedy calls "giant industrial combines" like U.S. Steel, Ford, and General Motors, and was hit hard by the Depression. The Steinways were forced to do everything but shut down for nearly two years after piano shipments dropped by 90 percent. "The business really fell apart pretty badly," Henry Z. Steinway recalled. The company bragged about selling to companies that contributed to the piano industry's free fall—180 Steinways went into the radio studios of NBC and CBS in New York.

What saved Steinway was another small piano, smaller than the Model M. The Model S was a grand that Henry L. Ziegler had all but designed before World War I. It had the voice of a larger grand, but did not take up as much room. Nor did it cost as much. It fell to Paul Bilhuber, a relative who had once worked under Ziegler, to sift through Ziegler's sketches and models and finish the designs.

Ziegler was the son of Heinrich Engelhard's daughter Doretta, who had married the boy next door on Hester Street, where the family lived when Steinway & Sons began. One of the stories passed down through the generations holds that Henry L. could draw a perfectly straight line exactly one meter long without a ruler. He was formal and old-fashioned; his own son called him "the governor." But Henry L. said no to his father when deciding on a career. Jacob Ziegler wanted Henry L. to follow him in the Zieglers' furniture business, which his grandson Henry S. said made "awful General Grant stuff—mahogany with too many carvings." But Henry L.'s Steinway uncles offered what would later be called a signing bonus of fifty thousand dollars. Those were the days when the cash was flowing, and Henry L. lived well. A trotting-horse enthusiast, he liked to ride through

Central Park on his way to work. He was wealthy enough to em-
ploy a groom to bring the horse to his town house near the
Fourth Avenue factory and pick it up when Henry L. arrived at
Steinway's showroom on Fourteenth Street. Henry L. hated new-
fangled motorcars even as William Steinway invested in them.

In the years when he dominated the company's research
and design process, Henry L. had a habit of scribbling, on the
door to a closet in his workroom, mathematical formulas he consulted regularly. Not realizing that the closet door was Henry L.'s
version of a bulletin board, an overeager employee painted it clean.
Henry L. was "apparently a bit of a thundercloud," his grandson
said, "so the response was predictable."

Henry L. and his Steinway cousins, Charles H. and Frederick, dominated the company for twenty-nine years after William's
death. They passed the company to William's second son from his
second marriage. Theodore E. was so devoted to the ideal of the
tradition-bound, family-run company that he lived in an apartment building on the site of the Fourth Avenue factory. He paid
rent, just like the other tenants; Henry Z. Steinway, born in that
apartment in 1915, said his father did not arrange a sweetheart
deal for the apartment when the family sold the factory.

The demolition of the factory cleared the way for the transformation of Fourth Avenue into Park Avenue. The railroad
tracks were paved over, the neighborhood became fashionable,
and the apartment house into which Theodore E. moved was
filled with neighbors who were presidents of this company or
chairmen of that. For Theodore E., keeping up appearances was
important. Years later, as the bubbliness of the 1920s gave way to
the grimness of the 1930s, a certain wealthy slice of New York
treated the Depression as an inconvenience. The Steinways
entertained as always. They sent the fourth generation to prep
schools and Harvard, and Theodore E. "never gave any hint how
bad things were," Henry Z. Steinway recalled.

Worse, for Henry Z. Steinway, 1937—the year he started at
Steinway & Sons—"was one of those down years when the

market fell out of bed." The Model S had helped sales, but not enough. Steinway decided, as he put it, "to go back aggressively into making uprights."

That was not the only change in his first few years at Steinway. Under pressure from the city's health department, Steinway stopped making the cast-iron plates for its pianos. The foundry had been the Steinways' first building on William's land in Queens, and for nearly seventy years workers had followed the same routine, pouring molten metal into a mold packed with sand and peeling the pattern away later. What was left was a slate-gray plate that could resist the tremendous amounts of tension generated when the strings are looped over the tiny pins at its far end.

The problem for Steinway was that there was a silicosis scare in the late 1930s. Silicosis, a pulmonary ailment caused by inhaling sand, was said to afflict foundry workers, though Steinway reported that no one at the Queens plant had symptoms. The city persisted in its efforts to stop Steinway from making the plates on the premises, and Steinway shut down the foundry, turning to a subcontractor, as it would seventy years later for the plate for K0862.

This was something of a turning point for Steinway, which had built its reputation on the idea that it made everything that went into its pianos, just as Henry Ford bragged that his River Rouge plant took in raw materials at one end and shipped out completed cars at the other. By the 1990s, some piano tuners would say that the old Steinway foundry plates made old Steinways sound better than newer ones. It is another argument that does not go over well on management row. The executives counter that tuners have a vested interest in bad-mouthing new or middle-aged Steinways—to stay in business, tuners have to convince owners that something needs to be worked on.

⚜

A year after closing the foundry, Steinway stopped making more than plates: It all but stopped making pianos. The government

would not allow nonessential products like pianos to be manufactured in wartime, at least not with the wood that was stacked outside William's plant—wood that had been bought and delivered
before America entered World War II. The way Henry Z. Steinway
remembers it, the government inspector rejected what Steinway
had on hand, saying, "Your wood is not good enough, you have
to buy according to government specifications." Steinway did the
only thing it knew to do: "We went back to the same wood suppliers we always used," he recalled, "and said, 'Can you sell us
wood according to government specifications?' "

Even after taking delivery on government-certified wood,
Steinway needed to find something to do besides finish the pianos
that had been working their way through the factory. It found two
things. One was to make wooden parts for stubby-looking gliders
like the ones used in the Normandy invasion. Steinway arranged a
subcontract with one of the prime contractors responsible for delivering the gliders yesterday if not sooner. They were strange
looking, these motorless aircraft with fuselages of fabric-covered
steel tubing and teardrop-shaped wings that measured eighty-
three feet from tip to tip. "The Air Force has never owned anything as ugly," one aviation historian wrote, "or as efficient."

The CG-4A, as the gliders were known, carried the tools of
battle—howitzers, jeeps loaded with ammunition, and a handful
of gunners and drivers. They were designed to fly at the end of a
three-hundred-foot-long rope. At the other end was a cargo
plane that would pull the CG-4A almost to its destination, release
the towline, and let the pilots aboard the glider figure out how to
touch down. The result was what one military historian called
"controlled crash landings." Only a handful of gliders survived
the war undamaged; most were abandoned where they came to a
stop. John E. Pike, a defense consultant who directed a number
of research projects for the Federation of American Scientists,
noted that they were "unavoidably unpopular" with soldiers but
were the "best of a bunch of bad options" for generals planning
an attack. According to Pike, "you were either going to kill a

small number of soldiers in glider accidents or a larger number of soldiers because they were scattered all over the place, one parachute at a time."

Steinway was responsible for making all the wooden parts for the CG-4A—the wings, the tail surfaces, the nose in which the pilot sat, the benches for crew members, and what Henry Z. Steinway remembers as "an elaborate floor." As production of the gliders began in 1942, Steinway handed over its third plant to the prime contractor, which had nowhere else to marry Steinway's wings to fuselages that were made elsewhere. Steinway had a more immediate problem. It had to translate the army-approved blueprints into patterns and the patterns into wings. The clock was ticking toward the deadline, but despite nine decades of experience in sawing and shaping wood, Steinway could not figure out what needed to be done. Henry Z. Steinway remembers that the blueprints were "terrible" and that the solution finally came in an unexpected way, thanks to a factory worker who told the Steinway bosses, "If you fellows just leave me alone for a day, I'll figure it out." He did.

Steinway made the wings the way it made pianos, even though the government said it did not need them to be perfect, it just needed lots of them. Joshua Stoff, the curator of the Cradle of Aviation Museum on Long Island, said that Steinway's "rate of production was so slow" that the air corps eventually turned to another subcontractor, a company that had made wooden crates. "[Steinway] was using old-world craftsmen and building glider wings like they were fine furniture." Its replacement "had people cranking them out and they didn't look like Ethan Allen furniture."

Steinway also managed to sell several thousand pianos to the army—its standard forty-inch upright, painted olive drab. The historian Richard K. Lieberman points out that many of them were retrofitted pianos that had been made in the 1930s but never sold. For army duty, these pianos had their two front legs removed—too delicate for the battlefield—and now wore celluloid keys. The original ivory would have disintegrated with exposure to weather at the front. Always quality conscious, Steinway sent along instruction manuals and tools for soldiers to tune them.

For Steinway, the gliders and the G.I. pianos became patriotic obligations—"We didn't make money on any of this stuff," Henry Z. said more than sixty years later. Nor did Steinway ask to be reimbursed for the wood on hand when the war ended, wood it could not use for pianos. So that wood went into, of all things, caskets.

❧

Henry Z. Steinway claimed he took a million piano lessons and went to thousands of concerts. But, he said as he approached ninety, "I still don't know which is Beethoven's this or Beethoven's that." Unlike William Steinway and others in the family, the only keyboards that Henry Z. was good on were the ones on typewriters and adding machines. He enjoyed Broadway musicals and "Ethel Merman belting out the songs"—without rock-and-roll amplification.

He began his career by working in the lumberyard, as his father and uncles had. "The instructions were, if you were a Steinway, you were really supposed to familiarize yourself with how the piano is made. They let us make cases, and soon we found out how hard it was to do." It was an important lesson for someone who had "gotten by" at Harvard. At the factory, he explained, "I learned a respect for work that is actually done. Making a case, it took me a day and a half to do what they do in four hours. I only did two or three cases. I had to be checked out by the guy next to me. I think I was driving him crazy. You really have to learn it." Practice did not make perfect for him. "These guys bend a spring a couple of times, and they get it right. I was bending the spring all over."

He worked for Frederick A. Vietor, a cousin who was the vice president and general manager, and Henry Z. assumed that Vietor would take over the company. But Vietor died at fifty, in

1941, and Henry Z. had the Steinway name. As he told Richard K. Lieberman in the 1990s, people "started looking to me to answer questions, and pretty soon I started answering them." He "more or less drifted into the factory management, because there was a great big fat vacuum there."

He was drafted as an army private in World War II and assigned to Governors Island in New York, investigating officer candidates. His eyesight—"I can really only see out of one eye," he said—kept him out of combat.

After the war, he was given the title of factory superintendent and was responsible for converting Steinway & Sons from gliders and caskets back to pianos. He was an insider, a familiar figure at the factory, where, among other things, he dealt with the union that had been organized around the time he joined the company. He served as a go-between, shuttling between union officials and his father—and, when his father rejected the union's demands, coming up with a counterproposal that both sides could accept. His brother John preferred to play the social circuit outside the factory walls and, with the impresarios in Steinway's concert department, hobnobbed with the famous pianists who performed on (and sometimes complained about) the instruments the company made.

Henry Z. was commanding—at six feet two, he was taller than anyone else in the family—and conservatively dressed in his Brooks Brothers suits. But he was fiercely determined to keep Steinway & Sons alive. "It was a tough job to get it going again," he recalled, "and business wasn't all that great, after the initial burst. My father was having no fun." It may or may not have been a sign of how Steinway & Sons had faded that when Henry Z.'s sister Elizabeth, known as Betty, married Schuyler Chapin in 1947, *The New York Times* mentioned her great-aunt, a Roosevelt; the best man, a Biddle; and her bouquet of orchids and sweet peas—but not that her father was the president of Steinway & Sons.

Henry Z. was soon named to the company's board of directors, and eventually spent much of his time at Steinway's office in

Manhattan, handling problems that went well beyond the scope
of a factory manager. He mastered corporate politics and elbowed
out a cousin, Paul Bilhuber, who had been trained by Henry
Ziegler. They got on each other's nerves; Bilhuber resigned in
1947. Henry Z. took over the company eight years later, when his
father called a board meeting to order, announced that the company needed a president who was not facing health problems,
and walked out. The directors created a new title for Theodore E.
Steinway—chairman—and named Henry Z. president.

The company he inherited was foundering—there had been
no more eight-thousand-piano years, and Steinway seemed to be
missing out on the great postwar boom that turned farmland into
densely populated suburbs. More worrisome for Steinway was
another development. Radio, which the Steinways blamed for the
piano industry's earlier declines, was itself being overtaken by
television. The number of households with television would surge
from 3.8 million in 1950 to 45.75 million in 1960. Two calculations
by the Steinway biographer D. W. Fostle put television's surge
and the speed of mass production into sharp relief: In less than
three weeks in 1953, more television sets were made than the total number of Steinways made in the hundred years since Heinrich Engelhard and his sons started the company. And,
underlining what a slow process piano making was, at least for
the Steinways, Fostle figured that if those pianos had been put together as rapidly as televisions, the entire output of Steinway &
Sons from 1853 to 1953—about 340,000 pianos—could have
been finished in thirty-seven minutes.

For his part, Henry Z. was a modern inheritor, determined
to do it his way. His way was the old-fashioned model of an inde-
pendent company, while his era was one of big-money conglom-
erates. But Steinway & Sons was anchored in the past, and in
1953, the company celebrated its hundredth anniversary with a
concert at Carnegie Hall—ten grand pianos and the New York
Philharmonic—and a book called *People and Pianos*. The text,

largely written by Theodore E. Steinway (who called it "a good propaganda item"), was relentlessly sunny. It was true that Steinway no longer managed concert artists' careers, Theodore E. wrote, and Steinway Hall "has long since been superseded by Carnegie Hall." He did not say that Steinway & Sons had a lower profile on the New York scene than it had had in his father's day, when it functioned as an impresario and owned the stage on which many of its clients appeared. He put the best face on the changes, saying they let "the family and the firm . . . devote their energies to the piano." Steinway & Sons had built "one-third a modern factory and two-thirds a craftsman's shop. Not that the firm is reluctant to use machinery as such," Theodore E. wrote, "but the art of piano making puts definite limits to mechanization; it is still basically a hand operation."

But the hands at the factory did not have enough to do in that centennial year. Steinway had the space and the equipment to make nine thousand pianos a year, but orders came to only three thousand. Henry Z. pressed for the changes he had advocated for years, changes that would save money. His strategy was to downsize the faltering company. In 1955, Henry Z. moved most of the company's administrative operations, and his own office, out of Steinway Hall in Manhattan—"that expensive space," as he called Fifty-seventh Street—and into one of the three factory buildings in Queens. Henry Z.'s economizing became legendary. In a story attributed to Van Cliburn, it was said that "you'd walk by at night and all the lights were turned off because they wanted to save electricity. They didn't care if people couldn't see the pianos in the showroom."

Even at tradition-bound Steinway & Sons, some traditions were abandoned. Henry Z. ordered David Rubin, the vice president who dealt with concert pianists, to enforce a decision that artists to whom Steinway had lent pianos had to return them or buy them. "It was not an easy thing to do, to have to call and say, 'Steinway wants to bring that piano back, but you have the option to buy it,' " recalled Rubin's successor, Peter B. Goodrich.

True to its roots as a high-end company, Steinway did not give serious consideration to starting a lower-priced line or to making pianos with some other name on the fallboard. Henry Z. knew that the company's board would never go for it—his father had long opposed the idea, just as he had resisted offers to license the Steinway name for everything from refrigerators to loud-speakers. There would be no diversifying Steinway. So Henry Z. proposed closing the two newer plants in Queens, after calculating that doing so would lower the company's overhead by several million dollars. Pianos had been varnished at one of the plants that he wanted to shut down, and Frederick Steinway's widow, Julia, remembered hearing stories about the humidity at the one he planned to keep, on William's original waterfront site. "You're going to have terrible trouble with the varnish," she warned. Henry Z. replied, "Well, we don't use varnish anymore, we use lacquer. We think it's going to dry just fine down there." He sold the two plants for $1.6 million. One became a warehouse for a department store chain, the other a shopping center.

Many executives in Henry Z.'s situation would have left New York City for a site large enough to hold a more modern factory—if not somewhere in the South, then perhaps the former Roosevelt Field airstrip on Long Island, only fifteen miles away, which was being divided up and sold. Steinway could have built a one- or two-story plant with a more efficient layout there, and its workforce could have followed without the disruptions of a move to the Sun Belt. But Henry said that land prices at Roosevelt Field climbed beyond Steinway's reach before anyone thought to look into a deal.

Steinway & Sons stayed at William's site, but there was not enough space in the jumble of separate sheds and buildings there. Henry Z. hired a contractor to build large workspaces to connect the old buildings. The connectors created "a much better lay-out," Henry Z. said, though the workers "still had to have eleva-tors and schlep stuff up and down from floor to floor." But, he explained, "We thought, that's what we're stuck with." A couple of years later, he also arranged to sell Steinway Hall to the Manhattan Life Insurance Company, whose president was a cousin of his, for $3 million. "We came out free and clear," he told the historian Richard K. Lieberman. "We were out of the banks for the first time since 1930."

%❧

By the late 1960s, Steinway & Sons was successful again. But Henry Z. was troubled about the future. "It was the hippie time," he recalled years later. "Nobody in the next generation . . ." His voice trailed off without finishing his thought: The fifth generation of the family was not prepared to run the company after he retired. "He felt very lonely," recalls Lee Morton, a New Hampshire technician who is also friendly with Henry Z. Steinway's cousin, Henry S. Ziegler. (Ziegler, a lawyer who never worked at Steinway & Sons, is the grandson of Henry L. Ziegler, who had followed C. F. Theodore as the firm's chief designer.) Morton remembers Henry Z. Steinway's worries that no one was offering to support the company; no one was saying, "Can we put any money back in the factory?" Morton also remembers hearing Henry Z. complain that the family rarely talked about anything other than quarterly projections, dividends, and "how do I get money out to continue the lifestyle to which I'm accustomed." Morton adds, "It was a burden for him."

So in 1972, Henry Z. Steinway and the board arranged a stock swap with CBS—essentially, a sale—that was valued at slightly more than $20 million, about $1.4 million more than the value put on the company by the investment bank he had hired the year before. There was a snob factor on the Steinways' part: CBS had been nicknamed "the Tiffany network" despite lowbrow hits like *Gunsmoke* and *Mister Ed* and *The Beverly Hillbillies*. There was also a patriotic stubbornness: Steinway would not go the way of Everett, a Michigan-based piano company that sold out to the growing Yamaha conglomerate at about the same time. Between the wars and again in the 1950s, Everett had dominated the market in upright pianos. It held a number of patents on the design of uprights, and many Steinway dealers had sold Everetts as the lower-priced line Steinway never offered.

The decision to sell out split the family. Henry S. Ziegler was solidly in favor of the deal with CBS, but Henry Z. Steinway says his mother considered it "a betrayal" and would not tell him before the stockholders' meeting how she planned to vote. Two of Henry Z.'s nephews—Theodore Steinway Chapin and Samuel Chapin, the twin sons of his sister Betty and her husband, Schuyler Chapin—wrote to other stockholders, taking issue with his claim that no one of their generation was interested in the company. Henry Z.'s brother John agreed with the Chapins that the sale was regrettable. "My own feelings on the CBS acquisition," John Steinway wrote to them, "are that it is a bloody shame, but apparently unavoidable. Some . . . are more interested in making a fast buck than in the preservation of a tradition of four generations. I feel a little like an unwilling funeral director. Such, I am afraid, is life."

In the end, everyone in the family, including Henry's mother, voted for the sale, under which CBS paid $367 a share.

Henry Z. argued that "in 120 years, the strength of Steinway was its owner management." Now there were no Steinways in the company's top management who were younger than Henry Z.'s brother John, who had joined the company in 1939. (Henry's oldest son, Bill, was hired after the sale to CBS and worked at the factory, in the engineering department, until shortly after CBS removed Henry Z. as president, naming him chairman. Henry Z.'s replacement, Robert P. Bull, fired Bill. Bull left Steinway several months later and Bill was rehired, but quit after less than eighteen months to attend business school and become an art dealer. The Chapins, who had held summer jobs at the factory while they were in college, felt that only Steinways need apply—a throwback to the company's earlier, male-dominated ways.)

Henry Z. Steinway was also concerned that Steinway's pockets were not deep enough. The factory had stayed in New York in what he called "an atmosphere hostile to manufacturing" while their U.S. competitors had gone "where they appreciate manufacturers"—primarily southern states with right-to-work laws. The costs of doing business in New York were punishing. The Hamburg factory had become Steinway's major profit center, but it needed modernizing. And Steinway had set its sights on selling pianos in Japan; CBS had a stake in piano maker Kawai. "Everyone could see the sense" in the CBS deal, Henry Z. said. Noting that CBS was a large corporation that provided more generous benefits, he added, "It was better for the employees."

Henry Z. has never regretted the sale, and his nephew Theodore Chapin, who by 2003 was the president and executive director of the Rodgers and Hammerstein Organization, came to see it as the right move. By then, Chapin had told his uncle that Steinway & Sons "would be out of business" if he had not sold it.

But the sale made Steinway a different company. At first, Henry Z. Steinway, as president of Steinway & Sons, reported to a CBS executive who oversaw a portfolio of musical brands that included the electric guitars that snarled and wailed for the Beatles and Jimi Hendrix, and the legendary "Leslies," the speakers for the electronic organs that are to blues virtuosos what Steinways are to concert pianists. Workers say CBS poured money into Steinway, installing equipment that had been deferred when the company was still family owned. But the tap was slowed, if not turned off, when CBS executives saw that the improvements did not translate into higher productivity and higher profits, and within a few years Henry Z. felt frustrated by the CBS bureaucracy. "We went through all these idiotic things like sending reports to California," where the executives to whom he now answered were based. The reports would end up at CBS headquarters, five blocks from Steinway Hall.

He met William S. Paley, the chairman of CBS, only once, as the sale was being finalized. The only connection—"if it can be called that," as Henry Z. put it—between the family and CBS was through the marriage of his sister Betty to Schuyler Chapin, who had worked briefly for Goddard Lieberson, the longtime president of CBS's Columbia Records. But by the time of the sale, Chapin had left Columbia. Preparing for the meeting with Paley, Henry found a photograph of Paley's original radio studio, which had been in Steinway Hall. He handed it to Paley, saying, "You might recognize this." Paley did. But Steinway received no special treatment once it became a part of CBS, and Paley did not want special treatment from Steinway. When Paley's secretary called to arrange to have the piano in his apartment tuned, she gave explicit instructions to send a bill. "We would have fixed it for free," Henry Z. recalled.

The CBS deal called for Henry Z. to remain with the company until he retired, although CBS replaced him as president in 1977—"They found me less than perfect as a C.E.O.," as he put it—and named him chairman. Henry Z. gave up that title in 1980, when he turned sixty-five, but never really left Steinway & Sons. Through the 1980s and 1990s and into the twenty-first century, he remained Steinway's goodwill ambassador, a reminder of the days when America was piano crazy and piano making was big business—and, among other things, he autographed pianos for buyers who wanted to have the Steinway name in more than just gold letters above the keyboard. He signed the cast-iron plate with a felt-tip pen, the way Leonard Bernstein signed Bösendorfers.

Thirty years after the sale, Henry Z. Steinway was mellower. He had become the last link between the name on the pianos and a business that began as a nights-and-weekends project in his great-grandparents' kitchen-turned-workshop. He remained a fixture at Steinway Hall, where he answered his correspondence on a manual typewriter. He also had a record he could look back on with pride. D. W. Fostle said that in Henry Z.'s first sixteen years as president—the time before the sale to CBS—he managed to increase the company's value an average of almost 17 percent a year. But during CBS's ownership, pianos had not regained the economic preeminence they had enjoyed in his grandfather's time. "One of their executives said, 'We didn't do much for it, but we didn't ruin it, either,'" Henry declared in 2003. "And that's about it. The conventional wisdom, people say CBS ruined the piano, but they didn't really."

❧

In 1954, the year before Henry Z. Steinway became president of Steinway & Sons and began downsizing the company to keep it going, the leadership of another family-owned piano company passed to a new generation. Genichi Kawakami transformed his father's company, Yamaha, in part by doing something that the Steinways did not—diversifying into a billion-dollar conglomerate. He started making motorcycles in the 1950s and audio equipment in 1968, ventures that gave Yamaha the capital to expand and make more pianos in a week than Steinway makes in a year.

A few months before Henry Z. Steinway turned ninety, he landed a television commercial. At a time when television viewers were watching pop icons like Mick Jagger pitch discount mortgages, Henry Z. straightened his bow tie and faced the camera as Steinway workers polished pianos in the background. It was not, however, a commercial for Steinway & Sons, but for a bank that showcased Steinway as a small business.

8

Playable

October 3: Trimming and drilling the hammers for the piano's bass

Johann Sebastian Bach declared that there is "nothing remarkable" about playing a piano. "All you have to do," he
wrote, "is hit the right notes at the right time, and the instrument plays itself." That was easy for him to say; he was a virtuoso.
But the remarkable thing about a piano is that it plays at all, that
something actually happens when you hit a key. What happens
inside the piano, a foot and a half away from your finger, is a jitterbug of tiny, hidden parts. Some physics is involved—this
dance is about transmitting power from the keys to the strings.
Some geometry is involved, too—this dance is about executing
tight moves in a tight space. Together, the dancers—pieces of
wood, cloth, and metal that have been trimmed to almost impos-
sibly tiny, close dimensions—form a mechanism known as the action. Without this maddening arrangement of parts that slide into
or pivot around one another, the piano would not make a sound,
unless you strummed it like a guitar.

It is this contraption, the action, that will give K0862 an important element of its personality, the part a pianist can actually
feel. The action does what the steering mechanism does for a car.
Auto magazines talk about "road manners" and the moment-to-
moment sensations that are conveyed through the steering wheel—
nervous and jumpy, loose and wobbly, tight and precise. A right
turn in an old car is a muscle-flexing workout; with power steering, parallel parking is a cinch. If the action is sluggish, a pianist
will have to pound K0862. If the action is too light, it will not deliver what the critic Harold C. Schonberg beguilingly called
"sprays of notes . . . volleys of fortissimos [and] streaking octaves." If the action misbehaves, it will mangle the ornaments—
the repeated notes—in the opening of Brahms's Handel variations
or the trill that sends the last movement of Beethoven's Opus 11
trio off in a different direction.

A responsive action will react to a surprisingly slight pressure on the keys. How slight? At the heart of the action is the

hammershank, a pencil-sized piece of wood with a hingelike tail, called a flange, that is an inch and a half long. "The amount of force needed to move that is supposed to be two grams, plus or minus a gram," John Marek, a foreman in Steinway's action-assembly department, explains. "Not much at all. The amazing thing to me, not being a piano player, is people can tell the difference, high or low."

But they can. The piano that felt good to Vladimir Horowitz would not have felt good to Arthur Rubinstein. The action that pleases Martha Argerich would leave Alfred Brendel grumbling. The way the hammershank flange is adjusted is only one reason. There are fifty-four action parts for each note on the piano—4,752 in all. And all of them are made in Marek's room, the most Dickensian corner of the factory.

It is one of the few places at Steinway that seems as pressured as a conventional assembly plant, with clattering machinery turning out dozens of parts hour after hour—towering drill presses and whirling saws and slicers. Here, the fingerwork must be as careful as a pianist's, but there is no talk of that, no talk that languid melody lines and beelike staccatos would be impossible without the parts manufactured in this room. Practice and memorization, the demons of a pianist's life—they too figure in what goes on here. The labor that is demanded is exact—centering a hole three-sixteenths of an inch in diameter in a piece of wood seven-sixteenths of an inch wide, for example. "When I came in here," says Marek, whom Steinway hired in 1997 after a twenty-year career making pumps and valves for water treatment plants, "it was overwhelming. There were so many processes and parts."

Now Marek spends his days looking over shoulders, peering into balky machinery, solving problems. His eyebrows always seem to be raised in a quizzical expression. He has the build of a fireplug, with a thickish neck sprouting from the vastness of his shoulders. His dark hair, more black than brown but not the black of a lacquered Steinway, is combed back. To make himself heard, Marek talks over the drone of a vacuum that draws sawdust from the action-assembly room and the precise *putt-putt-putt* of drill-like machines that punch holes through pieces of felt the size of a coat button. On close inspection—and everything in Marek's room involves close inspection—you will notice that the hole is not circular, like the hole in a life preserver, but oblong. Eventually it will surround an oblong spindle, on which a key will ride up and down.

Marek's room smells of wood—the shavings on the floor around the saws can be so thick that you can stamp your footprints in them—and of something burning: solder, it turns out, being melted to assemble the basketlike contraption that holds the hammers. The look of the room emphasizes the monotony of the work. The cinderblock walls are painted white, as is the ceiling. Not the pristine, icy white of a dust-free computer factory or a germ-free operating room, but a weathered white that seems almost creamed. The machines around the room have faded hulls, but there are splashes of bright color. Parts of the action are made with felt as red as Santa's. The bushings with the oblong holes are holiday green. The centers of the hammers are purple.

Like the hammershank and the hammershank flange, most action parts have names pianists have never heard of—the fly, the tender, the backcheck, the underlever, the knuckle. The knuckle, as it happens, is about the size of an eraser on a pencil and is covered with buckskin. It absorbs the full impact every time a pianist strikes a note—hard, fast, or slow.

There is nothing simple about this assortment of parts or the way they work together. It looks like something Rube Goldberg might have sketched out. Marek has learned that describing the action can lead to a pileup of subordinate clauses and phrases like "in turn." He is not one to clown around the way the Depression-era big band musicians who dreamed up "The Music Goes Round and Round" did. In his vocabulary there is no deedle-dee-ho-ho-ho. Nor is there the kind of Ella Fitzgerald magic that would keep eyes from glazing over. Marek's approach is all facts and physics, action and reaction: Press the key, which pivots like a seesaw, and something called the capstan screw pushes up against a group of interlaced parts called the wippen, which is connected to a highly sensitive lever called a balancier, which in turn pushes against the knuckle, which is attached to the bottom of the hammer. Just like that, the hammer swings up toward the string. But that is not all that happens. The key also raises the damper wire, which lifts the damper on the string, which frees the string to vibrate when the hammer finally gets there. And as soon as the hammer does, the damper falls back, deadening the string. The music goes round and round; the action just goes up and down.

The action—as devised by Cristofori, modified by Erard, and modified some more by C. F. Theodore Steinway, his nephew Henry Ziegler, and a Steinway cousin, Frederick A. Vietor—can be tightened and loosened, twisted and pulled, tweaked and retweaked. As the social historian Arthur Loesser wrote, it is what makes possible "the smaller, quicker shadings on the piano, the breathless ultra-pianissimos, the delicious swoon of a high note suddenly whispered and the plastic relief of prominent and subordinate voices in closely woven tone-textures." It is precise and essential. "Other than a soundboard not being put in correctly, this is the most important part of the piano," says Steve Drasche, a piano technician and rebuilder whose father had Marek's job in the 1960s and 1970s. "You can have tuning pins at a wrong angle and get away with that, or strings that are not put in right. There, you're not dealing with the sound and the feel."

When Loesser described the piano playing made possible by an exceptional action, he was not thinking specifically of Horowitz's playing, but it is because of Horowitz that Marek's crew builds the action the way they do. Henry Z. Steinway credits Horowitz with changing not only the way the piano was played, but also the way the action was constructed. Horowitz favored a fast, responsive action, one that was fixed so a key "only had to come halfway up [after being struck] for [him] to give it a full blow down again."

When Horowitz became a star in the 1920s, everyone wanted what he wanted. Vietor and the pianist Josef Hofmann—"working together and talking mechanically," in Henry Z. Steinway's words—figured out the modifications, and Steinway gave the result a Madison Avenue name: the accelerated action. As the patent makes clear, Vietor set each key on its own helmet-shaped, felt-covered piece of wood called a balance rail. Until then, the keys had risen from, and returned to, a flat surface. The change speeded the ascent and descent almost imperceptibly, but that hundredth of a second mattered—or seemed to.

⁊⊙

Marek's crew is also responsible for a very visible part of every note: the hammer—pear-shaped for the bass notes, bullet-shaped for the treble. Eleven workers make the hammers. On Monday, October 3, 2003, Anthony Rios starts work on K0862's hammers by slicing a sheet of wool into long strips. Each strip is wrapped around a core that contains two elements: a layer of felt and eighty-eight finger-sized pieces of wood that will become the tails of the hammers. The package looks like a miniature loaf of bread, the felt a crust and each piece of wood a slice. Emilio Lareo glues it together and runs it through a press that firms it up in a couple of minutes. His practiced casualness might seem to confirm the suspicions of pianists who complain that Steinway makes more than its share of hammers that have to be replaced. But Andy Horbachevsky, the manufacturing director, maintains that Steinway draws upon the skill and experience needed at this stage. The action parts are machined to within two-thousandths of an inch. "Point zero zero two," says the foreman, Marek, looking back on his experience making pumps and valves. "There, I was machining metal. Here, it's wood. As long as you can make the parts to tolerances, they'll work."

At the next workbench, Michael Cabrera scrubs off the excess glue before Clement Hart slices the loaf of wood, felt, and wool with a guillotine-like cutter, creating the hammerheads. After more trimming, drilling, and inspecting, the hammerheads—looking like giant teeth with wooden roots—are taken to a storage room where a meter shows the humidity to be 43.7 percent. The idea is to cure them in a relatively dry place before mating them to the other action parts of K0862.

The hammers will rest against a metal frame. Across the room, Robert Bravo, who, after working in a piano factory for twenty-one years, says jokes about encores have worn thin, heats his soldering iron to begin work on the frame. Marek explains that the process is not the same as it always was. The flux has been reformulated to be "environmentally O.K.," according to Marek. "There's no lead in it. You could splash it on your food and eat it. The solder's lead-free, too." Later the frame will be painted to match the "Steinway gold" of K0862's plate.

Once the hammerheads have dried, Marek's crew twists them onto the wooden hammershanks as if they were little propellers. The result is a hammer that does not lie flat on a table. It is bent, to strike each string at exactly the right spot. The hammerhead is only thirteen thirty-seconds of an inch wide. If it goes into the bass section of K0862, it will have an easy life: It will have to make contact with only one or two strings. In the treble section, a hammer has a harder job. There are three strings for each note.

❧

How good K0862's hammers are remains an open question. Piano technicians say it is impossible to judge a set of hammers without breaking them in, playing them for a while—weeks, maybe months. Some technicians who specialize in rebuilding pianos have given up on buying replacement hammers from Steinway at all. Too many duds, they say. They have tracked down European action makers whose hammers they consider more reliable and, when broken in, they believe sound fuller, more listenable. Certainly the hammers' character—their ability to deliver the thunder or the quiet that a pianist wants—cannot be judged in their present condition: They will be rubbed with files and hardened with lacquer before K0862 leaves the factory. Some pianists complain that Steinway relies on the lacquer known around the factory as "juice" to compensate for "cotton-ball hammers" made of too-soft material.

Action problems bedeviled Steinway for years. It outsourced its actions for seven years starting in 1984. "Our equipment until the eighties was in need of dire help," manufacturing director Michael Mohr says. "It was not updated, not upgraded." Outsourcing actions was nothing new in the piano business. Arthur Loesser points out that shortly after the Civil War, three Steinway workers struck out on their own and soon became the country's largest action maker, selling to other piano companies—but not Steinway.

Steinway's biggest headache with the action began in the 1960s and involved the bushings, which are tiny sleeves that hold even tinier metal pins that function like axles. Nineteenth-century piano makers packed the sleeves with thin cloth. But cloth, like wood, expands and contracts with the weather. And in parts this small—the pins are 0.051 inch in diameter, making the bushings about the size of a lowercase *o* in type this size—even tiny changes in temperature and humidity can make the action stick. Steinway's efforts to overcome that problem led to something that pianists of a certain age still shake their heads about: the Teflon bushing fiasco.

In 1962, Steinway patented a bushing made of nonstick Teflon, the "Permafree" action bushing assembly. At the center of the Permafree bushing was not something soft, like a piece of cloth, but hard—a piece of Teflon, which looked like light-colored plastic. Steinway began putting the Teflon bushings into pianos in 1963 and completed the changeover in 1964, when it used the last of its cloth bushings.

The Teflon bushing was the brainchild of Henry Z. Steinway's brother Theodore, who was known by his childhood nickname, Teed. He had inherited the job held by C. F. Theodore—and later Henry Ziegler—as engineer and product development specialist. "He's the one who was obsessed with Teflon," recalled Henry. "The Teflon thing, he said, 'Oh, it's simple, it's simple.'" But Teflon had its appeal to Henry Z. Steinway's cost consciousness. The Teflon bushings would reduce labor costs because they did not have to be trimmed by hand in the factory. As a man-made product, Teflon also promised consistency and, in turn, the end of Steinway's perennial headaches about the quality of the felt for bushings—headaches that had become more acute with the consolidation of suppliers after World War II.

But the Teflon bushings were no panacea. When the wood expanded, it squeezed against the rigid Teflon. That made for actions that were tight. When it shrank in the winter, the action seemed loose. Worse, pianists could hear what was going on. "The Teflon made clicking noises and drove everyone crazy—technicians, pianists, everyone," the pianist Charles Rosen said. The pianist Eugene Istomin said the distraction was unbearable. Rosen and a number of other performers switched to pianos made at Steinway's Hamburg factory, which never stopped using felt bushings.

Even some Steinway employees realized that Teflon was trouble. Rosen remembers an encounter with Franz Mohr, the company's head tuner at the time, who oversaw the grands the company set aside for concert artists to try out in the basement at Fifty-seventh Street. "Franz said softly, so that no one else could hear him, 'I've just taken all the Teflon out of all the concert pianos down here,'" Rosen recalled.

The New York plant went back to woven wool bushings in 1982. But it still considers Teflon an antidote to heat and humidity—so much so that there is Teflon in K0862. The workers soak the wool for the bushings in liquid that contains Teflon.

"It's absorbed in the felt," says Michael Mohr. "We think it does make a difference."

꒰ఞ꒱

While John Marek's workers are building the action and marinating the bushings so they will not stick, K0862 is upstairs, waiting. It stands in a kind of midway, a wide, open area where pianos come and go. They wait there, curve to curve or keyboard to keyboard, away from the windows, away from the tools, until the worker responsible for the next phase of the piano's development is ready. The waiting time lets K0862 adjust to its new soundboard, weighed down by the cast-iron plate and tensed up by the strings.

K0862 has company. Another concert grand is working its way through the factory, shuttling from workbench to workbench a day or two ahead of K0862. Also killing time on the midway are smaller grands; one has a rim of light-colored satinwood, not the basic black lacquer. The tight, jittery pattern of its grain looks like a seismograph's careful portrait of a small earthquake. Another neighbor has the reddish brown look of rosewood, with dark swirls and long veins that look purplish under the midway's fluorescent lights. They could not look more different from K0862 with its even spray-coat finish.

Pianos ride around the factory on metal frames Steinway calls trucks, industrial versions of the Y-shaped carriers used by some concert halls. These are rusty where those are shiny, but both are designed to keep a piano's legs from touching the floor. The factory trucks are bigger than the ones in concert halls. They are intended to provide more of a cushion against the broken surface of the floor than the piano's own legs.

Despite all the work so far, pianos on the midway are still carcasses. Lined up with their tails facing you, they look like completed instruments, their plates shining pleasantly, their strings in place. All they appear to lack are tops. On the other side, they all sport empty grins that say *Fooled you—not one of us has a key-board.*

The job of filling that wide space in K0862, of marrying the action stack to the keys themselves, falls to two woodworkers named Michael Farrell and Reuben Sookhai. Their workbenches are only a few steps from the midway, but the light in their area is softer and the atmosphere different. They seem less driven by time and numbers. Farrell—who has the height, and the economical moves, of a basketball player—is decidedly easygoing.

Farrell's work begins with three short trips around the room, each not more than a few paces. First he strides over to the midway, finds K0862, and pushes it to his workbench. Then he walks to a cart at the opposite end of the room that is loaded with cardboard boxes containing keysets—each keyset comprising the eighty-eight keys and the wooden tray on which they will ride inside the piano. Which box Farrell takes from the cart is up to him—all Model D keysets are, in theory anyway, the same. They are made in Germany by Kluge, a company Steinway bought in the 1990s, around the time it bought its plate supplier, O. S. Kelly.

Back at his workbench, Farrell slides the keyset out of the box. The keys look like seesaws, some with long white seats at one end, some with long black seats.

Fifty-two white and thirty-six black: The keys on a Steinway piano have been arranged in the same way since C. F. Theodore and Henry L. Ziegler locked them in more than a century ago. Other piano makers have experimented with more keys. Bösendorfer added three below the lowest bass notes, to accommodate the nineteenth-century firebrand Ferruccio Busoni, who ran out of room at the far end of the keyboard. Only once, in the 1920s, did Steinway make a piano with more than 88 keys. It had 148 keys, to be exact, but it was not the piano-factory equivalent of a double-wide trailer home. Its dimensions were the same as any other concert grand's, but it had two keyboards, one above the other, like a two-manual harpsichord. The second keyboard had only five octaves.

The idea of visual contrast, of making the keys for sharps and flats look different from the ones for naturals, goes back all the way to the invention of the pianoforte. Cristofori used boxwood for his naturals and darker rosewood for his "accidentals." English and French instrument makers followed his lead, making the naturals from "white material" and the sharps or flats of "dark wood"—stained material or ebony veneer. The convention was the opposite in Germany and Austria, where the naturals were the dark keys, the sharps and flats the white ones.

The keys lined up on Farrell's workbench are made of plastic. Steinway made its last batch of white keys out of ivory in 1989, and for thirty-five years before that, only concert grands had the ivory and its off-white, swirly look. Steinway put plastic keys in its smaller pianos after it decided, in the 1950s, that ivory was too expensive (it is now, of course, illegal). In the 1960s the company experimented with several types of plastic until it found one it considered suitable for concert grands. "We tried it out on Horowitz and others and they said, 'Fine, it's O.K., we can live with it,'" Henry Z. Steinway recalled.

But some screamed—Gary Graffman, for one. Lifting the lid on a concert-division piano he played regularly, he noticed immediately that the ivory keys had been removed and "cheap false teeth" installed. Steinway put the ivories back on that piano but interrogated him as a secretary took down every word. Henry Z. Steinway "grilled me on how I was able to detect the replacement of [the] keyboard," Graffman wrote in his autobiography. Graffman said it was easy: The plastic keys were "glaring, shiny, synthetic-looking, artificial—in short, plastic!—cold and slippery, slimy like the skin of a greased eel, and not what I am used to."

And those, Graffman acknowledged, were "some of the more acceptable" words that came out of his mouth.

❧

Farrell makes his third trip to another fully stocked cart, from which he chooses an action stack. Which one is, again, up to him. It is just after lunch on Friday, October 3, 2003.

To pair the action stack to the keys, Farrell bolts the metal frame that holds the action onto the wooden frame that holds the keys. He will also make sure that the whole keyset glides in and out smoothly—something technicians will have to do when K0862 needs work later in its life. The hammers cannot brush against the lower edge of the case cornice, one of the long trusses of wood that Senad Beharovic built in. It lies just above where the keys will sit.

Farrell's measurements tell him that the newly formed unit—keys, hammers, and other parts—is too tall. Too tall, in Farrell's terms, is a matter of hundredths of an inch. He makes the action assembly fit by lowering Beharovic's keybed, the wooden foundation at the front of the piano that the action and the keyboard tray slides into. Farrell also changes the shape of the keybed, giving it a tiny peak under middle C to hold the keyboard tray in place. "We're trying to create a high spot in the center—one thirty-second of an inch," explains Jim Lefflbine, Farrell's foreman, who has stopped by to watch him work. "Over the two-foot depth of the keyboard, it's a slight, slight slope, but that tapering will help." A thin curl of wood rolls out of Farrell's plane with each careful stroke. "You forget how small the measurements are here until someone comes in and applies for a job and says, 'I've been working construction the last twenty years,' " Lefflbine says. "He'll think an eighth of an inch is close."

Lefflbine, chatty where Farrell is quiet, adopts the role of play-by-play announcer, explaining the details of Farrell's sixteen tasks on K0862, each involving these smallest of measurements. Lefflbine also mentions several facts that Farrell probably would have left unsaid. Farrell's plane is not your ordinary plane. He points out that it is a miter frame plane cast in bronze, a design the Stanley Tool Company stopped mass-producing years ago. There is no better plane, Lefflbine says. It costs five hundred dollars. In a company that is careful about budgets, there is always money for tools. Farrell also has the newest bench in the factory, but that is more than a status symbol. An uneven surface could throw off his measurements, and his measurements are too important. The pairing of action and keys is "a love affair that's got to last," Lefflbine explains. "We can't just take another action off the rack and put it in the case."

In a quieter voice, Lefflbine turns his talk to Farrell. Steinway has competent woodworkers, Lefflbine says, and good ones. "Mike takes it to a whole other level from there," Lefflbine observes. "He doesn't feel it's right when I say that. He's modest. I've told him I feel he's really one of the best. I'm here eight years. I've seen a lot of guys come and go."

Farrell's attention is now devoted to settling the marriage between keyset and keyboard. He planes a hollow that will keep the screws on the bottom of the keyset tray from scratching the keybed as the keyset slides in and out. Farrell runs his hand over the hollow and feels more than the contour. "It's like when you shave without soap," Lefflbine says. "There is still some stubble there." Farrell rubs the keybed with kerosene, as a lubricant, and sands away the last inconsistencies.

Farrell stamps the piano's case number—K0862—on the keybed with a large rubber stamp. Using a caliper-like device, he measures the distance from the keybed to the strings. He must fit nine support blocks made of walnut beneath the keyset tray without pushing it any higher. He planes and sands while Lefflbine talks.

Lefflbine and Farrell, foreman and woodworker, are about the same age—early thirties. Farrell lives a mile and a half from the plant. Lefflbine lives sixty-seven miles away, in Connecticut; his odometer registers more than thirty thousand miles a year, driving to and from the factory. Lefflbine started as a helper, moving just-arrived shipments of items like lacquer and screws "just to make a couple of bucks." But Lefflbine is a Steinway legacy: His father is an accountant whose office is on the floor below management row. "One is a bean-counter," Lefflbine says as Farrell finishes up, "and one makes the beans."

≿⊘

For all that Farrell did, K0862 is still not ready to be played. It is up to Reuben Sookhai to make the adjustments to Farrell's work so the jitterbug will unfold the way it is meant to—smoothly, quickly, elegantly. He begins by twisting the capstan screw, a mushroom-headed shaft well past the midpoint of the key. Its shiny brass top is, Sookhai remarks, the only point of contact between the key and the other parts of the action that drive the hammer to the string. If the capstan screw is too low or too high, everything else will be off. The capstan screw, when he and Lefflbine talk about it, is always singular, not plural. There are, of course, eighty-eight capstan screws on a piano. Sookhai will twist and turn every one.

"It varies with different pianos, how much he has to adjust," Lefflbine says.

"This is no more than usual," Sookhai replies, reassuringly.

K0862 has reached the point where the action is inside the piano. To raise or lower the capstan screws, Sookhai must do what tuners will do for years to come: grab the edges of the keyboard and slide the entire assembly—keys, hammers, and all the parts in between—out of K0862's mouth. It is tempting to compare him to a dentist making a set of dentures comfortable. But he is too busy touching things up to kid around. The G below middle C appears out of line. "I want to see how high that was," he says. He slides the action out and twirls that capstan screw and others in the neighborhood.

"It all goes back to plate setting," Lefflbine explains. "The plate was set higher so the action stack needs to be set higher, because it's all about the hammers striking the string at almost a ninety-degree angle. If we set all the plates to the same height, you couldn't be sure you'd get that contact." Sookhai checks the measurements with a straightedge that isn't really straight—it rises toward the middle, matching the way Farrell planed the keybed around middle C.

Finally, K0862 makes its first sound. Sookhai presses a bunch of the keys below middle C with the palm and fingers of his left hand—half a dozen keys, maybe eight. The chord is a jumble of out-of-tune harmonics—imagine a church basement piano that has not seen a tuner in years—but Sookhai is not listening. His concern is the distance from the hammer to the string. "The G below low C is still riding high," he says. He tinkers. If he were listening, what he would hear is a ghostly noise, because the piano has no dampers, nothing to stop the open strings from vibrating. It would drive a pianist crazy. The keys go up and down, but there is no consistency from note to note. Middle C feels fine. The D next to it seems to hesitate. Going up the scale, some notes won't sound unless they are whacked. Some feel as if they have to be pushed all the way to the floor. Others play with only a tap. K0862 is a mishmash.

Sookhai has a rainbow of paper punchings at his workbench—green, blue, brown, and tan. The colors denote different thicknesses of paper, to be used in leveling the keys. The differences are small and uneven, not like steps—a fraction of an inch here, a millimeter or two there. The paper punchings, which look like the gummed circles used to reinforce the holes in notebook filler paper, raise the keys that fall short. Sookhai places a punching under the bushing at the end of each errant key. He puts the thickest level of punchings under the lowest B, C, and E. The C below middle C and the D next to it get thinner ones, and the E next to them a thinner one still. Sookhai is chewing his gum faster than when he started.

Sookhai heats the hammers with a torch of low-temperature alcohol. Heating the wood makes it supple, so that he can manipulate it very slightly. He is trying to get the hammers to rise and fall without hitting one another. The D below middle C is leaning to the left. He burns, pushes, and taps. "It's centered," he announces, satisfied, as the quitting-time whistle sounds.

While the workers punch in the next morning, Jim Lefflbine pulls out a wide black plank that he has parked on the floor in his office, behind the desk. "We're running short on D fallboards. I wanted to make sure we had one." The fallboard is the piece of wood that closes over the keys. One side, the side the world will see when it is open, carries the Steinway logo in gold letters half an inch tall. That side, smooth and wide now, will someday carry the battle scars of a well-used piano. Pianists who pounce on the keyboard—reaching too far forward as if they are clawing at something—will nick the fallboard.

Vijay Sakhicand installs K0862's fallboard, along with the blocks that sit inside the Sheraton arms and frame the keyboard, in about twenty minutes. Sakhicand takes measurements and drills holes—four measurements, four holes, done. He planes the edges of the fallboard so it will close without gouging the arms. With an artist's brush, he retouches the spots he has planed with black lacquer, then puts the fallboard aside to dry. Lefflbine says that Sakhicand makes the job look easier than it actually is. "He's very smart with the geometry that's required, which, in turn, requires a lot of finagling," Lefflbine explains. "In the up position, it has to be far enough back that it doesn't fall down and smack your knuckles."

Michael Mohr, the manufacturing director, walks by as Sakhicand adds his name to the "operator certification card" that is K0862's permanent who-did-what record. With Sakhicand's signature spilling out of the inch-wide space, half of the form has now been filled in. Mohr knows how much work remains. "Thirty days left," he says.

❧

The first recognizable melody played on K0862 is a surprise for a piano whose ancestors inspired the slogan "the instrument of the immortals." Inside a soundproof booth barely long enough for

K0862, Eric Thompson plays the opening of the theme from *The Simpsons* and smiles, even though the notes sound flat. His job is to tune not-yet-finished pianos like K0862 a bit lower than normal, as a precaution against tightening the brand-new strings too quickly. "This is a prelude to the first tuning," he says, so the tuning fork he uses is not the tuning fork of a piano technician making a house call. On that tuning fork, the A above middle C, the note the oboist sounds when the orchestra tunes up, vibrates at 440 cycles per second. Thompson's tuning fork vibrates at 430.

Thompson, a keyboardist and bass player who was not born with perfect pitch, works his way along K0862, octave by octave. On the notes above the bass, he mutes two of the three strings, tuning only one, leaving the other strings to be tuned later. By his judgment, K0862 will turn out fine. "Yeah, this is going to be a nice piano, actually, because I mean, the tone right now rings out, even if I go softer."

After Thompson plays the *Simpsons* theme, K0862 is wheeled from his booth to another, where it is broken in by a machine that pounds the keyboard four times a second. Four times a second is the tempo of "Chopsticks" played very fast, but the two-note harmony does not change on the seventh note, when you expect it to.

K0862's time in the pounding room—a soundproof booth like Thompson's—is clocked by a man who is happier at Steinway than he was in his last job, as a detective at an athletic-shoe store. "I didn't like that," Nelson Cruz says, recalling his days of collaring shoplifters and worrying that they would pull guns or knives on him. "A lot of risk for little pay."

Here, Cruz is intrigued by what happens when he flips the switch, even though most of the time he walks away as soon as the pounding machine gets going. "Chopsticks" would be hard to listen to day in and day out, and this would be harder. But Cruz is proud that he puts every piano through its first endurance test, for that is what the pounding machine does. "Usually, whatever wasn't done correctly, anything that was done loose, anything that wasn't tight, this machine will show what needs work," he points out. "That's basically it. Twenty, twenty-five minutes and it's done."

The sound of K0862 is still the strange, ethereal noise that Reuben Sookhai did not listen to—the sound of an unfinished piano. A finished piano has dampers, triangular pieces of felt that rest atop the strings, stopping them from vibrating. The dampers on K0862 (and the damper pedal, the one on the right, which lifts all the dampers at once) are put in by Earl Baldwin, who says the jabs about being a Baldwin in the Steinway factory have "kind of faded out" with time.

Baldwin has worked at Steinway since 1988 and has permanent bruises on his arms just below his shoulders, from reaching deep inside thousands of pianos. Before dealing with the dampers, he fits in a felt-edged slat that will keep the keys from bouncing and clacking. The one that goes into K0862 is the second one he pulled from a bin. As with the soundboard and the keyset, the choice is his, but he rejected the first one as too thin. His explanation echoes something Andy Horbachevsky said earlier in the life of K0862: "Somebody's going to spend a hundred thousand dollars to buy a piano. You don't want the piano to start making noise."

Next he installs the damper-pedal mechanism, and then the seventy-one dampers themselves. (There are only seventy-one, not eighty-eight, because the notes at the treble end of the piano do not have dampers.)

As he is finishing, Lefflbine points to a hole on the brace, a piece of metal that crisscrosses the cast-iron plate, where a screw should be. To reach the dampers, Baldwin had to remove the brace.

"Can't find the other screw," Baldwin reports.

Lefflbine disappears into his office, a bright room beyond the midway. When he returns to Baldwin's workbench, he hands him a gold screw. Then Lefflbine jokes, "Look at that. You can grab any screw off the floor, and it fits."

Baldwin sends K0862 around the corner, where it picks up perhaps its most esoteric part, the sostenuto pedal. This center pedal, when pressed, holds up the dampers of the keys being played at that moment, so those notes continue to sound.

In Lefflbine's view, Leon Anantua, the sostenuto pedal installer, is a good worker who has learned to be a better worker. They get along well, and the two of them can turn an end-of-the-day conversation into a demonstration of teaching and learning, of how factory workers hand down the unwritten secrets of their jobs. "Each person you have to teach slightly differently," says Lefflbine, who supervises Anantua. "That's something I think you learn in school. Some people don't learn as much from one teacher as they do from the next, but in this environment, we don't have that luxury, where I can just say, 'I give up on this guy because he doesn't understand me.' I have to go and find another way to teach him or her."

Take the pounding machine, which is supposed to break in a piano faster and more evenly than a pianist could. "I can say, 'You like cars?'" Lefflbine explains. "'You like engines?' The pounding machine is similar to an engine. It has a camshaft and pistons. I can say: 'The pistons are what move the car. Well, it's the same thing that pounds the piano.'"

Anantua, who has worked at Steinway for twenty years, has to insert a rod that will connect the pedal to the piano's action. He also has to fit a device called the sostenuto monkey next to the hammers at the bass end. When the pianist releases the sostenuto pedal, the rod and the monkey are supposed to drop the dampers smoothly. Not smoothly enough, Anantua says as he tries the sostenuto pedal he has just installed on K0862. He tinkers for half an hour.

"He could leave that till final adjustment, but he won't," Lefflbine says. "He's a quick study. When we went over this his first couple of days on this job, he said: 'I got it. I'm perfect.' I said, 'Those are words that shouldn't leave your lips yet.' One piano, I made him go over it for an hour and a half, because there were small tweaking motions that needed to be done. Leon felt it was good enough, but I felt he was not up to my standards. One part moved a little fast, and that could cause other parts to fail.

"This," Lefflbine concludes, "is the difference between eighty-five percent and one hundred percent."

9

A Fresh Personality

November 12: Tone regulator Bruce Campbell slides in the piano's keyset.

The worker responsible for turning K0862 into something—
something more than a long lacquered hull loaded with
parts that have been glued, bolted, or squeezed in—looks
like a scruffy teenager in a rock band, which he once was. He
wears Emerson, Lake & Palmer T-shirts in his soundproof booth
at the factory. He keeps a photograph of Frank Zappa above his
workbench. But after fifteen years at Steinway, Bruce Campbell is
one of the factory's most experienced workers. He describes himself as "the guy who does the Ds"—the 8-foot-11¾-inch Model
D concert grands like K0862, which rolls into his booth on
Wednesday, November 12, 2003.

Though the foreman who supervises Campbell says Steinway puts the same effort into all of its grands, the company clearly
pays special attention to Model Ds, in part because the Ds are the
pianos on which Steinway's reputation was built and on which it
still largely depends. Unlike smaller grands that end up in living
rooms or music school practice rooms, Model Ds are more likely
to be played on concert stages and in recording studios. Carnegie
Hall, for example, has four Model Ds—two for the main stage
and one for each of its smaller recital halls. Avery Fisher Hall at
Lincoln Center, the home of the New York Philharmonic, has
two. But their length is not the only thing that sets the Ds apart
from, say, Steinway's second-largest grand, which is twenty-five
inches shorter than a D (and costs about $30,000 less): The Ds
have more strings than Steinway's smaller grands, the better to
project the distinctive, thunderous sound Steinways are known for.

So a lot is riding on Campbell, who will spend between
twenty and twenty-five hours with K0862, more than anyone else,
even Ante Glavan in the belly department. Campbell is a tone
regulator, the worker who sizes up the personality of a piano and
develops it, makes it bigger and more appealing. He does not
tune pianos—he works on the action, not on the strings. His is a

job that Heinrich Engelhard Steinweg said went to the "aristocrats of the factory."

For all his informality, Campbell knows how tradition-bound Steinway is. Nowhere in K0862's ride through the factory has Steinway's history been as powerful. Campbell's booth is in a section of the factory built when Henry Z. Steinway consolidated the company's three plants in the 1950s. From his workbench, centered against the back wall of the booth, he can see the mansion that William Steinway purchased with the factory's land. The Steinways would not have built themselves anything so showy. Its cupola still crowns what an architectural historian once called "an imaginative combination of classical and medieval elements." From Campbell's bench, the temptation is to daydream, to imagine the double-arched windows gleaming like an Italian villa's, to picture Steinways whacking croquet balls on the lawn and chattering in German and posing for photographs between the cast-iron columns on the porch, to listen for horses clip-clopping along roads named for Steinway sons—Albert Street or Theodore Street.

Campbell's view is indirect. He looks outside through two openings that have not seen a window washer in a while. Usually when he opens the squarish pane on the back wall of his booth, he is trying to let in some air. The booth can feel stuffy when visitors crowd in, and when you are the guy who does the Ds, they crowd in often. The other opening is a window on the factory's outside wall, a few feet beyond the back wall of Campbell's booth. That window stretches from the waist up, and Venetian blinds fall from the ceiling down. Sometimes, when the sun is in his eyes, Campbell leaves the booth, scampers into the narrow no-man's-land between the booth and the outside wall, and tilts the Venetian blinds. Sometimes he just squints.

He knows how easily the mind can wander from work this tedious and repetitive. "On a warm summer day, this is the kind of job that will put you to sleep," he says. "You're relaxed, you're sitting down." But K0862 has arrived in his booth when the colors outside his window have the dense simplicity of Vermeer's Delft. Reality has replaced whatever reverie there was in the blue haze of August. The Steinways sold the house long ago. New streets were laid too close, and the old ones were depersonalized: Albert Street became Astoria's Forty-first Street; Theodore Street became Forty-second. The block is now packed with garages and machine shops. From time to time, upbeat newspaper articles mention the idea of restoring the mansion, of turning it into something other than the centerpiece of a small-time industrial wasteland. It is someone else's daydream, not Campbell's.

Inside his booth, a fly circles on a slow and lazy flight path. It passes over Campbell's scarred workbench. Like Glenn Gould or Awadagin Pratt—pianists who were, or are, famous for sitting on what look like flea-market finds—Campbell perches on a piano bench that is battered, its finish worn. The seat is a couple of inches higher than that of an ordinary piano bench. When he pulls the action out of a piano and is reaching deep into its mouth, he is grateful for the difference.

Campbell loves basketball. He was a teenager when the New York Knicks won their first National Basketball Association championship, in the spring of 1970, and he still marvels at Walt Frazier's flashy playmaking and at teammates like Dave DeBusschere and Willis Reed. At five feet nine, Campbell is on the short side, and he is so slim the word "wispy" comes to mind. But he played pickup basketball until he was twenty-one, when he broke his hand. "I got tripped up," he says, "and when I went down, I punched the court." That kept him away from another pursuit for a while: He was the keyboard player in a number of rock bands on Long Island, where he grew up. "Keyboards are all well and good, but there's nothing like a piano, that's for sure," he muses. "I haven't played anything that comes close to the feel of a piano."

That is his way of signaling that he has work to do. K0862 is waiting.

The word he uses to describe K0862 after he has played a few chords is "metallic." That would turn out to be a first-rate diagnosis.

❧

Before K0862 was wheeled into Campbell's booth, it was tuned by Athanasios Kotsis, who is known as Tommy. He also checks the strings, to be sure they are level. On each note above the bass, the hammer has to hit all three strings at once. (In the bass, there are only one or two strings.) If a hammer is off by even a minuscule measurement—a "hair," a "whisker"—it will hit only two. "The hammer's got to hit them perfectly," Kotsis explains, twisting a tool that looks as if it began life as a screwdriver and has been jerry-rigged for use on the strings. His boss, who is also Campbell's boss, a foreman named Mark Dillon, says that this kind of tool is not unusual at the factory. "A lot of the older tools, you'll find the guys made them themselves. They kind of copied the last one they had. Every job I've been at, there are improvised tools." Dillon knows the factory well: His father-in-law works in the restoration department, rebuilding customers' pianos. Two brothers-in-law and a nephew also work at the factory. His wife's grandfather worked there, too.

Standing outside Kotsis's booth, Dillon describes the characteristics of tuners, their particular combination of mechanical and analytical skills. "Tuners are usually lonely creatures," Dillon notes. "They don't work with an audience." And it is easier for a tuner to be isolated than it once was. "When I was doing this job," Dillon says, "I was out on the floor. There were no rooms." In those days, in the 1980s, a tuner had to learn to hear the piano he was working on above the noise of everything else in the factory. Dillon listens long enough to give K0862 a commendation. "If I was to determine that this piano didn't have the body to be a concert piano," Dillon says, "we'd take the hammers out and do them over again." But K0862 is coming along fine.

Yet the felt hammers come out anyway, as they always do

when Kotsis finishes, not to be redone, but to be turned upside down on Paul Salvodon's workbench for sandpapering—the first real step in voicing—and for their first taste of the "juice," the lacquer hardener that Steinway applies to its hammers. Some performers maintain that the hardener is overused and makes the pianos sound brittle. Salvodon's brother, Eddy, fitted the plate on K0862, and the brothers are not the only Salvodons on the payroll—Paul's wife works in the action assembly department.

Like everyone else in the voicing department, Paul Salvodon announces his verdict on K0862 in no time at all. "The bass section, I can make it better," he declares after playing K0862 with one finger, hitting each note twice. He has heard K0862 for only fifteen or twenty seconds. How can he tell? "When the sound is O.K., I know it's O.K.," he says as he dribbles a drop or two of hardener onto each hammer. He is careful not to aim for the top of the hammer, but low down, far below the shoulder. "You don't want to put any juice up where the strike point is," Salvodon says. He knows that a good hammer will spring apart if you snip the striking point with a pair of scissors, and juicing the striking point will upset the hammer's structure. The felt is like a sponge, he says, and the lacquer percolates through the felt. If he puts the juice where it will harden the shoulder and the hammer's tiny waist, the whole hammer will be stronger.

Now Salvodon can turn to prevoicing, or tailoring the piano's timbre and dynamic range. His job involves shaving a tiny amount of wool from each of the eighty-eight hammers. In all, he will take away about two ounces. He keeps handy a picture showing the shape a hammer should be. "If it's not perfect when it goes to voicing, they'll have to do it there," he says. And he will hear about it. He will also hear if he is too aggressive. He has sandpaper of increasingly fine grain—60, 80, 100; the higher the number, the finer the grain. He cuts a sheet of No. 100 and works on the tops of the hammers.

"A regulator is almost like a mechanic," Dillon says. But a mechanic does mental calculus in ones, fours, sixes, and eights— one transmission, four wheels, six or eight cylinders. Salvodon has eighty-eight notes to worry about. He marks the C-sharp above middle C after plucking the strings. It is hitting unevenly, he says.

In a couple of hours, when the juice dries, K0862 will be ready for Bruce Campbell. In that time, the last important bit of furniture making takes place: Antonio Cordero makes the piano's top, the big piece of wood with the curve that matches the case. Someday audiences will watch as stagehands prop it open or close it. In its shiny underside, they will see reflections: the pianist's face, perhaps, or the long gold plate.

Like the soundboard and the keys, the particular top is chosen at random from a rack of possibilities. Soon Cordero is drilling holes for the hinges. On a Model D like K0862, there are three hinges. On Steinway's smaller grands, there are only two. Cordero uses a thirty-inch screwdriver and dips the tips of the screws in "soap"—a lubricant. "If you don't, you'll never get them in there."

Ravi Badri helps Cordero flip the lid over. Dillon mentions that in his time at the factory, no one has ever weighed a top—the workers just know it is too heavy to be turned over by one person. Badri and Cordero align it atop K0862. Cordero marks where on the case to drill holes for the hinges. He joins the top to the hinge and raises the lid. His head is in a danger zone if the stick—or one of the hinges—gives way. "It hasn't happened yet," he reports.

He blows the piano with an air hose to clear away shavings that might have fallen inside. He writes "K0862" in his notebook.

"I've spent eight years just doing this," he says. "Every day, it's faster."

❧

On a shelf in Campbell's booth is a plastic bucket that was a Father's Day present. "Dad's paino tools," his son Aaron, then age ten, wrote on the front. Campbell smiles sheepishly as he reaches for it. "I didn't have the heart to tell him that's not how you spell 'piano,'" he says.

It is Thursday, November 13, the morning after Cordero had made the top. Campbell was still working on another piano when Salvodon's juice dried, and was not ready for K0862. The tools in Campbell's bucket are for tiny adjustments he hopes will correct problems he hears or feels: a brassy note, a sluggish key. Campbell taps and twists and tinkers with the keys and the action until the piano no longer feels mechanical. His goal is to make K0862 as uniform as possible: the spaces between the hammers, the gaps between the dampers, the distances between the strings, the angle at which the hammers rise and fall, the speed at which the keys descend and return. He may slide paper under a hammershank to change the angle, or heat it with an alcohol flame so he can bend it. He will sand parts that rub or chafe—just a stroke or two with sandpaper finer than Salvodon's. All of that falls under the definition of regulation, the adjustment of the individual components of the action assembly for which Campbell is responsible. There is a lot to regulating a piano. In Arthur A. Reblitz's authoritative manual on servicing and tuning pianos, the chapter on regulating runs fifty-two pages, about a sixth of the book. In the index, the entries and subentries for "regulating" and "regulating procedures" fill almost two-thirds of a page. After mastering the items described in the book, a regulator can merely slide the action into the mouth of the piano and try the notes. The rest is in the hearing. More often than not, Campbell hears something that needs work. "I'm pretty much known for hearing things in a piano that other people don't hear," he says.

Among his co-workers, Campbell is known for being careful. "Not everybody has Bruce's feeling of perfection," declares Victor Madorsky, a tuner who works in a soundproof booth near Campbell's. "He will not leave a piano if he feels it's not good enough." Madorsky himself was trained as an oboist at the St. Petersburg Conservatory. He says it is appropriate for an oboist to take a job tuning pianos—it is, after all, the oboist who plays the A when an orchestra tunes up. Madorsky also feels that being a tuner was his destiny in life; his grandfather was a tuner, and Madorsky inherited his tools.

At first, Campbell does not think that K0862 needs much work. "I was very lucky with this action," he says as he shakes the hammers, checking to see if they wobble. "It's nice." But as he pulls the action out and pushes it back in and flips the hammers up and down, his assessment darkens.

He taps the keyframe—the wooden tray on which the keys ride—as it sits in the mouth of K0862. He is listening the way a doctor does when palpating a patient who may have appendicitis. Campbell hears a hollow sound that tells him there is a gap between the keyframe and the keybed, the wooden shelf at the mouth of the piano. He decides to sand the keyframe—the underside, the part that is supposed to ride smoothly on the keybed. "The slightest splinter, someone like myself will hear a little scraping," Campbell explains as he lifts off the keys, turns the keybed over, and reaches for his sandpaper.

After an hour's work, after planing the keybed inside the piano, Campbell starts to express doubts about K0862. "This is definitely one of the more difficult ones," he says. "Usually, this is about ten or fifteen minutes." Things are getting bogged down. The problem seems to be with the crown in the keybed under middle C. He is sure that the keybed is higher at the ends and slouched in the center, instead of the reverse. The rise at the edges and the dip in the middle involve, at the most, millimeters.

As he brushes away some wood shavings, he talks about his training at Steinway. "The way they taught me was basically the old-fashioned way, apprenticeship," he explains. He spent nearly a dozen years voicing pianos—shaping the hammers on uprights and smaller grands—before he started working on concert grands. He also learned the art of regulating, tailoring the many tiny interacting parts in the action. He found regulating difficult.

"I wasn't used to the mechanical things," he says. "Voicing, it was more objective. You could hear it. Regulating, there's no taste involved." There are specifications, absolutes, measurements, and the procedures are interdependent: If a regulator sets a hammer to the wrong height, other things will go wrong. Campbell's boss, Mark Dillon, the foreman, calls tone regulating the moment when a piano becomes a musical instrument.

Campbell says that he learned tone regulating from the men who did the job when he was young. "How I personally learned, I got friendly with the guys who did the Ds, just because they were nice guys," he remembers. He keeps a photograph of Raymond Parada on the wall. It was Parada who did the Ds in the 1980s. "I've heard talk that the older guys wouldn't tell you their secrets," Campbell says. "I never ran into that. I asked so many questions, they had to give it up."

❧

The next morning, Campbell is checking spacing—between the strings, then between the hammers. "This is the kind of stuff that causes trouble with weather," he says. "It gets humid, the bushing expands. We're dealing with weather conditions. That's why they say to keep a piano away from the radiator. Even the tone can be changed by humidity. The hammers, it sounds a little duller. Downstairs in the selection room, they leave the air-conditioning on all the time. These are very sensitive instruments."

He lights a small alcohol lamp and holds the flame against the hammershank of the highest G on K0862. "I don't like the way it's going up and down," he says. "It's not straight. It's twisted." He heats the hammershank just enough to make it pliable, and bends it straight.

As he puts the alcohol lamp down, he points out that the hammers are different than they were when he started at the factory. "The hammers were larger and softer then," he explains, "so there was more work. The hammers were a lot rounder, and we had to spend more time getting them right." He felt time pressure. "The whole job—regulating, voicing, and prevoicing—was done in roughly four hours," Campbell recalls. That was a throwback to the days when all the regulators, including the one who did the Ds, were on the piecework pay scale. Even though Steinway abolished piecework shortly before Campbell was hired, tone regulators were still expected to have a piano ready in four hours. "If you weren't doing it in four, you weren't making the money you needed, probably," Campbell says.

Something bothers him about the E above middle C on K0862. The spacing is not right when the hammer rises. He takes the note apart. "There's paper under there," he discovers. A single piece of scrap paper made the hammer just uneven enough for him to notice.

Satisfied, he slips the action back into the piano and announces the next task: "set my hammerline," or the height of the hammers in relation to the strings. Steinway issues tone regulators a plastic gauge that shows the distance, but Campbell has learned over time that he likes to set the height a whisker less than the gauge says. He then attends to the let-off, and after that to the aftertouch, the distance the hammer drops after it has struck the string. Without aftertouch, K0862 would feel underpowered.

Campbell is not among those who insist that precise measurements must be followed—0.025 to 0.060 of an inch for the aftertouch, according to Reblitz's textbook. "It's not a scientific thing," Campbell declares—at least, it is not a scientific thing to him. "I'm not even sure what the measurement is," he says. There is a gauge to measure the distance, just as there is a gauge for the hammerline, but Campbell does not bother to use it. "I just know when it feels right and when it doesn't. Some pianists might like a little less. We're trying to set it to a specific and let the customer work it out the first time the technician comes into his house."

Campbell finishes the natural keys before lunch, the sharps
and flats after. Then he "dry lubes" the knuckles, the eraser-sized
shock absorbers, brushing on a powdered white lubricant. It
changes the yellow felt to the color of a manila file folder. As he
is putting the bottle of lubricant away, Campbell stares at
the label. "It doesn't have the ingredients on it," he reports.
Then, reading from the label: "Helps prevent squeaks in wood
flooring."

He vacuums his workbench. The quitting-time buzzer
sounds. His second day with K0862 is over.

※

It turns out that in regulating a piano, you adjust the aftertouch
before you adjust the touch. The next morning, Campbell checks
what is called the touch weight, which is exactly what the name
says: the amount of weight needed to depress the key. Campbell
begins by placing small weights on the hammer keys—fifty-one
grams at the bass end, forty-six grams at the treble. The hammers
are not supposed to spring up as Campbell lays on the weights.
He marks the ones that do; later, pieces of lead about the size of a
dime will be pressed in the bottoms of those keys to make them
heavier. "The tiniest little weight makes so much difference," he
explains as he lowers the fifty-one-gram weight onto K0862's
lowest F. With a shrug that says he knows just how arcane an outsider might find what he does day in and day out, he adds, "This
is really the most exciting part of the job."

He lays the weight on the lowest B-flat and talks about the
evolution of the parts he adjusts every day. "On pianofortes, the
hammers were like Q-tips. But you didn't get the velocity from
the hammer, and the string wasn't as long, so you didn't get the
volume. That's something that's always amazed me. These composers a hundred or two hundred years ago wrote this big music,
that big sound, for these rinky-dink pianos." A pianoforte, he
says, "is kind of like a toy piano."

He lays the weight on the D-flat and changes subjects. "I miss Johnny Carson," he says.

He works his way up the keyboard.

"This is the halfway point," he says when he finishes—the halfway point in his time with K0862.

The holes for the lead plugs are drilled by Gwendolyn Falls, who talks about her long, precisely painted fingernails—"They're mine, they're not fake"—while half-listening to Jerry Springer's talk show on a radio that receives the audio portion of television broadcasts. "I'm sorry I can't see it," she says. "Sometimes this can stress you out bad."

She divides the keys like a stack of cards, naturals in one pile, accidentals in the other. She sighs. "Eighty-eight keys. Every one of them is a person. They're all different. Every one of them has a mind of its own."

Falls mentions a famous cousin, the former New York Mets outfielder Mookie Wilson ("He's bad," she says, without elaboration), and two brothers-in-law who work in the factory. As she pushes in the last of the lead touch weights, Mark Dillon, the foreman, walks by. "Hey, Mark, eight-sixty-two?" she says.

"Eight-sixty-two," Dillon replies, and pushes the piano to Campbell's booth.

"That was quick," Campbell says. Campbell checks the touch weights and then sends K0862 to Victor Madorsky's booth for another tuning. Madorsky tries some fifths, some fourths, some octaves. He reports that K0862 sounds flat. "I'm making it a little bit sharp on purpose," he says. "It's going to drop." He plays a few bars of Tchaikovsky. "It sounds more or less decent," he declares. Then, explaining why he did not stick to intervals, he adds, "The music helps me a lot with the tuning."

K0862 goes back to Campbell, who runs through some chords. "Wow," he says. "Strange. It's loud. Louder than usual." He starts regulating the piano all over again, putting color-coded paper punchings under a handful of keys that seem particularly

loud—a low G, an F, a C-sharp, and a D-sharp. The punchings—
which go under the spindle each key rides on, and under Frederick Vietor's balance rail—will level the keys, even them out.

He can also insert smaller scraps torn from the dry end of
strips he puts in his mouth. "I look like Huck Finn," he says with
a shrug.

The green punch he puts under the low G does the job. The
F needs two, the F-sharp and G-sharp one each. "I feel for the aftertouch, you feel it in the key," he explains. "That's one thing
with these electronic actions that's hard to simulate, and that's so
much of playing the piano." He tests the sharps purely by feel,
but the naturals he wants something "a little bit less . . . I want it
to be—what's the word? You could say shallower."

When Campbell reaches the highest G-sharp, he is puzzled.
"It feels like it needs something, but when I put another green in,
it's too much." This time he is working not with the colored paper
punch but with a cloth one. What's its name? "I call it 'that green
thing,'" he says. He pulls out the chart. It is No. 5, and its name
is a mouthful: "Keyframe front rail cloth punch." The green
thing, however, does the job. Satisfied, he announces, "It's juice
time."

He has decided to end the day by putting more lacquer on
K0862's hammers. He uses almost a full bottle, eight ounces. "I
could put twelve ounces in there, but I don't want to overdo it,"
he explains. Now he does not think the piano needs that much
work. "It's got the power that I'm looking for. The brightness is
pretty much there." He goes on. "This is going to be a good
piano."

❧

The next morning, Campbell arrives at the factory wearing a New
York Yankees T-shirt with Paul O'Neill's name on it—"the consummate team player," Campbell says. He tries a few chords on
K0862, and there it is again, that metallic sound. With the hammers dry and back inside the piano, Campbell hears "something

that to me sounds like hitting a garbage can." He looks up, breaking into a grin. "Maybe that's a crude way of putting it."

Like so many workers before him, he pulls out a notebook and jots K0862's serial number inside. "It's just in case somebody calls me down and says, 'There's something wrong with this piano.' I can look back and go, 'Did I work on it?'" he explains, adding, "I haven't been called down yet."

He checks the soft pedal and says it feels spongy. The remedy is to adjust the damper stop rail, which was too high. Two dampers look ragged and do not sit right on the strings. He tells Dillon that K0862 needs John Valenti, a repair technician who floats through the factory and attends to pianos with small problems.

Campbell checks again to be sure each hammer is hitting all three strings of each treble note. "You can go real crazy doing this," he says, almost apologetically. Working alone in a soundproof room—"your own little bubble"—a tone regulator hears the slightest noise. And noise is what he is hearing from K0862. He plays a few more chords followed by an arpeggio. "You know what it is? I hear metal. There's plenty of metal involved here, but I hear it in the notes that needed fitting."

He sends the piano out for another tuning—not to Victor Madorsky this time, but to Shying Yee Tsao, a younger technician who grew up in Hong Kong and goes by the name Raymond around the factory. On Tsao's wall are two photographs taken before he emigrated. In one, he is at the wheel of a BMW. "Somebody said I looked like a Chinese James Bond," he says by way of explanation. In the other, he is seated at a Steinway. At the time the photograph was taken, "I didn't know this name," he says quietly.

As he tunes K0862, he explains that he is leaving for Hong Kong in two weeks to marry. His bride's immigration papers have not been approved. He expects to return to New York after the honeymoon by himself. He plays arpeggios, then the theme from *Love Story,* then "Ave Maria." He is the first person to play K0862 sitting down.

"It's a new piano," he says. "It needs to make a statement."

Tsao pushes K0862 back to Campbell, who makes one last round of minor adjustments. He still hears "an excess of metal," but sends K0862 to Dillon for inspection. Dillon gives the piano a workout and marks four hammers, five strings, and ten notes for more work. He also sticks K0862 with a Post-it note reading "touch in treble." It is shorthand. The touch there is too shallow; he wants more of a kick after the keys hit the strings. "I felt the evenness of touch started to disappear up there," he explains. "If somebody played it, they'd feel like they were running uphill."

Campbell is surprised by how many keys Dillon has marked. "He really went to town," Campbell says. "I thought he liked me."

What Campbell does not say is that Dillon is new in the foreman's job. A few months earlier, he replaced one of the factory's legends, a longtime foreman who retired after more than thirty years of supervising the tone regulators. Dillon has to establish his authority. But that is not his only concern. "We came out of the summer, we had a problem with tight keys," Dillon points out. "I'm doing a gentle reminder to everyone."

Campbell spends another couple of hours on K0862 before sending it back to Dillon. This time, it passes muster.

Its next stop is Valenti, the technician, who carries a green-and-brown bag stuffed with tools. K0862 has been pushed into the midway on Dillon's floor, the open area outside Campbell's booth. "This job is all about being patient. I am, by nature," Valenti says. He was a gardener whose interest in pianos began when a customer threw out a Wurlitzer spinet. "I decided to take it because a neighbor of mine worked here. He fixed it. I decided to start taking lessons from him. Not too long after that, I found a Steinway upright in the trash." This was in a dump in the Bronx where he was dropping off leaves he had raked at a customer's house. He called his friend. "He told me to take the wippens out, he would fix them. He had me working on it. By the time I finished, I was going, 'I like this, can you get me a job?'" (Wippens, which Steinway calls repetitions in its grands, are wooden parts that rock back and forth as the action assembly does its work.)

Now, though, he is thinking of leaving. His wife, who once worked as a secretary at Steinway, already has. On weekends, Valenti runs a limousine service on Long Island, where he lives. He drives wedding parties from the church to the reception, bridal couples to the airport, partied-out parents home. He started with an eight-door Checker Aerobus. It is boxy, like a New York City taxicab, and has row after row of seats. He has made enough money to buy a 1956 Cadillac and a 1966 Lincoln. He hires other drivers when he has the bookings.

For the moment, though, his mind is on K0862, and whether another damper needs a quick repair. "Even though something looks right, sometimes it doesn't work right," he says. "There are so many variables."

10

Finding the Screw

January 12: Dominick Iovino tunes K0862 one last time—and discovers a problem.

H aving been put together, K0862 is sent downstairs and
    taken apart.
          No one at the factory puts it that way. Anyone who
believes there is something funny about disassembling a just-
finished piano keeps a straight face. Michael Mohr, the manufacturing director, is as earnest as ever. Pianos that have been tuned
and regulated and voiced and retuned always go to the piano
world's equivalent of an auto body shop, where K0862 receives
touchups for nicks, dings, and blemishes—the little things that
can pop up on the ride from floor to floor, from workbench to
workbench. Here it is eyes that matter, not ears, and Mohr—
though he is not a flashy dresser around the factory—is not one to
underestimate looks. "The guys here are dealing with what the
customer is going to see," he explains. "The very first thing when
the customer takes it out of the box, they're not going to play it,
they're not going to hear the voicing, the regulation. The first impression, it's cosmetics."

On Monday, January 12, 2004, K0862 enters the world of
Jorge Diaz, the foreman who supervises the sixty-two men in the
factory's polishing department. Before he and his men undo
everything that has been done to K0862, he writes a code, a string
of numbers and letters, on a piece of masking tape and presses it
on the hinge. The code is 862-D-EB. Diaz explains how to break
it: 862 is short for K0862, the piano's case number; D is the
model; EB is the finish, ebonized—as if anyone would make the
mistake of applying mahogany highlights or walnut stain. Few
Model Ds are anything but black.

On the far side of Diaz's midway is a machine that buffs piano tops. It is the height of a pool table, but far longer. Its nozzles
look eerily like the ones on an exterminator's wand, and its rollers
move back and forth in long narrow strokes, then shift one
row over for more long narrow strokes. There is a formula here.
It is: up, back, up, back, over; up, back, up, back, over—boring,

repetitive, and essential. "Over" is a cue for a worker named Jean François to push a button and turn on the spray.

To do that—indeed, for his top-polishing machine to operate at all—a piano top must be laid on the long flat surface. George Perez goes to work on K0862, removing the temporary hinges. Two pop out easily. The third does not. Diaz, Perez, and another worker spend several frustrating minutes with their screwdrivers and mallets. Finally they push it out. As Perez delivers the top to François, Diaz puts the hinges in a gray box and marks "862" on a strip of masking tape on it. Then he pulls out the action stack—the keys, the hammers, and the mechanism that Bruce Campbell worked on only to have his foreman, Dillon, order him to work on it some more. Diaz parks it on a wagon marked "key polishing."

Key polishing is the realm of Mario Villalobos, and soon he is pushing the wagon and action stack to his workbench. Yes, people ask if he is related to Heitor Villa-Lobos, the composer who wrote *Bachianas Brasilieras* as an homage to two *B*s—Bach and Brazil. No, Villalobos is not related.

He notices hairline cracks in two keys, the D and the A two octaves below middle C. They could have been caused by almost anything, he says—jostling in the crate on the way over from Kluge's key-making factory in Germany, changes in temperature and humidity, even Nelson Cruz's key-pounding machine. Training his eyes to see tiny imperfections in the glare of the factory's fluorescent lights was a challenge. "You have to learn what you're looking for," Villalobos says. "There were things I could never see. It took me a while." In his years at Steinway, he has worked his way around the polishing room, refinishing legs and benches. Before that, he worked downstairs, polishing shiny brass pedals and swaddling them in felt covers—booties for pianos.

As for keys, the most he has ever had to fix on one piano is thirty. On K0862, he repairs the A and decides he will have to replace the D, using heat to separate the original plastic top from the Bavarian spruce base. With a router, he trims the replacement top, sending white plastic flakes flying like artificial snow. "Most people will be unable to tell it's been replaced," he says as he files the key's "hips," the indentations that make room for the flat and sharp keys next to them. On a D key, the hips flare out from the center like a hoop skirt. A D, like a G or an A, is a middle key, so it has a pair of hips. The other naturals have only one, and wider waists (their other side is straight).

Of all the workers who have had anything to do with K0862, Villalobos is the only one to mention safety in the workplace. He has not been active in the union, and brings up the safety issue conversationally, almost in passing, as he switches off the router. As a newly hired worker in 1988, he noticed that "there were a lot of guys working around here with one finger missing." He says that management is more concerned about safety than it once was. Still, he adds, "Guys have accidents. When I was in the action department, there were some big machines. One of them caught me." He holds up his middle finger. The injury was too slight to be noticeable. "It only nicked me."

While Villalobos works on the keys, another worker, James Zotales, raises the rest of K0862 on a hydraulic jack. Where Villalobos is serious, Zotales is glib, tossing off lines like "How do you change the tires on a piano?" Zotales removes the left leg and replaces it with a metal bar. He repeats the ritual with the right leg and then the tail leg, and pushes K0862 to a workbench by the far wall.

The flap—the rectangular piece of wood that is hinged to the curving lid—is parked atop sawhorses that are covered with little black stalagmites formed by drips of touch-up lacquer and a liquid containing a mineral solvent. The sawhorses belong to George Perez, who runs what everyone at the factory calls the thirty-pounder. It is a machine that looks like a sander, but is heavier and would buck like a bronco if Perez did not hold it steady with both hands. It breaks the surface of the lacquer on the flap, but only slightly, before one last polishing.

After running the thirty-pounder back and forth for five minutes, Perez moves the flap off the sawhorses, and he and Robert de la Rosa lift the lid on. Perez swabs it with the solvent and turns on the thirty-pounder. He pushes the machine around the curve. It sprays drops that will enlarge the stalagmites on the sawhorse. After ten minutes, he and de la Rosa turn the lid over, and the thirty-pounder bumps over the other side.

The next day looks to be another dirty one for K0862. The case, waiting at Enrique Rosado's workbench, is due for the same kind of facial, but the treatment is somewhat less aggressive—Rosado, a wiry man of medium height, cannot control the thirty-pounder on the curves. So, after laying a canvas cover over the strings to protect them against splashes and pulling on green rubber gloves, he picks up a piece of sandpaper and begins breaking the surface by hand—"getting the paint down," as he puts it. "The piano has that imperfect surface," he says. "Well, we smooth it down."

His is exacting work, but it involves long, repeated strokes, and there is time to talk about his off-hours passion, cars—fast cars. He has a Corvette calendar on the wall behind his workbench and dreams of a 1963 Corvette, the classic with the headlights that flip up when they go on. Rosado hopes to make enough money restoring and selling lesser cars to afford a '63 Vette someday. He spent his last vacation rebuilding a 1969 Chrysler and a 1956 Chevrolet. Rosado, who came to New York in 1996 and decided to stay, is a newlywed, but he has staked out his territory. "I told my wife, when we get a house, there will be a car in the garage."

He evens out barely perceptible "waves" on the side of K0862, north and east of the gold letters that spell the company's name, explaining, "This is what tells you the piano was not made by a computer." A bubble about the size of a capital *O* catches his attention. "The only reason you noticed it is I showed it to you. It's a millimeter deep in the wood." He runs his hand over the flaw before rubbing it away with fine sandpaper. "You have to have a really good touch to feel that," he says.

He applied for work at Steinway after meeting a foreman in his neighborhood in the Bronx. "I fell in love with the place"— and there is still wonder in his voice. He pats K0862. "You look at a tree, and you could never imagine a piano."

&

The next morning, K0862 has been pushed across the room to another workstation. Jean-Daniel Jean, a tall man with long arms and a hat emblazoned "Pooh" on his thin head, is preparing to dance his way around K0862 with steel wool, sandpaper, and water. Looking for nicks, he marks Xs on the case in white chalk—he finds about a dozen trouble spots on the top of the rim alone. He files them down and fixes them with a "burning stick," a lacquer crayon that he heats in an alcohol flame. That softens the tip of the crayon, and he drips one or two drops of lacquer on each nick. Some fast sanding follows. "Some pianos are good and some are bad, and you take a lot of time because there can be a lot of damage" to the finish of the cases, he says. "This one's in between." He glides around, sitting on a wheeled stool, and sees nicks on the tail where the leg attaches. He is concerned that the crayon is too black, and that his repair will stand out. "I've got to make it the same color as the piano," he explains. He does.

He then polishes the case with long soaring strokes, starting on the treble side. His long arms reach into the curve and beyond, and he does not break his rhythm even when he talks. "If you can't move, you can't do this job." He grins. He learned the job from Carlo Valentin, who works at the next bench and has been whistling "Yankee Doodle Dandy" as Jean pirouettes. Valentin has twenty-four years of experience at the factory, but Jean's moves are his own. "I know everything now," Jean announces. He flashes another grin. This one says he did not mean that the way it sounded.

❧

When the go-to-work buzzer sounds on Monday, Diaz is nowhere
to be seen, so Michael Mohr steps in. This is the day the quality
control inspector will look at K0862, and Mohr does not want
things to be delayed because K0862 is in disarray. He rips off the
masking tape on which Diaz has written the piano's polishing
code, 862-D-EB. Workers begin reassembling K0862, finding the
action on a rack near Villalobos's bench and the top on a rack
across the aisle. Battery-powered screwdrivers whir as they reat-
tach the hinges of the lid. They are all but done when Diaz walks
in, about fifteen minutes late. "Traffic, and a little late start," he
says sheepishly.

Soon the inspector, Maria Hatzinikolaou, is gliding around
K0862, leaning in close, bending, twisting, peering. As she hunts
for reasons to reject K0862 and send it back to Diaz's men, she
talks about how the factory has changed in her thirty-four years
there. "Years ago, it was like a family, with the three brothers,
Henry, John, and Teddy Steinway," she says. She started in the action department, before the sale to CBS. She was eventually
trained as a tone regulator. Then her job was eliminated, and she
was told to return to assembling actions. She refused to go.
"Freddie [Drasche, then the chief technical supervisor] talked to
the Steinways, and they offered me this job. They used to have inspectors, and then they let the pianos go without inspecting them
for years. So I became the quality control department."

Hovering over K0862, she concentrates on the finish that
Rosado had worked on and Jean had polished. She sees nothing
that requires sending the piano back for a do-over, so she signs a
form and Diaz loads K0862 into an elevator for the ride to the
first floor, where it will spend its last days at the factory. The air is
cold when Diaz steps out—the loading-dock door has been left
open—but K0862 does not yet feel the shock. It is stuck. The
wheel of its truck is caught in the gap between the elevator and

the floor. Someone brings Diaz a jack, and he raises the truck, freeing the wheel.

One indication of how much trust Steinway puts in its workers comes that afternoon. The two workers who are, in effect, the final quality control inspectors on the mechanical workings of every piano are the union men: Dominick Iovino, a tuner, is the shop steward, and Walter R. Boot is the brother of the union's president. But they are also two of Steinway's most senior employees. Iovino has worked at the factory since 1963, Boot even longer, since 1960. "These guys, they find anything wrong, boom, we stop it, we fix it," says Ron Penatzer, Steinway's top manufacturing official, who stops by before Iovino wheels K0862 into his booth. "You can have noise on a note, minor stuff. You just don't want it to go out like that."

Noise on a note is what catches Iovino's attention—metallic noise, the same thing that bedeviled Campbell. He believes he knows why: "There's something on the soundboard," he says. "We're going to have to search for it." Iovino, in a black sweatshirt and jeans, opens the door to his not-quite-soundproof booth— even with the door closed, the hiss of an air hose in the workroom outside comes through loud and clear. He calls Boot in with a question: "You got time for a fishing expedition?" From long years together Boot knows what Iovino has in mind, and brings a magnetized shim with him. As Iovino watches, Boot feeds it toward the soundboard through one of the holes in the plate. He flicks it back and forth. A screw rolls into view, and Boot fishes it out. It was the screw that Earl Baldwin had lost months before while installing the dampers. Boot had expected the culprit to be a tuning pin, from when the strings had gone in. "It's a common occurrence," Iovino explains as he finishes tuning K0862. "The piano travels all through the factory."

A few minutes later, K0862 travels into what once was an identical booth next door. In Boot's long residence, it has become a fantasy world. The walls are lined with grandfather clocks he has built and dollhouses he has repaired. With a piano in place, there is barely room to squeeze by without bumping something. He is one of the factory's larger-than-life characters. His workaday outfit is a T-shirt without sleeves, as if he were a motorcyclist with outsize tattoos to show off. "I don't do tattoos," he says flatly, but he does owns a motorcycle, a vintage Triumph; some years it gleams in the photograph on the holiday cards he sends out. "When I got married, I bought that as a wedding present. Thirty years later, same wife, same motorcycle." His hair is still sandy, and he looks younger than a man in his late fifties. But he is authoritative. His have been the last ears and fingers to go over every Steinway for more than twenty years. Stepping behind K0862, Boot voices the piano, punching hammers with a two-pronged needle to make notes that sound too loud blend in better. He talks about the advantages of three-pronged needles, and then mentions that at Steinway Hall "they use *one*"—that is, a needle with only one prong. What's the difference? "Experience," he says, looking over his half-frame glasses with a grin.

For the ten months before K0862 arrived, Walter Boot has had an extra duty. It has nothing to do with how the pianos sound or function, but for someone who has worked at the factory for as long as he has, it is freighted with meaning. He is assigned to put a small round medal commemorating Steinway's sesquicentennial into the case of each almost-completed piano. "One hundred and fifty years . . ." he says as he drills the holes for the medal into K0862. There is a catch in his voice. The sentence trails off.

Back at the keyboard of K0862, Boot starts playing. In five minutes he runs through most of his repertoire: a snippet of a Rachmaninoff prelude; the opening of the *Moonlight* sonata; a bit of the *Elvira Madigan* Mozart concerto; the opening of the second movement of Beethoven's *Pathétique* sonata, familiar to radio listeners as the theme for the music appreciation program *Adventures in Good Music*. After forty-three years in a piano factory, Boot is finally learning to play. Of more than four hundred workers at the factory, he is oboist-turned-tuner Victor Madorsky's only student.

§

Jean-Claude Petion zips through K0862's final cosmetic touch-ups before Maria Hatzinikolaou inspects it again. K0862 does not pass on the first try. She marks four of the eight portholes—"rosettes"—in the cast-iron plate. "They're rough," she says. Petion rubs them with sandpaper and spray-paints them using the aerosol can labeled "Steinway gold."

More inspecting brings more headaches. Hatzinikolaou tells him to repaint the part of the plate where the serial number will go, as well as the *S* of the Steinway name on the plate. K0862 will not be finished today, because the paint will have to dry overnight.

Then someone notices a little bubble on the arm of the piano. Petion is certain of the cause: an earlier touchup that did not cure right. And he has had enough. "She should not have sent the piano down here" after the earlier inspection, Petion says. "When it comes down here, it should be ready to go." He feels that Hatzinikolaou should have noticed the problems when she checked K0862 on the second floor, and should have raised her objections there.

The next inspection does not go any better. "Jean," she says, "don't forget." She puts another chalk mark on the plate, a few inches from the *S*. He sprays the plate. Hatzinikolaou sees two more tiny nicks. He fixes them. He closes the lid and pulls the plastic cover over K0862.

"Done," he says.

"Not so fast," she says. Hatzinikolaou opens the lid and sees dirt. Petion swabs it away. Someone else notices a scratch on the keyslip. As Petion rubs it, he notices two others.

"If I miss anything," he says, sighing, "it's not because I want to."

11

Temporary Identity

February 9: Steinway's chief concert technician, Ronald F. Coners, sizes up K0862.

Over eleven months, it has been shaped, spray-painted, polished, worked on, tuned, inspected, and worked on some more. In all that time, everyone—workers, foremen, executives on management row—has referred to it as K0862, or simply "eight-six-two" (as in "Where is eight-six-two now?"). In three minutes on Monday, February 9, 2004, its last day at the factory, K0862 gets a new identity. It is given a six-digit serial number, No. 565700. That number designates it as the 565,700th Steinway ever made.

A worker named Davendra Viran stencils the number onto the edge of the cast-iron plate, a few inches above the keyboard, just under the music rack. Viran, who goes by the name Roy, is a Guyanan who has worked at the factory for ten years. Unlike the rim-benders who christened K0862 with the wrong case number, Viran has never stenciled in the wrong serial number. Ask him if he has, and he will shoot you an indignant look, a how-dare-you look, a look that says, "Only an incompetent would make a mistake like that."

Its new number in place, No. 565700 makes a fast getaway. Within half an hour, Viran and four other workers have pried off two of its legs. They have wrapped the case in gray flannel, flipped it on its side, and strapped it inside the back of a truck. No. 565700 fills the right-hand side of the boxy space, its keyboard over the back wheel, its still-attached leg sticking out toward the center. Warren Albrecht, the wood technologist, looks in and sees only one leg lying next to the piano. "Don't forget the other leg," he says. He need not have worried. It was already on board, swaddled in a drop cloth as thick as a blanket. The truck pulls away from the loading dock and ambles over to Steinway Street. Joe Ragusa is at the wheel.

Ragusa spends most days driving back and forth between the Steinway factory in Queens and Steinway Hall, down the block and across the street from Carnegie Hall. Usually, Ragusa has a couple of pianos and, as he did on this run, a couple of plastic tubs containing interoffice mail. But pianos and memos are not the only things Steinway has loaded into its trucks. Once, when an ailing Vladimir Horowitz wanted to go to Connecticut, he fretted that the neighbors would spread rumors if an ambulance pulled up in front of his Manhattan town house to pick him up. According to Glenn Plaskin's biography of Horowitz, the Steinway truck, outfitted with a bed, pulled up to Horowitz's brownstone, as it had many times before. No one noticed that what ended up in the back of the truck was not Horowitz's piano, but Horowitz—or at least no one tipped off the gossip columns.

Driving toward Manhattan with No. 565700, Ragusa hits a few potholes—the usual, he says. It is a sunny day, mild for February, and Ragusa says the stop-and-go traffic is heavy for midmorning. No. 565700 leaves Queens via Steinway Street, a block from the factory—the spine of what was once William's company town. These days, Steinway Street is a direct but slow route to the Queensboro Bridge. After rumbling across the East Side, passing the Plaza Hotel and squeezing past some double-parked cars, Ragusa backs into a loading dock at the Steinway showroom's back door. Two movers trundle No. 565700 past old upright pianos that rest, all but abandoned, beside a freight elevator barely wide enough for a nine-foot grand, sideways. Ragusa hands over the leg Albrecht had worried would be forgotten.

The news is that No. 565700 is about to get still another identity. Steinway has chosen No. 565700 to be one of the three hundred or so grands in the fleet of pianos it lends out for concerts, recitals, recording sessions, and television programs. Steinway assigns those pianos still a third ID number, beginning with the letter C, for concert. So No. 565700 becomes CD-60—the D stands for the model. And its destination is not the first-floor showroom at Steinway Hall, with the wide window looking out on West Fifty-seventh Street, but the hall's basement.

※

Among pianists, the Steinway basement is both a semisecret realm and a storied place, a destination that confers status. There, lined up beneath fluorescent lights that hum and steam pipes that hiss, is what may be Steinway's most important asset, a roomful of long black pianos (except for CD-980, the long white one that went to Billy Joel for a recording project and later to a John Lennon tribute at Radio City Music Hall). Everyone from Moriz Rosenthal (one of Liszt's last pupils) to Charles Rosen (one of Rosenthal's last pupils) to Glenn Gould to Mitsuko Uchida to Alfred Brendel has gone there to pick what he or she considered the perfect piano to borrow and play in public. In the 1960s, Leonard Bernstein, who played Baldwins and Bösendorfers at concerts, sneaked in to choose a Steinway for recordings, or so Steinway officials say.

The Steinway basement is where Sergei Rachmaninoff was introduced to Vladimir Horowitz in the 1920s. They played a two-piano version of Rachmaninoff's Concerto No. 3, and Rachmaninoff is said to have declared, "That's the way it should be played." Other Russian pianists gathered there, as much to play cards as to practice. In the 1950s, Gary Graffman catnapped in the basement while Leon Fleisher practiced on their favorite piano, and vice versa. Graffman called the pianos in the basement "ladies of the evening" because they were, "to put it crassly, available for one-night stands."

Emanuel Ax remembers the first time he saw the basement, as a teenager in 1965, a few weeks after Vladimir Horowitz's first public recital in twelve years. "For most of us students who were there, it was as though this guy had come back from the dead," Ax said. "Everyone had a story: His piano is souped up." There, in the basement, was Horowitz's piano. Ax got to try it out, and discovered it was not a hotrod. "It was a very live instrument, with lots of power, but it was just a piano. It was, in a way, reassuring, and in a way, very, very humbling, to realize that all of that stuff was his ear and his imagination."

In the 1970s, Ivo Pogorelich marched in and let his leopard jacket—it *was* the 1970s—fall to the floor, as if he expected someone to pick it up. This was before Pogorelich became famous for not winning the International Chopin Competition in Warsaw (Martha Argerich, one of the jurors, walked out to protest the vote that sent him packing). Peter B. Goodrich, then a junior executive at Steinway and a dark-suit-and-tie type, picked up Pogorelich's jacket, thinking, "Is this guy the most obnoxious, arrogant of artists?" Then Pogorelich began playing. "I thought, this guy is extraordinary. I'll pick up his jacket anytime."

In the 1980s, Rosalyn Tureck slipped and fell in the basement, and sued. Steinway has not varnished the floor since.

There are pianists who say the pianos in the basement communicate with one another. There are pianists who say the pianos have friends and enemies in their own ranks, and don't put out their best sound if they are placed next to one they don't like. If that is so, one can only wonder what the pianos make of pianists.

That kind of talk, of course, only enhances the basement's otherworldly reputation. "My wife jokes that I've worked at Steinway for close to thirty years and she's never been in the basement—'I'm not allowed to go in there'—but it's thought of as being this mecca," says Goodrich, who by the time of CD-60's arrival was Steinway's vice president in charge of dealing with concert artists, a job that involves coordinating the schedules of the pianos the artists want—the pianos in the basement.

The basement enclave came about by accident. In Steinway's earlier building, on East Fourteenth Street, the concert pianos were, according to Henry Z. Steinway, "mixed up with everything else." When Steinway & Sons moved uptown, the plan was to separate the loaners from Steinway's retail pianos and wheel them into a small room on the second floor for tryouts. The executives' offices (and a small recital hall) were on the third floor. Ernest Urchs, who had Goodrich's job in those days, considered the second floor second-class. "He wanted to be on the third floor, with the big shots," Henry says. And the retail salespeople were worried about distractions on the second floor, telling Henry Z. Steinway's father that "they"—famous pianists— "can't be dropping through here all the time."

The only place with space that was not spoken for was the basement, so the concert pianos ended up there, in a room that could not be more different from the rest of Steinway Hall. It has plain-looking cinderblock walls, like the factory. Upstairs, the carpeted showrooms are filled with paintings or photographs of pianists who play, or played, Steinways. On the wall in the basement is a yellowed etching of the factories in Queens from the days before Henry Z. Steinway consolidated operations into one plant. Upstairs, the salespeople sit at small wooden desks that are polished and elegant. In the basement, the desks are utilitarian, made of metal. Even the pianos in the basement are different from the ones upstairs. These pianos are not for sale.

But they all have numbers. Like CD-60, a single Steinway can have as many as three sets of numbers. The case number, a letter followed by four digits—K0862, for example—is assigned when the rim is bent and is used to track the piano at the factory. The letter changes at the beginning of each year. Two thousand three was a K year; in 2004, the case numbers began with L, and in 2005 with M. (I and O are not used, because those letters could be confused with ones and zeros. Nor are there Q, X, Y, or Z years. The Q could be mistaken for an O or a zero; as for the others, Steinway has just never bothered with them.) Steinway's serial numbers, in comparison, are for finished pianos, continuing the sequence supposedly begun by Heinrich Engelhard Steinweg back in Seesen.

Unlike the serial number, a concert division number is not permanent. Concert division pianos are typically retired from the fleet after five or six years. When that happens, the concert division number is taken off, the six-digit serial number is stenciled on again, and the concert division number is assigned to another piano, though not immediately. The last CD-60 was retired in the 1990s.

Some Steinway buyers find decommissioned concert division instruments and snap them up. CD-18, the onstage favorite of Rachmaninoff and later Horowitz, became the living room piano in Eugene Istomin's apartment after it was retired from concert life. The conductor Skitch Henderson bought CD-199, once a favorite of Istomin, Graffman, and Fleisher. The broadcaster Charles Osgood bought CD-30, which spent its early days at a studio where it was used for dozens of classical recordings as well as the "Sing Along with Mitch" LPs.

Another Model D in the fleet was stationed in Milwaukee. It became a favorite of John Browning's. When Alexander Toradze arranged to buy it, Browning was incensed. He argued that great concert pianos should not be sold, they should stay in the concert inventory. Steinway went ahead and sold the piano to Toradze, and a couple of years later, Browning fell in love with its replacement. He decided that he wanted to buy it for his summer festival and had no qualms about asking Steinway to take it out of concert service. Peter Goodrich says he reminded Browning of what he had argued earlier, that great concert pianos should not be sold. "He said, 'This is different,' " Goodrich recalls, "as it always is."

CD-60's transformation from No. 565700 is completed by Jorge Maldonado, who has been a polisher for ten of his nineteen years at Steinway. The job is easier on New York Steinways than on Hamburg Steinways, with their glossier finish—"When it's broken, it's like crystal," he says. Mostly, he does touchups. "Little chips, little things," he said. "It's not the fault of the movers. A piano's heavy."

But he also does the concert numbers. He rubs off Viran's 565700, using a dull, spatula-like knife he has brought from home. As at the factory, some of the best tools are improvised. Then, using the same kind of dry-transfer lettering that Viran had used, he stencils "60" onto the same spot on the gold plate.

He notices a ding in the black finish. He repairs it, but only after doing something else to establish the piano's new identity.

He places two gold numerals onto the lid, giving them a final slap with the palm of his hand: a six and a zero.

᠂᠂᠂

These days, the basement is the domain of Ronald F. Coners, Steinway's chief concert technician. "I could never figure if this was piano heaven or piano hell," he says. "It's both. There are so many pianos down here, some people look at it as wonderful, some look at it as a heck of a lot of work, and some as a heck of a lot of mess."

Coners's take on which it is depends on what kind of a day he is having, on what the latest crisis is, on whether he can rearrange his itinerary to add another stop and take care of another piano on another stage at another performing arts center. Having racked up a million and a half frequent flier miles, he can sound world-weary, as when he says, "I tell people I fly all around the world to stick needles in pieces of felt." When he is in the basement, he often seems overworked and overscheduled. But he is not one to lose his cool, and he can deliver one-liners with perfect timing. Don't call him the head tuner, he says: "I don't tune heads."

Horowitz once walked through the dungeonlike door to the basement and asked, "Where's the big one?"—meaning Coners, who is six feet three inches tall. Coners's predecessor was a shorter man with a mustache who looked the part of a tuner, not a running back—maybe not a speed-burner but solid and powerful. "If you were going to sketch out what Ron Coners looks like, he wouldn't be what you'd sketch," says Leo Spellman, Steinway's vice president for marketing. "You'd probably come up with some professorial-looking person. He is the direct opposite in terms of looks." In the basement, Coners usually wears a white shirt—no tie—and khaki slacks. In chilly weather, he arrives in a windbreaker or a parka, but there is no blazer underneath. His appearance is so informal that many stage managers and impresarios, encountering him for the first time, assume he is a piano *mover*. But not superstars like Daniel Barenboim and Alfred Brendel, who want him in the wings wherever they play. Other pianists have been known to send his bosses angry letters when he could not find time for them.

Coners is unusual among tuners. He does not tune in private homes (except perhaps Cliburn's or, before his death, Horowitz's). He has a staff job (most tuners work for themselves and are paid by their customers) and spends his time working on pianos for the concert market (where most tuners find they can generate publicity but not income). Coners can line up six pianos for Brendel to try, but the ritual is almost unnecessary. Coners is certain which piano Brendel will choose before Brendel arrives. Coners is also certain that if he puts CD-60 in the lineup, Brendel will play a few notes, jump up, and move on.

Brendel wants something more seasoned, and Coners's assessment of CD-60—the first answer to the how-good-is-it question from outside the factory—is "It's raw." After playing a scale and a few chords, Coners says that the treble is "a little too bright," meaning that some of the high notes sound glassy, brash, and hard. It has potential but needs time to develop. Michael F. Huseman, a Steinway salesman who has wandered downstairs for a look at the new arrival, listens to Coners—and to CD-60—and sums things up in five words: "Mechanically complete, but artistically challenged."

There is hope, though. Unlike brand-new pianos that are sold as soon as Roy Viran has rubbed on the serial number, concert division pianos get help in the basement. Marvin Hamlisch calls the instruments in the concert division "couture pianos," because they can be custom tailored to fit a pianist's personality—and if a particular piano cannot be brightened up or toned down enough to please a particular pianist, the basement always has other pianos to try.

Coners redoes some things that had been done on CD-60, more than once, at the factory—marking problem notes, filing, fixing. "Some of this is because it's new," he says. He even argues that "redid" is the wrong word to use in describing what he is doing. "I'd call it 'rechecking.' You have to keep checking on a new piano." But he is doing more than that. He is making CD-60 palatable to a particular constituency, a constituency that knows

pianos, and that he knows better than anyone else. As he explains, "The guys at the factory have no reference point. We're
dealing with the artists. We get the feedback."

But even as he spends part of an afternoon realigning hammers and respacing strings, he says that CD-60 is proof that the
factory is turning out better pianos than it once did. "Twenty-five
years ago, the action—everything felt heavy," he says. "We had a
lot of tonal problems."

That is an understatement. In the 1970s and 1980s, after
Steinway put in the Teflon bushings, some pianists complained
that the magic had gone out of Steinway's concert grands. Some
worried that the company's standards were slipping. In the 1990s,
when Coners became the chief concert technician, he insisted on
choosing the pianos for the fleet himself. "There were too many
that weren't up to where we thought they should be," he said. After a year or two, he had to start taking pianos he had not tried
out. "It's not a problem," he said. "The consistency is so much
higher. That doesn't mean there's no variation, but we haven't
sent any pianos back lately."

Now, as then, problems with Steinway's concert pianos are
supposed to be corrected in the basement. As he sits down at
CD-60 and describes how brand-new pianos require much less
work these days, Coners sounds a bit like the lonely repairman in
the Maytag commercials. Still, he does a lot to CD-60, and later
admits that he thought about doing more. He says he considered
replacing the hammers, but decided to see how they responded
to his treatment. A week later, when the first of fifteen pianists arrives to play CD-60, its sound is more even, more focused.

"The whole problem with pianos is they're organic, constantly changing," Coners says. "Not like building a refrigerator
or something."

At the end of 2003, when CD-60 was still being tuned and voiced
at the factory as K0862, Steinway was making fewer concert

grand pianos than it once did. There are not many consumers with living rooms large enough for a piano nearly nine feet long. So Coners has no choice but to accept whatever Model Ds the factory sends him. If one does not come along that has the big, even sound he is looking for, he will tell Carnegie Hall or Lincoln Center that they will have to wait to replace the pianos they have.

There was also what he called "the juicing issue"—how much lacquer, or "juice," should be drizzled on the hammers at the factory. Coners maintains that Steinway has improved the quality of its hammers in recent years, so they need less juice than they once did. Even so, he said, at the factory "some of the guys still go through this routine of putting quite a bit of juice in." In Coners's opinion, CD-60 got too much juice, which left the treble too forward and too bright. His strategy is to dribble on a different kind of juice, a solution that will soften what the factory juice had hardened.

Coners, who was a couple of months past his forty-ninth birthday when CD-60 arrived in the basement, did not grow up imagining that he would spend his life tending concert pianos. He did not get very far with music as a child. "It was one of those things as a kid that I never really wanted to do. I could sight-read halfway decently, but I could never remember, memorize," he says. He did not play much football, either, despite his size: "My father wouldn't let us. He said there were too many guys hobbling around who'd been hurt." He survived intramural basketball without injury and landed at Steinway after attending Nassau Community College on Long Island, where, as he explains it, "I was always mechanical but signed up for civil engineering." He had also worked briefly as a housepainter.

Like so many workers at the factory, he applied because someone with connections to Steinway suggested that he do so. In Coners's case, the idea came from Elizabeth Mohr, Franz Mohr's wife and Michael Mohr's mother. The Mohrs knew Ron Coners from the church they attend on Long Island. At the time, in 1975, the factory had no openings that involved working on pianos, but hired Coners for its building maintenance department. After a month of painting stairwells and doing odd jobs, he was "miserable," and told Franz Mohr, the chief concert technician, that he was quitting.

But Franz Mohr arranged a transfer. Coners became an apprentice technician in the basement in Manhattan. It was an unusual move—unprecedented, as far as anyone could remember. Then as now, Steinway usually hired tuners with at least minimal experience. "They'd never taken anybody from scratch like that," Coners said. "It really was a unique thing."

On Coners's first day, he arrived late, because he had taken the wrong subway, and Mohr said they would go "across the street." Across the street meant to Carnegie Hall. On the stage, practicing, was Arthur Rubinstein. At eighty-eight, he was still a superstar, though easier to deal with than Vladimir Horowitz. Within a year, Coners was tuning at Carnegie Hall, and a year or two later, he went on tour with Emil Gilels, a pianist who was known for his technical control even as he rode triumphantly over orchestras in the warhorses of the Romantic concerto repertory. Coners became so close to Gilels, a Ukrainian who was the first Soviet pianist permitted to tour in the West, that Gilels would have Coners sit in the green room after his concerts while he greeted concertgoers. Coners jokes that some probably eyed him and wondered if he was with the KGB.

Coners credits Gilels with opening his ears, and his mind. "Most of what I teach everybody now, I learned from him," Coners said. "Not technical stuff, but what to listen for." But he also gives credit to Alfred Brendel, who puts a premium on the evenness of sound and thus on voicing. Coners won Brendel's favor in the spring of 1977, tuning for Brendel's Beethoven sonata cycle at Carnegie Hall. Telling this story as he works on CD-60, tools in hand, Coners is quiet for a moment and looks away, beyond the row of pianos that stand beyond CD-60. "Those two guys, I learned more about voicing from them than from anybody."

Coners does not have perfect pitch, and believes it is actually a detriment for a tuner. "We had a guy, a Korean conductor, who had perfect pitch. He thought he could learn how to tune. This is totally different, and I don't care who you are, it's going to drive you crazy."

Like many pianists, Peter Goodrich and Leo Spellman say that Coners's technical skill is not what sets him apart, good though he is at voicing and regulating. He is unusual because he can listen to the pianist as well as to the piano. "He understands what pianists mean when they describe what they are looking for in a piano or what they would prefer not to have in a piano," Goodrich says. "He has the patience and the confidence to know how to speak with a pianist. It's very tricky, because a great concert technician must understand how much to say—never say too much, but say enough to give the artist confidence, and then let his or her work speak for itself."

With CD-60, he changes the way the soft pedal shifts the hammers and all the parts that are between them and the keys. He works on a half-dozen notes in the bass that he says sound weak. And he reaches into a drawer, only to stop himself. "I'm still looking for tools that I don't have anymore." He went to tune for a recording session in Berkeley, California, and left a computer case containing his tools in the pianist's car on a side street. "He goes back to the car—'I don't want my sheet music stolen.' 'What about my tools?' 'Nobody'll know what to do with 'em.' We come back, the window's broken, the tools are gone." Coners wonders if someone overheard them talking and figured the tools were worth something.

He says the dampers on CD-60 are ringing too long, so he respaces some of them against the strings. To someone watching him work, that seems like doing a wheel alignment on an eighteen-wheeler: maddening. Coners makes it look easy. He uses a tool with a crook on the end, and pulls hard. "Some of us carry those medical clamps, things you clamp a vein with, like a long scissor," he says. The proper name for that surgical tool is a hemostat; some have small hooks on the ends of the blades, which are especially useful when yanking strings. Make that *leveling* strings, which can achieve the same result as filing the hammers. "When I started, Franz said, 'You've got to do the open strings,' but he didn't give me much instruction on *how* to do it. I was constantly taking felt off the hammers before I realized you could level the strings."

On K0862, the C two octaves above middle C is "fuzzy." Coners works on the strike point just by pushing against the action assembly. It moves a whisker—far enough. He is thinking of reshaping all eighty-eight hammers by the time he has worked his way to the high G. "There's no way you're going to get a full sound out of that."

Working his way up CD-60, hammer by hammer and string by string, he remembers onstage disasters. Once, André Watts was on *Live from Lincoln Center* playing CD-278, a piano close to ten years old at the time. Coners was backstage. A string broke during the performance. "I didn't have time to put in a new string," so Watts finished his concerto with only one string for that note.

Coners usually carries spare sets of everything—strings, hammers, felt, tools. But not always. Once, when Brendel broke two bass strings while playing with the New York Philharmonic, Coners discovered that he had no bass strings in his bag. He improvised by wrapping coils around a treble string and hoping it would hold. It did. In Toronto, Brendel rode the left pedal, and because something called the stop-screw was loose, the hammers moved too far and hit the next note.

Coners's progress on CD-60 is interrupted from time to time by telephone calls from those who know the number of the telephone at his workbench, not the one at his desk inside the soundproof tuning booth that he uses as an office. Calls to the line at his desk are answered by an assistant, who takes a message, or they go to voice mail. Coners answers the phone by his workbench himself, if he is nearby. Around the time that CD-60 arrives in the basement, Coners is deep in the hunt to buy a weekend house, so there are calls about mortgage rates and closing dates, and amid talk about overheated real estate prices and too-good-to-be-true profits, he guffaws that his new retreat is in a town called Speculator.

Coners continues his adjustments on CD-60, and in time, his assessment improves. "Basically, a very good piano," he says. It remains "a little too bright up here"—the notes in the two octaves above middle C. "It's got good body, though."

There are several options for CD-60. It could stay in the fleet in the basement, which would likely mean being selected for concerts in small halls and for television programs like *Good Morning America*. In the summer, almost every piano in the basement is sent to a music festival. "By the time they get back, they've soaked up humidity and have to be reworked again," he notes. "That's when we'll determine if it stays in stock or goes to a hall. The other track it could take is, it could go to a dealer."

❧

In the Steinway basement, a piano is only as good as a pianist thinks it is. Of the fifteen pianists who are asked to try CD-60 in February 2004, a few weeks after Coners has pushed it away from his workbench and parked it beside older basement pianos, the consensus is that it is quite good. And also quite young. Emanuel Ax's verdict is "nice" after playing Debussy. Robert Taub plays Chopin and calls CD-60 "tremendous." Brian Zeger plays Ravel, as did Katia and Marielle Labèque (but Katia Labèque found CD-60 not terribly brilliant—"yet"). Hamlisch plays "The Way We Were." Kenny Barron plays "The Very Thought of You."

When the music stops, the analogies begin. Stephen Hough, who says CD-60 still sounds "raw" despite the work Coners has put in, compares it to a shoe that needs time to be broken in. Lang Lang says it is like a car that begs to be driven fast and hard, "in sixth or twelfth gear." Erika Nickrenz compares it to a colt that is fun to ride. "It has a little kick to it," she explains, "but it doesn't have the ugliness to go along with it . . . sometimes, when you get the kick, you get the ugly." Hamlisch likens it to a flower that has yet to bloom.

But CD-60 sounds as if it has been built for Taub, who has a reputation as something of scholar as well as a first-rate performer. He is known for a repertoire that ranges from pieces written for him by Milton Babbitt to Beethoven's piano sonatas, about which he wrote a book that described, among other things, what he had learned from examining Beethoven's original manuscripts. After trying out CD-60, Taub would fly to London, where he would play Beethoven's "Hammerklavier" sonata—"the one that makes all pianists quake in their boots." His responsibilities as a visiting professor at Kingston University there include a recital series at Hampton Court Palace—though, to hear Taub tell it, not spending the night inside. After his last concert, he found that he had been locked in. "I was left wandering around inside the palace, trying to find a way out," he says. "All the corridors were dark, and seemed to be endless. Finally, one last guard made a final sweep through and was just as surprised to see me as I was glad to see him." A few weeks later, friends sent him clippings from London tabloids. The photos, taken by security cameras at the palace, showed a shadowy figure described in the captions as the "ghost of Hampton Court Palace." Says Taub: "I knew better." CD-60, he says, "has the kind of action which is effortless to play, completely predictable, completely uniform, and the way it's voiced, the sound is almost completely uniform, so that everything you are doing can be an artistic statement rather than a mechanical compensation."

One pianist's idea of bigness is different from another's. Lang Lang feels CD-60 has enough thunder to take on Carnegie Hall. Zeger, too, calls it "a big-hall piano." Ax, though, says it will probably do better in a smaller auditorium. For a concert at Avery Fisher Hall, "you might ask for something a little bit louder for a Russian concerto or something of that sort, and probably especially for Mozart, because in Mozart you need to cut through a little bit."

But he also says to wait awhile—it is still too soon to know how CD-60 will turn out because it is hard to judge a piano that is still so new. "I have a good feeling about it," Ax says. "I think it's going to do well."

12

~~~

Debut

April 26: Emanuel Ax tries K0862 in the basement of Steinway Hall.

On a bright, blustery afternoon in late April, Monday the twenty-sixth, a gangling young pianist named Jonathan Biss bounds onto a stage in Michigan. Biss begins hammering his way through a short, angry piece filled with dark chords and angular melodies that seems at odds with the primary-blue of the sky and the green of the lawn outside. And just like that, CD-60's working life begins, 614 miles from the basement.

For its public debut in Steinway's concert fleet, Ron Coners has sent CD-60 to the Irving S. Gilmore International Keyboard Festival in Kalamazoo, Michigan. The Gilmore, as it is called, is named for the department-store heir who endowed it. The Gilmore is something of a newcomer to the crowded schedule of competitions and festivals to which young virtuosos are invited. It began in 1989 and now commandeers half a dozen auditoriums in and around Kalamazoo for two weeks of recitals by hot young prospects and by well-known artists like Emanuel Ax.

CD-60's destination is an airy colonial-style chapel on a college campus. Biss, and CD-60, play to a sold-out house. The piano sounds good—somewhat small, but sweet. It does not sound overpowering. The spectrum of tone color is widest in the middle of the keyboard. The ends of the keyboard are a bit of a letdown. The bass only hints at the legendary Steinway thunder. The upper treble is still too bright, though not tinkly or tinny. All in all, CD-60's sound is honest. CD-60 sounds like what it is, a new piano that is being broken in.

Biss himself, a serious-looking young man with long hands and a surprisingly soft handshake, is breaking out of the pack of hopeful young pianists at the Gilmore. He is becoming a name. His first compact disc, a recording of Beethoven and Schumann, has just been issued. He had been tapped as a last-minute replacement by the Boston Symphony, playing Beethoven's Piano Concerto No. 5, the *Emperor,* when Andreas Haefliger called in sick. The reviews had been good, and he had chalked up the Boston appearance as another milestone in an extremely promising career. Isaac Stern had heard Biss when he was fifteen and made the calls that landed him a manager. Biss made his Carnegie Hall debut at nineteen, in 2000, and just four years later was playing concertos with the New York Philharmonic and the Baltimore Symphony.

Of course, Biss comes from a musical dynasty. His parents are the violinists Paul Biss and Miriam Fried; *The New York Times* mused that Biss was probably the only pianist to have made his Carnegie Hall debut *in utero,* when Fried appeared there with the Cleveland Orchestra. His paternal grandmother was the cellist Raya Garbousova, for whom Samuel Barber wrote his cello concerto. Garbousova also played chamber music with everyone from Nathan Milstein to Vladimir Horowitz to Albert Einstein, who, she maintained, was always slightly out of tune.

But Biss did not become another string player, and his parents did not pressure him to pursue music. The way Fried tells it, he pressured her. "He badgered me about playing the piano when he was three, I think," she recalls. "He kept badgering me, and when he was six, he started playing." He went on to enroll at the Curtis Institute of Music in Philadelphia, and to study with Leon Fleisher.

Biss is a blur at the Gilmore, always in motion, practicing, schmoozing with other pianists, checking his cell phone for voice mail messages. For all his seeming confidence, he has wrestled with self-doubt. At Curtis, he says he "was convinced that every single person at the school played better." He considered giving up his career after one master class with Fleisher "because there was no way I was going through humiliation like that again."

His repertoire is not just the well-known concertos. CD-60's solo debut comes in two pieces by Leon Kirchner, a modernist who is well into his eighties. Kirchner wrote the second piece, *Interlude II,* for Biss; Biss played its world premiere in London in 2003. Kirchner said the "seeds" of *Interlude II* came from poems by Emily Dickinson and Edna St. Vincent Millay. Kirchner provided detailed instructions for its performance, encouraging Biss to express the same kind of rhapsodic feeling as the poetry. After intermission, Biss is joined by his mother and her colleagues from the Mendelssohn String Quartet in the Brahms Quintet in F minor for piano and strings, Opus 34.

After the concert, Biss complains that CD-60 feels stiff, like a still-new Steinway he played at the Marlboro Music Festival when he was a teenager. He blamed that piano for his tendonitis. He says that he had to struggle to get the sound out of CD-60. At least he was only playing chamber music, he concludes: "Better this than the Brahms concerto."

CD-60's fallboard—the cover that closes over the keys—already had fingernail scratches by the time Biss sat down at the piano. Its first public performance had come three evenings earlier, on the Gilmore's opening night, when it was one of half a dozen pianos in an ambitious and demanding concert that kept the stagehands busy wheeling pianos on and off the stage. CD-60 was featured in a concerto for four pianos by Bach and in a piece for six pianos—*Hexaméron,* a rarely played extravaganza by Franz Liszt. Liszt stitched *Hexaméron* together using variations by half a dozen other composers, including Czerny and Chopin, and it was singularly appropriate for opening night at the Gilmore. Commissioned for a nineteenth-century benefit, it had, as the pianist Raymond Lewenthal wrote, "no pretension or intention of doing anything but entertaining a crowd of rich patricians who were to be relieved of a considerable sum of money for a worthy cause." That was exactly the crowd assembled in the festival's orchestra seats—benefactors and such luminaries as the governor of Michigan and United States senators. Though Biss took part in the Bach and the Liszt—as well as an encore performance, also with CD-60, of a six-piano arrangement of "The Stars and Stripes Forever" by John Philip Sousa—he was assigned to one of the other pianos on the wide stage. CD-60's first night in public came under the hands of Elizabeth Schumann in the Bach and Orion Weiss in the Liszt and the Sousa.

After the Gilmore, CD-60 settles into its itinerant concert life, and Ron Coners's assessment continues to improve. Now he maintains that CD-60 is a good piano but could be a great one in a year or so, after it has been played some more. But for a while, there is reason to doubt that CD-60 will ever be heard again. It simply disappears after the festival. No one files missing piano reports, and the piano world does not move at the speed of all-points bulletins and Amber alerts. At first its disappearance goes unnoted.

A couple of weeks later, in June 2004, the piano finally turns up. Coners pieces together what has happened. The trucker hired to bring CD-60 back from Michigan missed the pickup, and another trucker was hired. He saw "Steinway & Sons" on the manifest and read no further. He had driven pianos to Steinway & Sons before—to the factory. He did not realize that Steinway also shipped pianos to an address in Manhattan: Steinway Hall. The factory receives pianos all day long, so the workers on the loading dock took CD-60 off the truck without question. And there it sat, orphaned, until someone called Coners and said, "We think we got one of yours." Soon CD-60 is back on Joe Ragusa's truck and settled once again in the Steinway basement.

Its next stop is a piano competition. The founders of the New York Piano Competition, Melvin Stecher and Norman Horowitz, select CD-60 from the pianos in the basement. Stecher and Horowitz are duo pianists–turned–teachers, and after selling their music school, they started a contest for fourteen-to-eighteen-year-olds. The young pianists spend a week playing CD-60 while six judges, including Abbey Simon and André-Michel Schub, listen. Simon warms to CD-60. On the third or fourth day, he eats lunch quickly and disappears. It turns out that he has sneaked into the auditorium to play the piano.

Before long, though, CD-60 is upstaged by a laptop computer. The laptop belongs to John A. MacBain, the scoring guru of music contests. He has used it to score the International Violin Competition in Indianapolis and the Van Cliburn International Piano Competition in Fort Worth. He takes less than an hour to turn the numbers on the judges' score sheets into results. This is a sideline—his day job is as a research engineer in Indiana with the Delphi Corporation, the huge automotive-parts supplier. He maintains that scoring is fun for someone whose doctorate is in mathematics—though it is less than thrilling for everyone else.

Stecher and Horowitz try to level the field in other ways. They prescribe the pieces, within categories. A prelude and fugue from *The Well-Tempered Clavier* by Bach figure in the choices, as do a movement of a sonata by Beethoven or Haydn, a Chopin étude, and the first movement of a concerto. CD-60 handles them all. Its sound has grown more even since Gilmore—the bass and treble are no longer the question marks they had been for Biss. CD-60 is learning.

CD-60 waits out the rest of its first summer in the basement. Coners sends it to a recording session with "the five Browns," a quintet of young pianists who had already been profiled on *60 Minutes*. They have also been praised on the Web for looking like "the kid who mows your lawn, the nice young person who waits on you at the coffee shop, or the girl every boy has a crush on." Their debut album is CD-60's debut album as well. Of the eleven tracks on the recording, five feature all five Browns (the other arrangements call for the Browns to play in ones, twos, and threes). So CD-60 is heard in "Flight of the Bumblebee," "The Sorcerer's Apprentice," excerpts from *West Side Story,* and selections from *Peer Gynt*. By the time CD-60 is returned to the basement, no one seems to know which Browns played CD-60, or whether it was used in any of the two- and three-piano tracks.

❧

Eight is old when a piano has been played hard—pounded night after night, bumped and nicked and gouged by stagehands, tuned just before the lights go down. Eight is when a piano wears out from too much galloping over the craggy surfaces of various *B*s— Bach, Beethoven, and Brahms, not to mention Bartók, Barber, and Berg—and too much dawdling through Mozart middle movements so poky the audience could slip out for a martini between the notes. Eight is when a piano in the concert fleet needs more than another quick tuning, when it needs more, even, than the piano-world equivalent of a 100,000-mile checkup. Eight is a couple of years past retirement age.

Somehow, the Steinway at the Grace Rainey Rogers Auditorium at the Metropolitan Museum of Art has gotten to be eight. The Met's in-house impresario still loves the piano. But Steinway, as Coners puts it, "likes to keep new product in front of the public." The time has come to designate a replacement. That replacement is to be CD-60.

The Grace Rainey Rogers is one of a dozen or so concert halls in New York that rate the semipermanent loan of a concert division piano from Steinway & Sons. Carnegie Hall, Avery Fisher Hall, and Alice Tully Hall are among the other auditoriums with the same arrangement: The "house" piano is on loan from Steinway. That is, the piano is free. The halls promise to have them tuned by a Steinway technician before each concert (they also promise to pay for the tuning). At a large, busy hall like Avery Fisher, the pianos sometimes have to be tuned twice a day.

These pianos go back to the Steinway basement around Memorial Day, when the concert season ends, for what the people at Steinway call "summer camp" or "piano camp"—a going-over by Ron Coners and Steinway's other staff technicians, followed by a temporary assignment, a workout at a summer music festival.

Once the fall season opens and the pianos are back in their regular homes, pianists may borrow another piano from the basement, but most play the house pianos. So CD-60's new assignment means that it will be the piano heard in dozens of concerts during the 2004–05 season.

The idea of stationing CD-60 at the Met came up after it

returned from the Gilmore. Coners, reminding Steinway's concert relations chief Peter Goodrich that the Met needed a new piano, suggested CD-60 as a strong candidate to replace CD-212. The Met responded enthusiastically and requested CD-60. Coners thought the piano would do well in the nine-hundred-seat Grace Rainey Rogers despite its relatively dry acoustics. It is not the most hospitable home for smallish-sounding instruments.

Sending CD-60 to the Met solves a ticklish problem for Coners and Steinway: The house pianos at Carnegie Hall and at Avery Fisher Hall in Lincoln Center are also coming due. Coners has tried CD-60's younger siblings, the Model Ds that are now close to completion at the factory. He says that nothing in the pipeline would be suitable for those two halls. He wants to stall them, hoping the factory will send along a bigger-sounding piano in a few months. He does not want the Met, impressive though its lineup of concerts may be, to be in competition with America's two most important halls. He does not want a three-way squabble. And even with the Met taken care of, the prospect of replacing two important pianos at about the same time makes him roll his eyes.

Goodrich takes the CD-60 proposal to Hilde Limondjian, the general manager of concerts and lectures at the Met. She is enthusiastic, but asks to have CD-212, the piano CD-60 is to replace, sent back—just in case. Steinway agrees, and in the fall the moving van pulls away from the loading dock at Steinway Hall with both pianos on board—the rookie and the old pro. The van is not Ragusa's by now familiar truck. He does not deliver pianos to Steinway's customers. This van belongs to a piano moving company the Met has hired.

CD-60 does not make its entrance the way tourists do, by climbing the granite steps on Fifth Avenue and trudging into the bustling Great Hall. CD-60 arrives through the Met's basement. The Met's guards wave the van in, and soon CD-60 is on the loading dock, wrapped in movers' blankets.

Limondjian has come to greet the pianos. She and Mikel Frank, the stage manager of the Grace Rainey Rogers, lead the way through basement corridors to a freight elevator. Once CD-60 has been pushed inside, the elevator climbs slowly to the first floor, and when the wide metal doors spring open, CD-60 rolls through a corridor of rifles and revolvers toward an unmarked door—the stage door. The piano breezes through the wings. As its legs are reattached, Limondjian looks out at the nine hundred empty seats and says that the acoustics in CD-60's new home have improved with time. Its walls are made of light-colored korina, a wood that has a prominent, wavy grain and is often used for the backs of guitars. It is wood that Steinway, looking for long, straight grain, would have rejected for CD-60. But it has aged nicely, making the Grace Rainey Rogers more resonant than when it was new, in the 1950s. Limondjian sits down at CD-60 and whips off an arpeggio, then bits of Bach and Chopin. CD-60 has a different sound from CD-212's, with a sweeter treble and a less forward bass. But she seems pleased with the new arrival.

Its first real test comes a couple of nights later, at a concert by the Beaux Arts Trio with its pianist, Menahem Pressler. Biss plays CD-60 again in November 2004, when he and his mother, Miriam Fried, appear at the Met. CD-60 sounds more even than it did in Michigan, and Biss seems to have no trouble with the action this time.

Sixty other concerts take place in CD-60's first season at the Met. Pianists can perform on CD-212 if they prefer it to CD-60. No one does. Everyone chooses CD-60. Peter Serkin plays CD-60, as do Frederic Chiu, Anton Kuerti, Ruth Laredo, and the winners of a half-dozen international piano competitions. As the season ends, André Watts performs a program that calls for him to discuss a Beethoven sonata before intermission and to play that sonata after intermission. Watts, who had defected from Steinway to Yamaha in the 1980s and 1990s, has returned to playing a Hamburg Steinway in public, but that piano could not be

hauled to the Met in time for his appearance. On the morning of
his lecture-performance, he tries out CD-60 and CD-212, and se-
lects CD-60.

The Met's season ends a couple of weeks later.

❦

Being a New Yorker, CD-60 spends most of the summer of 2005
in the Hamptons. Steinway sends its concert division pianos to
music festivals around the country, including Tanglewood in
Massachusetts, Brevard in North Carolina, Aspen in Colorado,
and Pianofest in the Hamptons. CD-60 gets tapped for a festival
a few miles down the road from Pianofest, the Bridgehampton
Chamber Music Festival. There, CD-60 is played by a number of
pianists, most of whom are in their twenties and most of whom
play in concert. Only one plays CD-60 in the quiet of early morning. The festival's twenty-eight-year-old executive director, Maureen Angeles, arrives between seven and eight o'clock each
morning, letting herself into the Greek Revival church that is the
festival's home long before anyone else shows up and long before
the day's rehearsals begin. For an hour or so, she plays CD-60. It
is a perk that offsets the pressure of staging twelve concerts with
thirty-odd performers in three weeks. A Yale-educated adminis-
trator who was a serious pianist as a teenager—"I wasn't focused
enough to do it as a career"—she looks forward to her time with
CD-60 in the coolness of the sanctuary. It is a coolness the chamber music festival has paid for. The festival, not the Presbyterians
who built the church, pays to have it air-conditioned to keep
Steinway from worrying that the pianos it sends to Bridgehampton will be exposed to excessive humidity. On the morning of
CD-60's last concert, she works through a Brahms intermezzo.

A couple of hours later, her place at CD-60 is taken by a
pianist she had met ten years earlier, when Angeles was a teenage
student at another summer festival. Now Andrew Russo is six feet
four inches tall and bears the slightest resemblance to Nick Nolte
or John Tesh, the broadcaster–turned–New Age–composer. His

father was a minor league catcher and Russo grew up with dreams of playing center field for the New York Mets.

He has arrived to rehearse a wind quintet by Mozart and the "Dumky" trio by Dvořák for a concert that evening. Mozart and Dvořák are not exactly Russo's everyday fare. "I almost wonder why anyone would want to hear me play it," he says after the rehearsal. He has made his name playing modern music by the likes of the Pulitzer Prize winner George Crumb, John Adams, and a Dutch rock guitarist–turned–composer, Jacob ter Veldhuis. Ter Veldhuis's work includes "The Body of Your Dreams," inspired by an infomercial for a muscle-toning machine.

Some of the pieces Russo plays most often call for him to reach inside the piano, to places not touched since the piano left the factory, and pluck the strings. Russo has picked up pointers on how to do this from Crumb himself. Russo called Crumb after looking up his number in the telephone book. Crumb invited him to come by and talk about a piece of Crumb's that Russo was scheduled to play in California.

Russo played Crumb's *A Little Suite for Christmas, A.D. 1979* at the Van Cliburn competition. It earned him the distinction of being the first Cliburn contestant ever to generate sound by bypassing the keyboard. "What I was trying to do was say, you know, I am the American guy coming to represent the United States," he explains. "All the people who come from Russia for this competition usually play Rachmaninoff and Tchaikovsky. People come from Germany and play their Beethoven and Schubert. And then American guys show up and play Rachmaninoff and Schubert and we ignore our own music, so I decided to be the American guy who goes there and plays American music." It did not earn him a place in the semifinals. And, for the record, the American guy's biography is not all American. He spent much of his twenties in Paris, where, one night at a party, he met the woman he would marry. She is Russian.

In the Hamptons, Russo seems preoccupied, but not with the music. He asks to use Angeles's fax machine—he is worried

about missing the deadline for confirming an appearance in the
fall. Worse, he does not have the right jacket for the concert. Before heading to the Hamptons, he had not read the chamber music festival's contract carefully enough to notice that he was
supposed to appear in a white jacket. Russo does not own a
white jacket. "I usually play concerts where everyone is in all
black," he says.

Russo is staying in the weekend house of a retired investment banker—a house so close to the Atlantic Ocean that Russo
could have slammed a home run over the breakers and part of the
way to Scotland. Russo mentions the white jacket problem to his
host, who suggests calling—from this house that cost several million dollars in the days before *everything* in the Hamptons cost
several million dollars—a thrift shop. Russo makes the call. The
shop does not have his size, 42 long. Russo decides to mention
the problem to Angeles, who arranges for him to borrow a jacket
from another musician who is not playing that evening. The crisis
over, the rehearsal can begin.

After the Sunday worship services each week, festival vol-
unteers place vinyl cushions on the sanctuary's wooden pews, as
much to make reserved seating possible as to make the concertgoers more comfortable. Each cushion carries a row and seat
number that corresponds to the tickets Angeles and her staff have
sold. As the rehearsal begins, only one cushion is filled. Russo's
wife has taken a seat and opened a book, *How to Think Like
Leonardo da Vinci: Seven Steps to Genius Every Day*. She is reading the English version. She knows how it ends. She has already
read it in Russian.

On the stage, Russo trades the piano bench for the metal
chair that had been set out for the cellist, Edward Arron. The
bench—the kind that piano salesmen call an adjustable artist's
bench, with a tufted vinyl seat—sits too high for his tall frame,
and he cannot lower it far enough to fit his legs under CD-60. The
metal chair would be absurdly short for anyone else, but it puts
Russo where he wants to be.

Working through the Dvořák, Russo pushes his glasses up into his hair. He pounds the floor with his left foot. After a run-through, the trio goes over a couple of rough spots, and Russo beams that CD-60 has a "halo of resonance" that he likes. "It seems like a piano that is hard to get a harsh sound out of, which is helpful because you can put quite a lot of force into it," he says.

He knows about hitting pianos hard. Standing on the lawn before the concert in the evening is Paul Schenly, who counts himself as one of Russo's teachers. Schenly runs Pianofest, and Russo has been a regular there for several years. Schenly says that one of the things he tried to teach Russo was that it was not necessary to beat up the piano every time he sat down at the keyboard. Yes, Russo packs a wallop—Schenly remembers "feeling really sorry for the piano" the first time Russo performed at Pianofest. "I told him you can't club the piano—the idea is to use power, not force," Schenly recalls. Now Schenly adds a post-script: "If one doesn't go through that stage early on, then one can't become a great pianist."

Schenly's assessment of CD-60 is no less insightful. He says it sounds "like a rosebud that is lovely but hasn't fully opened up." He says the action has been beautifully regulated—Coners's work has paid off. The scales sound even, and Schenly finds in CD-60 the "toned-down" quality that some pianists, notably Alfred Brendel, like. Maybe if a good piano doesn't go through a rosebud stage early on, it can't become a great piano.

A couple of days after the concert, after Russo has left for upstate New York and after Angeles has picked up the cushions in the church for the last time, CD-60 goes back to the Steinway basement, a bit older, a bit more mature, a bit more sure of itself. The ritual is familiar: Coners gets it back in shape, says it is coming along fine, and sends it off for another year at the Met with the likes of Emanuel Ax, Marvin Hamlisch, Stephen Kovacevich, Frederic Chiu, and Ruth Laredo.

As a two-year-old, though, CD-60 will face new competition. In the truck alongside CD-60 is a Hamburg Steinway that the Met has requested. Suddenly there is the possibility of back-stage drama, of pianists trying both instruments and being torn as to which to play. Will CD-60 be more popular than its German cousin or will it be relegated to the sidelines? The pianists will decide.

Postlude

On Its Own

December 16, 2005: K0862—now known as CD-60—on the stage at the Metropolitan Museum of Art

In time, CD-60's voice became fuller and its action looser. In
its second year, there was no reason to complain about the
Terrible Twos: CD-60 no longer felt stiff, the way a brand-
new piano usually does. CD-60 had been broken in.

For most pianists, that is fine, and as things turned out, CD-
60 did not need to worry about being passed over for the new
Hamburg Steinway at the Metropolitan Museum. In the first
three months of CD-60's second season there, it was the choice of
every pianist who appeared but two. Sergey Schepkin, a Russian-
trained pianist who reminds some critics of a less idiosyncratic
Glenn Gould, tried both pianos at his rehearsal. He decided to
play the Hamburg Steinway for the first half of his recital—the
all-Bach half. He told the stagehands to wheel that piano away at
intermission and bring out CD-60, on which he played the all-
Brahms half. And Philippe Entremont chose the Hamburg Steinway when he appeared with the Munich Symphony, conducting a
Mozart concerto from the keyboard.

Jonathan Biss, who broke in CD-60 at the Gilmore Festival,
became the first pianist to play it more than once when he performed with his mother at the Metropolitan Museum. Biss also
appeared, by himself, at Zankel Hall, the new small auditorium at
Carnegie Hall. Reviewing Biss's performance, *New York Times*
critic Bernard Holland said that he was young and impetuous,
but added, "At 24 Mr. Biss is where he ought to be and a little
farther."

Ruth Laredo died on May 25, 2005, not quite three weeks
after playing CD-60 at the Met. She appeared with members of
the St. Petersburg Quartet in a quartet by Shostakovich and a trio
by Tchaikovsky and accompanied the soprano Courtenay Budd.
In introducing six songs by Rachmaninoff, including the famed
"Vocalise," Laredo told the audience, "It is the piano, not the
singer, who should be singing." Talking about the concert a couple of days later, she mentioned people who had been in the

audience, how her voice had sounded over the public address system, how well she thought the hard passages in the Scriabin had gone—in other words, she talked about everything but CD-60. "I didn't think about the piano for a minute," she said. "I guess that's the ideal."

৵৽

If CD-60 were to go back to the Steinway factory, it would find that some of the workers who figured in its early life have gone. Joe Gurrado, the foreman in rim-bending, left Steinway in 2005. Steinway replaced him by calling back his predecessor, Ralph D'Alleva, who had retired in 2002. Around the factory, the word was D'Alleva would do the job for a month or so, until a new foreman was promoted or brought in. Four months later, D'Alleva was still on the job.

Eric Lall, Gurrado's No. 2 in rim-bending, quit in 2004 and moved to Florida. Louis Auguste, who shaped the arms on K0862, retired in 2005, as did Maria Hatzinikolaou, the quality control inspector. Victor Madorsky, the Russian-trained oboist whose tuning booth was a few steps from Bruce Campbell's, left to be a tuner and piano technician at the Peabody Institute in Baltimore.

Ante Glavan, the bellyman on K0862, continues to glue in soundboards and bridges, but he has a new boss. Lou Begojna, the foreman of the belly department and Glavan's brother-in-law, became the manager of Steinway's restoration center, a separate unit that rebuilds customers' older Steinways. Its purpose is to compete with technicians who rebuild pianos.

There have been a number of changes on management row since K0862 left the factory. John Marek, the action assembly foreman when No. K0862 was being built, was promoted to manager of fabrication in 2005. He moved from the din of the action assembly department to the quiet of management row, to the office that had belonged to the plant manager, Ronald Penatzer, the general manager of manufacturing. Penatzer moved to a larger room that had been vacant. He liked the view from his new windows, which look out on the lumberyard and Building No. 88, until he retired in the fall of 2006.

Andy Horbachevsky, who was in charge of engineering development and fabrication when K0862 was being built, was named to succeed Penatzer. It was Horbachevsky's second job change since K0862 left the factory. In 2005, he became director of continuous improvement. That newly created position was, he explained, "about driving quality through the whole plant" and improving customer satisfaction. Michael Mohr, the manufacturing director responsible for assembly operations during K0862's time at the factory, became the director of shop operations and assembly. Warren Albrecht, the wood technologist, was named director of materials.

※

Henry Z. Steinway, the great-grandson of Heinrich Engelhard, turned ninety as CD-60's second season began—the only Steinway human to have lived through the four sets of owners in the company's century and a half.

In January 1973, less than five months after he completed the sale to CBS, CBS sold another non–broadcast unit in its portfolio—the New York Yankees, which it had owned since 1964. Some workers at Steinway worried that if CBS no longer wanted a big-money franchise like the Yankees, it would not bother to find a buyer for little Steinway—it would simply shut down the factory, sell the last of the pianos at bargain prices, and claim a tax write-off.

Their fears were unfounded. CBS held on to Steinway for almost thirteen years. The early promise of cash for capital investments gave way to corporate pressures and haggling over whether pianos could be made cheaper and faster.

Still, when CBS finally gave up on Steinway, it did not close the factory. Instead, it found a buyer, a group of investors led by John P. Birmingham, a Boston lawyer and automobile racing enthusiast, and his brother Robert. With the Birminghams came a new president, Bruce A. Stevens. His first decision was to reopen hundreds of pianos that had sat, unsold, in boxes inside the factory. Stevens ordered them inspected and tuned. He says it was an important step in showing the workers and Steinway's dealers around the country that the new management wanted to concentrate on quality. The new owners also hired Schuyler G. Chapin, a former general manager of the Metropolitan Opera who happened to be Henry Z. Steinway's brother-in-law, as vice president of Steinway's concert division. Chapin said he assumed when they approached him that "they were looking for a kind of hail-fellow-well-met to ward off complaints." Not so, he discovered: "They were looking for someone who would seize on the fact that splendid pianos were again being made in the New York factory as well as the factory in Hamburg."

In Stevens's first year in charge, Steinway made five thousand pianos, roughly the same number of grands and uprights it had made in CBS's first year. The rest of the piano business withered. Some 144,316 pianos were sold nationwide in 1985—42 percent fewer than in 1972. The decline continued, and the national total had dropped to 94,044 in 1995, when Steinway was sold again. This time, the buyers were Kyle R. Kirkland and Dana D. Messina, two investment bankers who had worked with Michael R. Milken when he led Drexel Burnham Lambert's junk bond operation. Now it was Henry Z. Steinway's turn to worry. "I thought, here we go up the flue for sure," he recalled. "Two hotshots from Santa Monica who are not yet forty? This is where we get liquidated for sure." Kirkland was thirty-three; Messina was thirty-four.

Like the workers who feared the worst for Steinway when CBS sold the Yankees, he need not have worried. Steinway & Sons was Kirkland and Messina's second music-related company. In 1993, they had arranged a leveraged buyout of Selmer, the No. 1 band-instrument maker in the United States. In 2001, they bought one of Selmer's main competitors, the No. 3 company, United Musical Instruments.

At Steinway, they inherited a strategy for competing with foreign manufacturers like Yamaha and Kawai, not by mass-producing less expensive Steinways, but by starting two lower-priced brands, Boston and Essex. Those were the first pianos in Steinway's history that it did not build itself. Boston pianos are made in Japan by Kawai, and Essex pianos in Korea by Young Chang. The company now sells about as many Boston and Essex pianos as Steinways, and analysts who follow Steinway say the new brands have paid off. Joseph B. Lassiter III, a professor at the Harvard Business School, credits the Boston piano, in particular, with halting Yamaha's gains in the American market.

Steinway also went upmarket, introducing a "crown jewel collection"—more expensive Steinways with more exotic cases than the one on K0862, whose retail price when it was finished in 2003 was $92,800. If it had been a crown jewel piano with a finish of real ebony—not black lacquer sprayed on maple—K0862 would have gone for $141,000. Steinway has also revived art case pianos—instruments with fancy decorated cases. One, copied from an 1880s Steinway painted by the extravagant Victorian artist Lawrence Alma-Tadema, sold for $675,000.

Kirkland and Messina took the company public under the stock symbol LVB, for Ludwig van Beethoven—all the possible combinations that began with ST had been taken—and won over Henry Z. Steinway. "When I go to the factory," he says, "there are happy faces where there used to be gloomy faces and guys telling me, 'Oh, you should buy the business back.'"

TOP

CAST IRON PLATE

SOUNDING BOARD

RIM

TUNING PIN — DAMPER

KNUCKLE — STRING

PEDALS

HAMMER

UNDERLEVER

BACKCHECK

BALANCIER

KEY

CAPSTAN SCREW

WRESTPLANK

Inside a Concert Grand

Notes

Prelude: By These People, in This Place

xii "The piano being a creation and plaything": Preface by Jacques Barzun to Arthur Loesser, *Men, Women and Pianos: A Social History* (New York: Simon and Schuster, 1954), p. vii.

xiv a "holy, distant and celestial Harmony": Alex Ross, "Four Hands," *The New Yorker,* February 28, 2005.

xiv "a squadron of dive bombers": Gary Graffman, *I Really Should Be Practicing: Reflections of the Pleasures and Perils of Playing the Piano in Public* (New York: Doubleday, 1981), p. 196.

xiv "powerful but rather strident": Angela Hewitt, "Vox in a Box," *The Times Literary Supplement,* November 11, 2005.

xiv onstage favorite of Rachmaninoff: Author's interview with Eugene Istomin and Tali Mahanor, April 21, 2003.

xiv and took it home: Author's interview with Peter B. Goodrich, March 23, 2004; e-mail to author from Peter B. Goodrich, November 2, 2005, and note, November 3, 2005.

xv old factory: Author's interview with Joseph Pistilli of the Pistilli Realty Group, November 5, 2005.

xvi In its first fifty years: The Steinways' ledger for pianos made in New York begins with the piano to which they assigned the serial number 483. The company says they simply continued the sequence they had begun in Germany.

xvii No. 300,000 is the Steinway that is still in the East Room: Elise R. Kirk, *Musical Highlights from the White House* (Malabar, Florida: Krieger Publishing, 1992), p. 116; e-mail to author from Elise R. Kirk, November 2, 2005.

xvii The basic design of concert grands like K0862 has gone unchanged: Author's interviews with Tali Mahanor, December 13, 2005; Lee Morton, July 19, 2005, and Henry Z. Steinway, June 7, 2005. See also pp. 109–13.

xvii on the market since the 1930s: Theodore E. Steinway, *People and Pianos: A Pictorial History of Steinway & Sons* (New York: Steinway & Sons, 1953), p. 59.

xvii lost 666,400 factory jobs: Author's interview with James Brown, principal economist, New York State Department of Labor, April 14, 2003.

xviii fetch buckets of beer: Author's interview with Ronald Penatzer, July 14, 2005; author's interview with Joe Gurrado, March 12, 2003.

1. A Familiar Curve

This chapter is based largely on the author's observation of manufacturing operations on the Steinway & Sons factory floor on the dates mentioned in the text. In addition, several Steinway employees provided numerous interviews to clarify the manufacturing process:

Author's interviews with Joe Gurrado, February 6, March 11, and March 12, 2003; March 18, 2005.

Author's interviews with Andy Horbachevsky, February 6, March 11, March 12, and May 9, 2003; March 11 and December 8, 2005.

Author's interviews with Warren Albrecht, May 8, 2003 and July 14, 2005.

7 But as for what comes: Author's interview with Bruce A. Stevens, May 8, 2003.

8 Another Steinway relative: Richard K. Lieberman, *Steinway & Sons* (New Haven, Conn.: Yale University Press, 1995), pp. 139–40.

8 The savings in labor: Author's interview with Henry Z. Steinway, November 3, 2005.

18 "when does a piano become a musical instrument": Andy Horbachevsky often says the same thing, and it has become a catchphrase of the rim-bending department.

2. An Elderly Mechanic

This chapter is based largely on interviews with Henry Z. Steinway in March 2003 and in March, June, November, and December 2005; on William Steinway's diary; on the accounts in Richard K. Lieberman's *Steinway & Sons,* D. W. Fostle's *The Steinway Saga,* and Cynthia Adams Hoover's *The Steinways and Their Pianos in the Nineteenth Century*; and on other sources including those identified below. In the nineteenth century, the newspaper now known as *The New York Times* variously called itself *The New-York Daily Times* or *The New-York Times.*

22 "an elderly mechanic": *The New York Times,* May 11, 1864, p. 4. Steinweg was probably not upset to be described as an elderly mechanic. At fifty-six, he had lived longer than the average New Yorker of his day, and in the mid-nineteenth century, the term "mechanic" denoted someone who would now be considered a mechanical engineer. Author's interview with Marc Rothenberg, editor of the Joseph Henry Papers, January 31, 2006.

22 Clara Barton to P. T. Barnum: Harvard University Art Museum, Announcement of *Mathew Brady's Portraits: Images as History, Photography as Art,* p. 1.

22 Brady had built his reputation: James D. Horan, *Mathew Brady: Historian with a Camera* (New York: Crown Publishers, 1955), p. 29.

22 he hired artists to retouch: Ibid., p. 21.

24 Steinweg's "masterpiece": "Henry E. Steinway," *Contemporary American Biography, 1895* (New York: Atlantic Publishing and Engraving Co., 1895), p. 8. Elbert Hubbard, *The Story of the Steinways* (East Aurora, New York: The Roycrofters, 1911), p. 15.

24 Julianne . . . was pregnant: Author's interview with Henry Z. Steinway, March 3, 2005.

24 As an adult, he petitioned: Ibid.

24 Karl Brand: Richard K. Lieberman, *Steinway & Sons* (New Haven, Conn.: Yale University Press, 1995), p. 10.

25 He suggested in 2005: Author's interview with Henry Z. Steinway, June 7, 2005.

26 "Musicians came from distant cities": Hubbard, *Story of the Steinways,* p. 17.

26 One story, repeated: Author's interview with Henry Z. Steinway, March 3, 2005, and examination of Henry Z. Steinway's copy of *Mitteilungen.*

26 "I think I invented": Author's interview with Henry Z. Steinway, March 3, 2005.

26 As for No. 483: Craig Collins, "Steinway: An American Saga," in *150 Years of Steinway Pianos* (Tampa, Fla.: Faircount, 2003.), p. 18.

26 It sold for five hundred dollars: This would translate to approximately $11,600 in today's dollars.

27 Hubbard, probably drawing on stories: Hubbard, *Story of the Steinways,* p. 19.

27 He wrote enthusiastic letters: Lieberman, *Steinway & Sons,* p. 14.

27 It took so long for mail: D. W. Fostle, *The Steinway Saga: An American Dynasty* (New York: Scribner, 1995), p. 11.

27 Hubbard's melodramatic account: Hubbard, *Story of the Steinways,* p. 20.

28 The parents and seven children: Henry Z. Steinway note to author, November 30, 2005.

28 But New York's mainstream newspapers: Peter Conolly-Smith, *Translating America: An Immigrant Press Visualizes American Popular Culture, 1895–1918* (Washington, D.C.: Smithsonian Books, 2004), p. 31.

29 an anti-German wage scale: Arthur Loesser, *Men, Women and Pianos: A Social History* (New York: Simon and Schuster, 1954), p. 493.

29 a city directory: Fostle, *The Steinway Saga,* p. 27.

29 There was nothing much: "News of the Morning," *The New-York Daily Times,* March 7, 1853. Some historians suggest that the Steinways may not have formed Steinway & Sons until a month or two later and, after they had become successful, gave March 5 as the founding date because it was William's eighteenth birthday.

30 The new partners guessed: They did not change their names legally until 1864. Dumas Malone, ed., *Dictionary of American Biography* (New York: Charles Scribner's Sons, 1935), vol. 17, p. 567.

30 Fostle calculates: Fostle, *The Steinway Saga,* p. 75.

30 From the beginning: Aaron Singer, *Labor-Management Relations at Steinway & Sons, 1853–1896* (unpublished Columbia University doctoral dissertation), p. 13n.

30 "First premium piano-fortes": *The New York Daily Times,* June 20, 1854.

31 "the meanest of workshops": "Opening of Messrs. Steinway's New Piano Store and Factory," *The New York Times,* May 11, 1864.

31 "the largest and best of factories": Ibid.

31 "North of Fiftieth Street": Adrian Cook, *The Armies of the Streets: The New York City Draft Riots of 1863* (Lexington: University Press of Kentucky, 1974), p. 6.

31 "The factory [formed] a standing advertisement": *Frank Leslie's Illustrated Newspaper,* September 22, 1860, p. 281.

31 guidebooks pictured: Moses King, *King's Handbook of New York City, 1892: An Outline History and Description of the American Metropolis* (Boston, Mass.: NP, c. 1892), pp. 876–79.

32 An engraving in *Frank Leslie's: Frank Leslie's Illustrated Newspaper,* September 22, 1860, p. 282.

33 photograph taken in Brady's studio: Steinway Photo No. 04.002.0116 in Steinway & Sons Collection, La Guardia & Wagner Archives, La Guardia Community College, Queens, New York.

33 The Fifth did Guard Duty: "Construction and Destruction: Union Occupation of Arlington, 1861–1865," National Park Service monograph; "The Civil War in Arlington," Arlington (Virginia) Historical Society monograph.

33 They were angry about a law: Cook, *Armies of the Streets,* pp. 51 and 52; Edwin G. Burrows and Mike Wallace, *Gotham: A History of New York City to 1898* (New York: Oxford University Press, 1999), pp. 887–88.

33 "Steinway was widely known": Annotator's note to Diary of William Steinway, July 11, 1863, Web site of the Steinway & Sons Collection, La Guardia & Wagner Archives, La Guardia Community College, Queens, New York. See: http://www.laguardiawagnerarchive.lagcc.cuny.edu.defaultc.htm

34 "It was a terrible scene": Ibid.

34 Charles gave the organizers: Diary of William Steinway, July 13, 1863.

34 "All business in the upper part of the city": Ibid.

34 William discovered "to [his] horror": Diary of William Steinway, July 15, 1863, and annotator's notes on the Web site of the Steinway & Sons Collection, La Guardia & Wagner Archives.

34 Within twenty-four hours: Diary of William Steinway, July 16, 1863.

34 The factory went back to work: Ibid., July 18, 1863.

34 soldiers went to the store on Sunday: Ibid., July 19, 1863.

34 He did not explain why: Ibid., July 19, 1863, and annotator's notes on the Web site of the Steinway & Sons Collection, La Guardia & Wagner Archives.

34 William was the junior partner: Author's interview with Henry Z. Steinway, March 9, 2005.

35 He worked on developing a bulletproof vest: Theodore E. Steinway, *Index to Diary of William Steinway,* summary for February 7, 1862, Steinway & Sons Collection, La Guardia & Wagner Archives.

35 If his timing had been better: Victor Boesen and Wendy Grad, *The Mercedes-Benz Book* (Garden City, New York: Doubleday, 1981), pp. 46–48; W. Robert Nitske, *The Complete Mercedes Story* (New York: Macmillan, 1955), pp. 11 and 121.

35 A lung ailment: Steinway, *Index to Diary of William Steinway,* summary for March 11, 1865.

35 Typhoid fever killed Charles: Ibid., summary for March 31, 1865.

35 Just how much of a celebrity: "William Steinway Ill," *New-York Times,* November 13, 1896, p. 1.

35 "the perfection of the instrument": Theodore E. Steinway, *People and Pianos: A Pictorial History of Steinway & Sons* (New York: Steinway & Sons, 1953), pp. 31–34.

35 "Mr. Music in America": Lieberman, *Steinway & Sons,* p. 5.

36 "His silence [was] more eloquent": "Success in Life," *New-York Times,* December 4, 1896, p. 4.

36 Hubbard's flowery magazine article: Hubbard, *Story of the Steinways,* p. 25.

37 And he called attention: "William Steinway," *Contemporary American Biography,* p. 4.

37 Henry Z. Steinway, recalled: Author's interview with Henry Z. Steinway, June 7, 2005.

37 Alfred Dolge explained: Quoted in John F. Majeski, Jr., *Steinway: A Century of Distinguished Family Enterprise,* booklet-sized reprint of articles prepared for the hundredth anniversary of Steinway & Sons (New York: *Music Trades* magazine, 1953).

38 They turned to an advertising agency: Singer, *Labor-Management Relations,* p. 20 n. 36; Craig H. Roell, *The Piano in America, 1890–1940* (Chapel Hill: University of North Carolina Press, 1989), p. 175; Philip H. Dougherty, "Raymond Rubicam, 85, Co-Founder of Largest U.S. Ad Agency, Dies," *New York Times,* May 9, 1978, p. 42.

38 "Wife tells me she is —": Diary of William Steinway, March 1, 1869, and annotator's notes on the Web site of the Steinway & Sons Collection, La Guardia & Wagner Archives.

38 the family "sort of stiffed": Author's interview with Henry Z. Steinway, June 7, 2005.

39 as the soloist James Wehli discovered: Howard Shanet, *Philharmonic: A History of New York's Orchestra* (New York: Doubleday, 1975), p. 129n.

40 "The damned artists": Quoted in Lieberman, *Steinway & Sons,* p. 48.

40 the Philharmonic's somewhat larger home: Shanet, *Philharmonic,* p. 166.

40 "Mayor Hoffman lays the stone": Diary of William Steinway, May 20, 1866.

41 "well-disciplined band": John H. Mueller, *The American Symphony Orchestra: A Social History of Musical Taste* (Bloomington: Indiana University Press, 1951), p. 34.

41 "attained European celebrity": Theodore Baker, *A Biographical Dictionary of Musicians* (New York: G. Schirmer, 1905), p. 582.

41 "Everybody is delighted with the acoustic qualities": Diary of William Steinway, October 31, 1866.

41 "the best concert then possible in the city": Quoted in Gerald Board-
   man, *American Musical Theater: A Chronicle* (New York: Oxford
   University Press, 1992), p. 19.

41 He "enchants all with his play": Quoted in Jennifer E. Steenshorne, "Diary of a Charmer," *New York Archives,* Winter 2004, p. 14.

42 "great crowd": Diary of William Steinway, November 29, 1867.

42 The *New York Tribune* said that Dickens: Quoted in Fostle, *The Steinway
   Saga,* p. 180.

42 "I think him splendid": Quoted in Steenshorne, "Diary of a Charmer,"
   New York Archives, Winter 2004, p. 14.

42 it needed the higher ticket revenues: Shanet, *Philharmonic,* p. 129.

42 The *Times* noted that the interior: "Interior Improvement of Steinway
   Hall—Outlay of Twenty-five Thousand Dollars in Decoration," *The
   New-York Times,* June 26, 1868, p. 8.

43 William merely carried out: Steinway, *People and Pianos,* p. 34.

43 "More remarkable piano-playing than Mr. Rubinstein's": "Rubinstein-
   Wieniawski-Thomas Concerts," *The New-York Times,* January 4, 1873,
   p. 4.

43 Liszt called him "Van II": R. Allen Lott, *From Paris to Peoria: How European Piano Virtuosos Brought Classical Music to the American Heartland*
   (New York: Oxford University Press, 2003), p. 175.

44 He played 215 concerts: R. Allen Lott compiled and posted Rubinstein's
   itinerary at http://www.rallenlott.com.

44 Wieniawski missed only one concert along the way: Author's interview
   with Henry Z. Steinway, December 5, 2005.

44 the "real reason" was vertical integration: Henry Z. Steinway memo to
   author, November 30, 2005.

44 "anarchists and Socialists": Quoted in "Features of New York: North Beach,
   Steinway, Long Island," *The New York Times,* July 12, 1896, p. 25.

45 "if we could withdraw our workmen": Ibid.

46 the taxes were among the lowest: Burrows and Wallace, *Gotham,* p. 938.

46 "Over 14 Acres of Waterfront": Diary of William Steinway, July 8,
   1870.

46 "All are delighted with the magnificent house": Ibid., July 12, 1870.

46 The first factory buildings went up within two years: Robert A. M. Stern,
   et al., *New York 1880: Architecture and Urbanism in the Gilded Age* (New
   York: Monacelli Press, 1999), p. 977.

47 William moved the key-making operation there: Fostle, *The Steinway
   Saga,* p. 29.

47 He commissioned plans for workers' houses: Stern, et al., *New York
   1880,* pp. 978–79.

47 "A. T. Stewarts new improvement": Diary of William Steinway, March 9, 1871.

47 But the Panic of 1873: Thomas Kessner, *Capital City* (New York: Simon & Schuster, 2003), p. 162.

48 On the Fourth of July in 1886: Diary of William Steinway, July 5, 1886.

3. Anti-Manufacturing

This chapter is based largely on the author's observation of manufacturing operations on the Steinway & Sons factory floor on the dates indicated, as well as interviews with Andy Horbachevsky on February 6, March 11, March 12, and May 9, 2003; and on March 11, December 8, and December 13, 2005; and these other sources:

50 C. F. Theodore . . . moved back to Germany: Henry Z. Steinway note to author, November 30, 2005.

50 Once, New York Steinways had rounded arms: Author's interview with Frank Mazurco, August 22, 2003.

54 The world around Steinway was changing: "The Sad Story of Baldwin's Bankruptcy," *Music Trades,* December 1, 2001, p. 122.

55 Kawai sells: Author's interview with Brian Chung, May 20, 2003.

57 Newer coatings contain: Author's interview with Robert Burger, May 9, 2003.

57 "In their scheme of things": Author's interview with Bill Wurdack, Jr., December 9, 2005.

59 For generations, Steinway hired: Author's interview with Michael A. Anesta, September 10, 2003.

68 Hamburg has filled: Author's interview with Werner Husmann, June 23, 2003.

4. Part No. 81

This chapter is based largely on the author's observation of manufacturing operations on the Steinway & Sons factory floor on the dates mentioned in the text and on author's interviews during a trip to Tacoma, Washington, and Vancouver, British Columbia, with Warren Albrecht on October 9 and 10, 2004.

84 until the Spaniard Juan Perez: John Valliant, *The Golden Spruce: A True Story of Myth, Madness and Greed* (New York: W. W. Norton and Company, 2005), p. 36.

84 "the last significant feature": Valliant, *The Golden Spruce*, p. 37.

84 "the toughest, meanest natives": Author's interview with Husby Forest Products employees, October 10, 2004.

85 Loggers have a different worry: Douglas Martin, "Canada's Wasted Woodlands," *The New York Times*, August 28, 1983, section 3, p. 4.

85 "the Brazil of the north": Quoted in Timothy Egan, "Struggles over the Ancient Trees Shift to British Columbia," *The New York Times*, April 15, 1990, section 4, p. 1.

85 they worry that the forests: Martin, "Canada's Wasted Woodlands," *The New York Times*, August 28, 1983.

85 Swift probably had the Queen Charlottes in mind: Valliant, *The Golden Spruce*, p. 38.

85 "perfectly suited to support life": Valliant, *The Golden Spruce*, p. 9.

86 has been known to exceed eighteen feet: Valliant, *The Golden Spruce*, p. 16.

86 Conifers will grow continuously: Valliant, *The Golden Spruce*, p. 9.

5. Descendant

The idea for a chapter about K0862's ancestors—instruments that marked the turning points in the development of the piano, and in Steinway's own history—came to mind at the very end of an interview with Henry Z. Steinway on March 5, 2005, when he said, "We just got the first Model D back. Want to see it?" He credited the notion that the piano, No. 51257, is, in fact, the first modern Model D to Roy F. Kehl of Evanston, Illinois, a meticulous researcher who has mined the company's own records and traced the development of the modern Steinway. Henry Z. said that No. 51257 had been noticed by Tali Mahanor, a New York–based piano technician who recognized the serial number from Kehl's chronologies and her own work. Her subsequent insights, in interviews, telephone conversations, and e-mail messages, were invaluable. By coincidence, Lee Morton, a technician who tends the piano of Henry Z.'s cousin Henry S. Ziegler was working on No. 52340, a Model D made a few months after No. 51257. He too was helpful in explaining how Henry S. Ziegler's grandfather Henry L. Ziegler improved on C. F. Theodore Steinway's original 1884 design. At Steinway & Sons, Margaret Wolejsza confirmed details from the company's sales records; Michael Megaloudas provided information on how the company came to reacquire No. 51257 in 2004; and Ronald F. Coners, Peter B. Goodrich, and Frank Mazurco filled in other elements of the story. Other elements of this chapter were drawn from the following sources:

94 a backwater Medici: Arthur Loesser, *Men, Women and Pianos: A Social History* (New York: Simon & Schuster, 1954), p. 29.

95 Richard Burnett calls "subtlety or guile": Richard Burnett, *Company of Pianos* (Goudhurst, England: Finchcock Press, 2004), p. 14.

95 the "noisiest gadfly": Quoted in James Parakilas, *Piano Roles* (New Haven: Yale University Press, 1999), p. 11.

95 Within that short distance is everything: See, for example, H. Wiley Hitchcock, *Music in the United States: A Historical Introduction* (Englewood Cliffs, New Jersey: Prentice-Hall, 1969), p. 67.

96 Johann Sebastian Bach endorsed the products: Eva Badura-Skoda, "Johann Sebastian Bach," in Robert W. Palmieri, ed., *The Piano* (New York: Routledge, 2003), pp. 37–38; Rosamond E. Harding, *The Piano-Forte* (Cambridge: Cambridge University Press, 1933), p. 53 n. 1.

96 One of Bach's sons played: Apparently, it was at least the third. There had been earlier concerts in Vienna and Dublin, but none with the Bach name attached. Jeremy Siepmann, *The Piano* (New York: Alfred A. Knopf, 1997), p. 11.

96 The musicologist Henry Edward Krehbiel: Henry Edward Krehbiel, *The Piano-forte and Its Music* (New York: Cooper Square Publishers, 1971), pp. 47–49.

97 "cowardly mastodons": Excerpts from Gottschalk's autobiography are reprinted in Richard Burnett, *Company of Pianos* (Goudhurst, England: Finchcock Press, 2004), p. 105 n1.

97 The pianist Melvyn Tan: E-mail to author, November 29, 2005.

98 "Erard was the ideal": Cynthia Adams Hoover, "The Steinways and Their Pianos in the Nineteenth Century," *Journal of the American Musical Instrument Society,* 1981, p. 7.

98 He found the action: Emanual Ax, "Chopin: Works for Piano and Orchestra," booklet with Sony BMG SK 63371, p. 8; author's interview with Emanuel Ax, November 27, 2005.

100 Arthur Loesser points out: Arthur Loesser, *Men, Women and Pianos: A Social History* (New York: Simon and Schuster, 1954), p. 476.

100 one of their pianos won a prize: "Gold Medal Grand, Square & Upright Pianos," Steinway & Sons flyer, c. 1864; also "Principal Medals Now at Display at Steinway Hall," undated memorandum in Henry Z. Steinway's files.

100 "one of the longest and most magnificent rooms in the United States": "The First Exhibition of the Metropolitan Mechanics' Institute" (leaflet advertising 1853 fair), Library of Congress portfolio 201, folder 6, digital ID rbpe 20100600.

100 the Smithsonian Institution's "new and splendid" building: "Second Exhibition of the Metropolitan Mechanics' Institute" (leaflet advertising 1855 fair), Library of Congress portfolio 202, folder 2, digital ID rbpe 20200200.

100 the pioneering physicist Joseph Henry: Michael C. Herndon, "Polkas, Anyone?" *Smithsonian Preservation Quarterly,* Fall 1992; Marc Rothenberg, et al., eds., *The Papers of Joseph Henry:* Vol. 8, *The Smithsonian Years, January 1850–December 1853* (Washington, D.C.: Smithsonian Books, 1998), p.10.

100 *The New York Times* called the musical instrument: "The Passage of the Passenger Bill in the House—The Texas Debt Bill—The Fair of the Metropolitan Mechanics' Institute," *New-York Daily Times,* February 23, 1855, p. 1.

101 "One by one the jurors": "Opening of Messrs. Steinway's New Piano Store and Factory," *The New-York Daily Times,* May 11, 1864, p. 4.

102 "No longer could Beethoven": Edwin M. Good, *Giraffes, Black Dragons, and Other Pianos: A Technological History from Cristofori to the Modern Concert Grand* (Stanford, Calif.: Stanford University Press, 2001), p. 207.

102 "It impressed us as being one of the most majestic instruments": "Amusements—Academy of Music," *The New-York Times,* February 7, 1863, p. 5.

103 Theodore had spent $80,000: Some piano historians say that Chickering equaled Steinway's spending. But the Steinway biographer D. W. Fostle maintains that the figure of $160,000 is "without certifiable accuracy" and that neither Steinway nor Chickering sold enough pianos "as a result of winning their gold medals" to offset their expenses in Paris. D. W. Fostle, *The Steinway Saga: An American Dynasty* (New York: Scribner, 1995), p. 149.

103 Another writer, "C.B.S.": "The Paris Exposition.—American Musical Instruments on Exhibition—Ocean Signal," *The New York Times,* May 22, 1867, p. 2.

104 Theodore sent William a telegram: "Local Intelligence–General City News—the Exposition Gold Medal," *The New York Times,* July 4, 1867, p. 2.

105 The budget is too tight: E-mail to author from Andreas Werz, professor, California State University–Fresno, July 16, 2005.

105 William tempted: Diary of William Steinway, December 30, 1875.

106 younger brother, Albert, called Frank Chickering "a loony fool": Ibid., June 8, 1876.

106 "a Chickering judge, a Steinway judge": Fostle, *The Steinway Saga,* p. 226.

109 "because of the payoffs": Author's interview with Henry Z. Steinway, December 5, 2005.

110 "female kiss-fender": Reprinted in Theodore E. Steinway, *People and Pianos: A Pictorial History of Steinway & Sons* (New York: Steinway & Sons, 1953), p. 70.

110 He whined about the "dangerous action": David Taylor, "Paderewski's Piano," *Smithsonian,* March 1999.

111 "our piano of today": Author's interview with Tali Mahanor, December 13, 2005.

110 "It obviously had some design flaws": Author's interview with Lee Morton, July 19, 2005.

112 Steinway realized that No. 51257: Author's interviews with Ronald F. Coners on June 7, 2005; Peter B. Goodrich on December 1, 2005; and Frank Mazurco on December 8, 2005.

6. Bellying

This chapter is based largely on the author's observation of manufacturing operations on the Steinway & Sons factory floor on the dates indicated. The section on plate making is based on an interview with Ronald Penatzer on July 14, 2005.

116 "I play more in Carnegie Hall": Author's interview with Franz Mohr, March 1990.

117 A devout churchgoer: Franz Mohr with Edith Schaeffer, *My Life with the Great Pianists: Horowitz, Cliburn, Rubinstein and Others* (Grand Rapids, Mich.: Baker Books, 1992), p. 162.

117 Franz Mohr took Michael along: Ibid., p. 52.

117 Over the objections of his father: Ibid., p. 165.

118 He started as a stringer: Author's interview with Michael Mohr, September 9, 2003.

118 Kelly, which made plates for Baldwin: Tom Stafford, "Had Foundry, Made Plates," *Springfield (Ohio) News-Sun,* August 13, 2001, p. 22.

7. The Company That Was

This chapter is based largely on the author's interviews and correspondence with Henry Z. Steinway.

132 manager of the American Marconi Company: Jeff Kisseloff, *The Box: An Oral History of Television, 1920–1961* (New York: Viking, 1995); Tom Lewis, *Empire of the Air* (New York, HarperCollins, 1991), pp. 116–17.

133 born in an apartment building: Author's interview with Henry Z. Steinway, March 5, 2005.

133 a grand piano introduced in 1912: Richard K. Lieberman, *Steinway & Sons* (New Haven, Conn.: Yale University Press, 1995), p. 129.

134 introduced at a cocktail party: Author's interview with Henry Z. Steinway, June 11, 2003.

134 lowering itself to the new mass market: Theodore E. Steinway, *People and Pianos: A Pictorial History of Steinway & Sons* (New York: Steinway & Sons, 1953), p. 64; Lieberman, *Steinway & Sons,* p. 133.

134 Steinway did so well: Lieberman, *Steinway & Sons,* p. 120; author's interview with Henry Z. Steinway, March 5, 2005.

135 which continued to rise: Lieberman, *Steinway & Sons,* p. 120.

135 It became more than an annex: Author's interview with Henry Z. Steinway, March 5, 2005.

135 boxy and modern looking: Steinway, *People and Pianos,* p. 64; author's interview with Henry Z. Steinway, March 5, 2005.

135 The company also built a new Steinway Hall: Steinway, *People and Pianos,* p. 64; Lieberman, *Steinway & Sons,* p. 147.

135 the city's preeminent concert theater: "New York Concert Halls," *The New York Times,* February 1, 1925, p. E6; "Old Steinway Hall, a Landmark, Passes; Owners Move from Building at Which Great Artists Had Appeared," *The New York Times,* June 16, 1925, p. 13.

136 "impressive dignity is most fitting": R.W.S., "The Sky-Line," *The New Yorker,* April 11, 1925, p. 28.

136 Thirty-five musicians from the New York Philharmonic: "Throng at Opening of Steinway Hall," *The New York Times,* October 28, 1925, p. 28.

136 The New York Philharmonic's offices: "New York Symphony Society Leases Steinway Hall Space," *The New York Times,* October 25, 1925, p. E19.

136 "the new vanguard of business": Sally Bedell Smith, *In All His Glory: The Life and Times of William S. Paley and the Birth of Modern Broadcasting* (New York: Simon & Schuster, 1990), p. 47.

137 "The business really fell apart pretty badly": Author's interview with Henry Z. Steinway, June 11, 2003.

137 The company bragged: Steinway, *People and Pianos,* pp. 65 and 83.

137 What saved Steinway was another small piano: Lieberman, *Steinway & Sons,* pp. 190 and 200.

138 He paid rent, just like the other tenants: Author's interview with Henry Z. Steinway, June 7, 2005.

138 "never gave any hint how bad things were": Ibid.

138 Worse, for Henry Z. Steinway: Ibid.

139 a silicosis scare in the late 1930s: Author's interview with Henry Z. Steinway, June 11, 2003, and June 7, 2005.

140 John E. Pike, a defense consultant: Author's interview with John E. Pike.

141 Steinway was responsible for making all the wooden parts: Author's interview with Henry Z. Steinway, June 7, 2005.

141 curator of the Cradle of Aviation Museum: Author's interview with Joshua Stoff.

141 The historian Richard K. Lieberman points out: Lieberman, *Steinway & Sons*, p. 228.

142 "We didn't make money on any of this stuff": Author's interview with Henry Z. Steinway, March 5, 2005.

143 As he told Richard K. Lieberman: Lieberman, *Steinway & Sons*, p. 239.

143 when Henry Z.'s sister Elizabeth: "Miss Steinway Wed to Schuyler Chapin," *The New York Times*, March 16, 1947, p. 59.

143 Henry Z. took over the company eight years later: D. W. Fostle, *The Steinway Saga: An American Dynasty* (New York: Scribner, 1995), p. 488; Lieberman, *Steinway & Sons*, p. 246.

144 He mastered corporate politics: Lieberman, *Steinway & Sons*, p. 239; author's interview with Henry Z. Steinway, November 30, 2005.

144 Two calculations by the Steinway biographer: Fostle, *The Steinway Saga*, p. 484.

145 "a good propaganda item": Ibid., p. 485.

145 But the hands at the factory: Ibid., p. 487; Lieberman, *Steinway & Sons*, p. 242.

145 "It was not an easy thing to do": Author's interview with Peter B. Goodrich.

146 So Henry Z. proposed closing: Author's interview with Henry Z. Steinway, June 11, 2005.

147 "We came out free and clear": Lieberman, *Steinway & Sons*, p. 264.

147 "It was the hippie time": Author's interview with Henry Z. Steinway, June 7, 2003.

147 "He felt very lonely": Author's interview with Lee Morton, May 31, 2005.

148 his mother considered it "a betrayal": Author's interview with Henry Z. Steinway, June 7, 2003, March 5, 2005, and June 11, 2005.

148 Henry Z.'s replacement, Robert P. Bull: Lieberman, *Steinway & Sons*, p. 308; author's interviews with Henry Z. Steinway, June 11, 2005, and with Robert P. Bull, January 16, 2006.

149 In 2002 Chapin had told his uncle: Author's interview with Theodore Chapin, June 7, 2003.

8. Playable

This chapter is based largely on the author's personal observation of manufacturing operations on the Steinway & Sons factory floor on the dates indicated.

154 "nothing remarkable": Quoted in John Amis and Michael Rose, *Words About Music: A Treasury of Writing* (New York: Paragon House, 1992), p. 186.

156 Depression-era big band musicians: Adrian Press and Nat Shapiro, *The Music Goes 'Round and Around: The Golden Years of Tin Pan Alley, 1930–1939,* booklet with New World Records 80248, p. 13.

157 "the smaller, quicker shadings": Arthur Loesser, *Men, Women and Pianos: A Social History* (New York: Simon and Schuster, 1954), p. 338.

157 "Other than a soundboard": Author's interview with Steve Drasche, July 13, 2005.

157 Henry Z. Steinway credits Horowitz: Richard K. Lieberman, *Steinway & Sons* (New Haven, Conn.: Yale University Press, 1995), pp. 201–02; author's interview with Henry Z. Steinway, June 7, 2005.

158 Vietor and the pianist Josef Hofmann: *The New York Times,* June 19, 1941, p. 21.

158 "working together and talking mechanically": Quoted in Lieberman, *Steinway & Sons,* p. 201.

160 Outsourcing actions was nothing new: Loesser, *Men, Women and Pianos,* p. 522.

160 the Teflon bushing: Author's interview with Henry Z. Steinway, June 7, 2005.

161 "The Teflon made clicking noises": Author's interview with Charles Rosen, April 9, 2003.

164 The idea of visual contrast: Robert Palmieri, *The Piano: An Encyclopedia* (New York: Routledge, 2003), p. 206.

164 "We tried it out": Author's interview with Henry Z. Steinway, June 11, 2003.

164 But some screamed: Gary Graffman, *I Really Should Be Practicing: Reflections of the Pleasures and Perils of Playing the Piano in Public* (New York: Doubleday, 1981), p. 192.

9. A Fresh Personality

This chapter is based largely on the author's observation of manufacturing operations on the Steinway & Sons factory floor on the dates indicated.

182 In Arthur A. Reblitz's authoritative manual: Arthur A. Reblitz, *Piano Servicing, Tuning, and Rebuilding: For the Professional, the Student, the Hobbyist,* 2nd ed. (Lanham, Md.: Vestal Press, 1993), pp. 149–201, 324–25.

10. Finding the Screw

This chapter is based largely on the author's observation of manufacturing operations on the Steinway & Sons factory floor on the dates mentioned in the text.

11. Temporary Identity

This chapter is based largely on interviews with Ronald F. Coners in February 2003 and on December 1, 2005. Additional material was drawn from these sources:

205 Once, when an ailing Vladimir Horowitz: Glenn Plaskin, *Horowitz: A Biography* (New York: Quill, 1983), p. 280. Henry Z. Steinway says he knew nothing about Horowitz's trip in a Steinway truck until this author mentioned the anecdote. Henry Z. Steinway speculates that David Rubin, who managed Steinway's concert and artist department, arranged Horowitz's truck trip. Henry Z. Steinway note to the author, November 30, 2005, and author's interview with Henry Z. Steinway, December 1, 2005.

206 Everyone from Moriz Rosenthal: Henry Z. Steinway points out that the irascible Rosenthal switched from Steinway to another brand— probably Baldwin, he said, although Rosenthal was also identified with Mason & Hamlin. But Rosenthal supposedly chose the 1927 Steinway Model B that is now in the author's living room. Rosenthal is said to have done this as a favor to his doctor, the author's wife's grandfather. Sometimes family lore cannot be disputed.

206 "ladies of the evening": Gary Graffman, *I Really Should Be Practicing: Reflections of the Pleasures and Perils of Playing the Piano in Public* (New York: Doubleday, 1981), p. 166.

206 Emanuel Ax remembers: Author's interview with Emanuel Ax, February 25, 2004.

207 Ivo Pogorelich: Author's interview with Peter B. Goodrich, March 23, 2004.

207 The basement enclave came about: Author's interview with Henry Z. Steinway, June 7, 2005.

209 Another Model D in the fleet: Author's interview with Peter B. Goodrich, March 23, 2004.

211 Coners is certain which piano: The author watched Brendel try six Model Ds, including CD-60 (K0862), on April 19, 2004. Brendel passed over CD-60 and picked the one that Coners had predicted he would choose.

12. Debut

This chapter is largely based on concerts and rehearsals that the author attended at the Irving S. Gilmore Keyboard Festival in Kalamazoo, Michigan; the New York Piano Competition in New York City; and the Bridgehampton Chamber Music Festival in Bridgehampton, N.Y.

220 He had been tapped: Author's interview with Angela Duryea, publicist for Jonathan Bliss, November 8, 2005.

221 Isaac Stern had heard Biss: Ibid., January 19, 2006.

221 *The New York Times* mused: Jeremy Eichler, "Young Pianist at the Ready to Believe in His Success," *The New York Times,* March 8, 2005, p. E1.

221 His paternal grandmother: *Los Angeles Times,* July 11, 2004.

221 The way Fried tells it: Question-and-answer session after concert, Irving S. Gilmore International Keyboard Festival, April 26, 2004.

221 For all his seeming confidence: Eichler "Young Pianist at the Ready to Believe in His Success," *The New York Times,* March 8, 2005.

221 Kirchner said the "seeds" of *Interlude II*: Gilmore Festival program notes, April 26, 2004, p. 2.

222 After the concert, Biss complains: Author's interview with Jonathan Biss, April 26, 2005.

222 as the pianist Raymond Lewenthal wrote: Quoted in Joe and Elizabeth Kahn, Gilmore Festival opening night program book, p.6.

223 Ron Coners's assessment: Author's interview with Ronald F. Coners, September 13, 2005.

225 But Steinway, as Coners puts it: Ibid., December 12, 2005.

227 that piano could not be hauled: Author's interview with Jennifer Wada, Metropolitan Museum of Art May 12, 2005.

228 On the morning of his lecture-performance: Author's interview with Mikel Frank, Metropolitan Museum of Art May 15, 2005.

228 A couple of hours later: Author's interview with Maureen Angeles, August 17, 2005.

229 Ter Veldhuis's work includes: "Pianist Andrew Russo Exposes Americans to Joys of Modern Works," *San Jose Mercury News,* December 12, 2004, p. AE7.

229 Russo has picked up pointers: Author's interview with Andrew Russo, August 17, 2005.

229 It earned him the distinction: Andrew Russo biography from Impresario Arts, L.L.C.

229 "What I was trying to do": Author's interview with Andrew Russo, August 17, 2005.

230 She has already read it in Russian: Ibid.
231 Russo packs a wallop: Paul Schenly e-mail to author, August 19, 2005.
231 Schenly's assessment of CD-60: Ibid., August 18, 2005.

Postlude

234 It was the choice of every pianist: Author's interview with Jennifer Wada, December 5, 2005.
234 Reviewing Biss's performance: Bernard Holland, "Young and Impetuous, But Firmly in Control," *The New York Times,* March 10, 2005, page E3.
235 "I didn't think about the piano for a minute": Author's interview with Ruth Laredo, May 9, 2005.
235 If CD-60 were to go back to the Steinway factory: Author's interviews with Andy Horbachevsky, March 11 and December 8, 2005, and Michael A. Anesta, November 15, 2005.
236 His first decision: Author's interview with Bruce A. Stevens, May 8, 2003.
237 Schuyler G. Chapin: Schuyler G. Chapin, "Steinway Pianos: Pursuing Quality" (letter to the editor), *The New York Times,* December 1, 1991.
237 Some 144,316 pianos (and other sales figures): "U.S. Piano Sales History," National Piano Foundation.
237 "up the flue for sure": Author's interview with Henry Z. Steinway, June 11, 2003.
238 Joseph B. Lassiter III: Author's interview with Joseph B. Lassiter III, June 13, 2003.
238 "When I go to the factory": Author's interview with Henry Z. Steinway, June 11, 2003.

Selected Bibliography

About Steinway & Sons

Chapin, Miles. *88 Keys: The Making of a Steinway Piano.* New York: Clarkson Potter Publishers, 1997.

Fostle, D. W. *Speedboat.* Mystic, Conn.: United States Historical Society and Mystic Seaport Museum Stores, 1988.

———. *The Steinway Saga: An American Dynasty.* New York: Scribner, 1995.

Hoover, Cynthia Adams. "The Steinways and Their Pianos in the Nineteenth Century," *Journal of the American Musical Instrument Society,* 1981.

Lenehan, Michael. "The Quality of the Instrument," *The Atlantic Monthly,* August 1982.

Lieberman, Richard K. *Steinway & Sons.* New Haven, Conn.: Yale University Press, 1995.

Majeski, Brian T. "The Steinway Story," *Music Trades,* September 2003.

Majeski, John F., Jr. *Steinway: A Century of Distinguished Family Enterprise* (booklet-size reprint of articles prepared for the 100th anniversary of Steinway & Sons). New York: Music Trades Magazine, 1953.

Ratcliffe, Ronald V. *Steinway.* San Francisco: Chronicle Books, 1989.

Singer, Aaron. *Labor-Management Relations at Steinway & Sons, 1853–1896.* New York: University Microfilms International, 1977 (Columbia University doctoral dissertation).

Steinway, Theodore E. *People and Pianos: A Pictorial History of Steinway & Sons.* New York: Steinway & Sons, 1953.

About Pianos and Music History

Amis, John, and Michael Rose. *Words About Music: A Treasury of Writing.* New York: Paragon House, 1992.

Bradley, Van Allen. *Music for the Millions: The Kimball Piano and Organ Story.* Chicago, Ill.: Henry Regnery Company, 1957.

Burnett, Richard. *Company of Pianos.* Goudhurst, England: Finchcock Press, 2004.

Closson, Ernest. *The History of the Piano.* Brussels, Belgium: Les Presses de Belgique, 1947.

Crawford, Richard. *The American Musical Landscape: The Business of Musicianship from Billings to Gershwin.* Berkeley: University of California Press, 2000.

Good, Edwin M. *Giraffes, Black Dragons, and Other Pianos: A Technological History from Cristofori to the Modern Concert Grand.* Stanford, Calif.: Stanford University Press, 2001.

Graffman, Gary. *I Really Should Be Practicing: Reflections of the Pleasures and Perils of Playing the Piano in Public.* New York: Doubleday, 1981.

Harding, Rosamond E. M. *The Piano-Forte.* New York: Da Capo Press, 1973.

Hinson, Maurice. *The Pianist's Dictionary.* Bloomington: Indiana University Press, 2004.

Hitchcock, H. Wiley, with Kyle Gann. *Music in the United States: Historical Introduction.* Upper Saddle River, N.J.: Prentiss Hall, 2000.

Kamien, Roger. *Music and Appreciation.* New York: McGraw Hill, 1976.

Kindall, Allen. *The Chronicle of Classical Music: An Intimate Diary of the Life and Music of the Great Composers.* London: Thames and Hudson, 1994.

Krehbiel, Henry Edward. *The Piano-forte and Its Music.* New York: Cooper Square Publishers, 1971.

Loesser, Arthur. *Men, Women and Pianos: A Social History.* New York: Simon & Schuster, 1954.

Lott, R. Allen. *From Paris to Peoria: How European Piano Virtuosos Brought Classical Music to the American Heartland.* New York: Oxford University Press, 2003.

Mohr, Franz, with Edith Schaeffer. *My Life with the Great Pianists: Horowitz, Cliburn, Rubinstein and Others.* Grand Rapids, Mich.: Baker Books, 1992.

Mueller, John H. *The American Symphony Orchestra: A Social History of Musical Taste.* Bloomington: Indiana University Press, 1951.

Oringer, Judith. *Passion for the Piano.* Los Angeles, Calif.: Jeremy P. Tarcher, 1983.

Palmieri, Robert. *The Piano: An Encyclopedia.* New York: Routledge, 2003.

Parakilas, James, et al. *Piano Roles: Three Hundred Years of Life with the Piano.* New Haven, Conn.: Yale University Press, 1999.

Plaskin, Glenn. *Horowitz: A Biography.* New York: Quill, 1983.

Roell, Craig H. *The Piano in America, 1890–1940.* Chapel Hill: University of North Carolina Press, 1989.

Rosen, Charles. *Piano Notes: The World of the Pianist.* New York: Free Press, 2002.

Schonberg, Harold C. *Facing the Music.* New York: Summit Books, 1981.

———. *The Great Pianists: From Mozart to the Present.* New York: Simon and Schuster, 1987.

Shanet, Howard. *Philharmonic: A History of New York's Orchestra.* New York: Doubleday, 1975.

Siepmann, Jeremy. *The Piano.* New York: Alfred A. Knopf, 1997.

———. *The Piano: The Complete Illustrated Guide to the World's Most Popular Music Instrument.* London: Carlton Books Limited, 1996.

About New York City

Ackerman, Kenneth D. *Boss Tweed: The Rise and Fall of the Corrupt Pol Who Conceived the Soul of Modern New York.* New York: Carol and Graf, 2005.

Burrows, Edwin G., and Mike Wallace. *Gotham.* New York: Oxford University Press, 1999.

Conolly-Smith, Peter. *Translating America: An Immigrant Press Visualizes American Popular Culture, 1895–1918.* Washington, D.C.: Smithsonian Books, 2004.

Keffner, Thomas. *Capital City: New York City and the Men Behind America's Rise to Economic Dominance, 1860–1900.* New York: Simon and Schuster, 2003.

King, Moses. *King's Handbook of New York City, 1892: An Outline History and Description of the American Metropolis.* New York: Barnes and Noble, 2001.

McCullough, David. *The Great Bridge: The Epic Story of the Building of the Brooklyn Bridge.* New York: Simon and Schuster, 1972.

Stern, Robert A. M., Thomas Mellins, and David Fishman. *New York 1880: Architecture and Urbanism in the Gilded Age.* New York: Monacelli Press, 1999.

About the Pacific Northwest

Lucia, Elias. *The Big Woods: Logging and Lumbering—from Bull Teams to Helicopters—in the Pacific Northwest.* Garden City, N.Y.: Doubleday, 1975.

Pike, Robert E. *Spiked Boots: Sketches of the North Country.* Woodstock, Vt.: Country Man Press, 1999.

———. *Tall Trees, Tough Men.* New York: W. W. Norton, 1967.

Valliant, John. *The Golden Spruce: A True Story of Myth, Madness and Greed.* New York: W. W. Norton, 2005.

About Expositions, World's Fairs, Marketing, and Consumer Culture

Cohen, Lizabeth. *A Consumer's Republic: The Politics of Mass Consumption in Postwar America.* New York: Vintage Books, 2003.

Giberti, Bruno. *Designing the Centennial: A History of the 1876 International Exhibition in Philadelphia.* Lexington: The University Press of Kentucky, 2002.

Gross, Linda P., and Theresa R. Snyder. *Philadelphia's 1876 Centennial Exhibition: Images of America.* Charleston, S.C.: Arcadia, 2005.

Leach, William. *Land of Desire: Merchants, Power, and the Rise of a New American Culture.* New York: Vintage Books, 1993.

Strasser, Susan. *Satisfaction Guaranteed: The Making of the American Mass Market.* Washington, D.C.: Smithsonian Books, 1989.

Acknowledgments

First things first: I'm grateful to K0862, known these days as CD-60. As main characters go, it turned out pretty well, I think.

My thanks to everyone who appears in this book, which began as a series of articles published in *The New York Times* under the rubric "Invention for 900 Hands." Jonathan Landman said yes to the idea instantly and recognized the possibilities even before K0862 began to take shape; Susan Edgerley championed the series and, later, the book; Anne Cronin saw that each installment in the series was tightly and carefully focused; Michael Kolomatsky designed irresistible pages; and Kyle Massie, Charles Knittle, and their colleagues on the metropolitan copy desk shepherded each part into print. Linda Lake tracked down obscure sources and factoids, as did Alain Delaquerriere, Sandra Jamison, Barbara Oliver, and Carolyn Wilder. On the photo desk, William O'Donnell, Roger Strong, and Robert Glass retrieved the archived images that appear throughout the book. Don Hecker, Joan Nassivera, and Arlene Schneider read early versions of the manuscript, and as deadlines loomed, Joe Sexton, Wendell Jamieson, and Diego Ribadaneira were wonderfully indulgent.

Alex Ward and, before him, Susan Chira provided guidance and advice on the Times' end of Times Books, as did Paul Golob and the indefatigable Robin Dennis at Henry Holt and Company. I'm grateful, too, to Emily DeHuff for sharpening and improving the text. Thomas C. Baker, Debra Kent, and Patricia Gutiérrez also read versions of the manuscript, as did my parents, James P. and Leirona Barron. They put me on the path that led to Steinway and K0862 by taking me to dozens of concerts and by saving enough money to buy No. 170359. To steal a line from Frank Sinatra, another product of 1915, it was a very good year.

Steinway & Sons agreed to let me watch their workers build one piano from start to finish. On the factory floor and on what I came to call management row, Steinway's employees explained and, when I didn't get it the first time, reexplained how and why they do what they do. This was especially true of Andy Horbachevsky, Michael Mohr, and Ronald Penatzer. Warren Albrecht was a knowledgeable tour guide in the Pacific Northwest. Ronald F. Coners was refreshingly frank in his basement domain. Frank Mazurco proved to be a fine pianist and an expert on any number of details. But no one can touch Henry Ziegler Steinway, the last member of the family to preside over Steinway & Sons. Time and again, Henry Z., as I have called him here, plumbed his files and, better yet, his memory of pianos, pianists, and relatives. So did his cousin, Henry Steinway Ziegler. Apart from their interchangeable names and gracious elegance, there's no confusing those two.

This book is not what the critic and composer Greg Sandow would call "history, the way a real historian would write it." I'm not a historian, and others have concentrated specifically on Steinway's past, notably Richard K. Lieberman (in *Steinway & Sons*) and D. W. Fostle (in *The Steinway Saga: An American Dynasty*). Professor Lieberman's work in making William Steinway's diary accessible on the Internet was invaluable. I also benefited from the work of Cynthia Adams Hoover and her colleagues at the Smithsonian Institution and, thanks to her, had the unexpected pleasure of trying Paderewski's piano and the original White House Steinway, No. 100,000.

Hilde Limondjian at the Metropolitan Museum welcomed CD-60 and was unfailingly encouraging. Mikel Frank, the stage manager, and Jennifer Wada coordinated things when there were photographs to shoot and concerts to attend. Similarly, the Gilmore Festival in Kalamazoo, Michigan, smoothed the way for me to watch CD-60's public debut, and the Bridgehampton Chamber Music Festival was equally generous in letting me sit in on rehearsals during the summer of 2004.

Fred R. Conrad, the consummate *New York Times* photographer, did more than capture K0862 at every turn, from raw wood to finished piano on a concert stage—he improved my understanding of what we were seeing. Fred is a weekend woodworker whose appreciation of tools and processes led to conversations with the pros at the factory that teased out details they take for granted and I wouldn't have known to ask about.

My agent, David Black, played so many roles as this book took shape—negotiator, adviser, advocate, hand-holder—that I can't put them all into words. As he knows, the series in *The Times* and thus this book came about, indirectly, because of something I heard on the radio. I was in Florida, on vacation, coming back from the beach one afternoon, and as I pulled into a parking space, *All Things Considered* was doing a story about a guy who was trying to figure out what made Stradivari's violins so special. I looked over at the other person in the car and said, "I could go watch Steinway build one piano, from start to finish." The other person in the car was my wife, Jane-Iris Farhi. She's remarkable. She's thought-provoking. She's become K0862's biggest fan. I could go on, and in a way, I already have. Take a look at the note for page 206.

Index

Note: Page numbers in *italics* refer to illustrations

About the Author

JAMES BARRON is a staff reporter for *The New York Times*. Over the past twenty-five years, his writing has appeared in virtually every section of the paper and has ranged from breaking coverage of the September 11 attacks and the 2003 New York City blackout to Christo's "Gates" installation in Central Park. An accomplished amateur pianist, he lives in New York City.